WORDSWORTH CLASSICS
OF WORLD LITERATURE

General Editor: Tom Griffith MA, MPhil

THE TRAVELS OF MARCO POLO

D0029331

The Travels of Marco Polo

❖

With an Introduction by Benjamin Colbert

WORDSWORTH CLASSICS
OF WORLD LITERATURE

The paper in this book is produced from pure wood
pulp, without the use of chlorine or any other substance
harmful to the environment. The energy used in its
production consists almost entirely of hydroelectricity
and heat generated from waste material, thereby
conserving fossil fuels and contributing little
to the greenhouse effect.

This edition published 1997 by Wordsworth Editions Limited
Cumberland House, Crib Street, Ware, Hertfordshire SG12 9ET

ISBN 1 85326 473 3

Typeset in Great Britain by Antony Gray
Printed and bound in Denmark by Nørhaven

INTRODUCTION

That *The Travels of Marco Polo* recounts one of the most remarkable ventures in the history of Western travel has been unchallenged as long as readers have turned to travel literature for a sense of the world beyond their firesides. The *Travels* vividly records one of the first encounters between a representative of European civilisation and the more ancient civilisations of the then mysterious and marvellous East, especially China and India. For medieval readers, this must have been momentous: the circulation of the *Travels* in over 119 manuscripts at the end of the thirteenth and throughout the fourteenth century provided them with one of the few first-hand accounts of places, peoples, and cultures known before then, if at all, through the hearsay of merchants, themselves dependent on reports from their Muslim counterparts plying the ancient silk and spice routes to the East. Before Marco Polo's travels, medieval maps (called T-O maps) often inscribed the three known continents within a circle around the spiritual epicentre of Jerusalem, with Asia occupying the hemisphere above the 'T' bar, and Europe and Africa the two lower quadrants. Older cosmographical ideas of doubtful currency but more accuracy include the ancient Ptolemaic picture of the world, which figured Asia as an undifferentiated land mass encircling the Indian Ocean in the south and rejoining the African continent (see Map 1). In both views, Asia remained an extensive but ill-defined space of otherness, the site of biblical, classical and fantastic races, places, riches, monstrosities; a space, in short, where the medieval imagination had gained a foothold in cosmography that would not readily yield to the empirical observations of travellers. Over and against this space, Marco Polo's writing fills in the details of Asia and traces its outlines with an accuracy often questioned since his times, but almost unprecedented before them (see Map 2). The *Travels* offers, as an early version's title puts it, a

'Description of the World', from the sphere of Venetian influence in the Mediterranean to the almost mythical islands of Japan, from the Persian Gulf to the 'Region of Darkness' in the Russian north. It is a description that is part travel narrative and part cosmographical treatise, part reportage and part romance, but always one that tirelessly supplies detail to the little-known or unknown regions of the world.

Yet although facts are his ostensible business, Polo's account shades into the world imagination that precedes it. It admits as often as it excludes the marvellous. Weaving stories of Christian miracles and eastern sorcerers, outlandish sexual customs and cannibalism, into the staid fabric of his catalogue of towns, peoples, customs, economies, Polo creates a narrative that blurs the boundaries between what we might call ethnology and mythology, observation and hearsay. At once empirical and imaginative, Polo's narrative opens itself up to criticisms of dishonesty; it proffers a description of the world but at the same time seems to be creating the world it would describe. To Polo's contemporaries there was less a problem with the matter of the *Travels* than its manner. Polo was distrusted not for his account of the dog-headed islanders of Angaman in the Indian Ocean, but for his disturbing celebration of the economic and cultural success and efficiency of the pagan Mongol empire that ruled most of the lands in which he travelled. To some, Polo earned the nickname of *Il Milione*, Marco 'Million', and a reputation for exaggeration, or worse, as a teller of tall tales. In our more empirical times, Polo's matter has received increasing scrutiny, as the title of a recent study by Frances Wood evidences: *Did Marco Polo Go to China?* Accumulated historical and geographical documents allow us now to compare Polo's data with reliable contemporary accounts, not only of travellers, but of medieval Chinese officials as well. The discrepancies between what Polo observed and what he might have (or should have) observed raise new problems with the accuracy and even the originality of his text.[1]

1 Doubts as to the authenticity of Polo's travels have been cast because of his failure to mention landmarks like the Great Wall of China or cultural practices like the binding of the feet of Chinese women. However, in a review of Wood's book, T. H. Barret points out that Polo's critics might be equally guilty of historical inaccuracies. The Great Wall, he asserts, had not yet been built when Polo travelled through northern China, and foot-binding may not have been obvious to outsiders. See T. H. Barret, 'Wall? I saw no Wall', *London Review of Books*, 30 November, 1995, p. 28.

Marco Polo's *Travels* belongs, then, to the story not only of Europe's contact with, but also its knowledge and imagination of the East as well. The latter, however, is intimately tied up with the former, for Polo's enterprise would scarcely have been possible in an earlier or succeeding century. While trade contacts with the East existed before the thirteenth century, in that century political conditions allowed the egress of Europeans into lands that had hitherto been the shadowy sources of goods increasingly demanded by the well-to-do: drugs, silks and spices. Trading through intermediaries, the prosperous Pisan, Venetian and Genoan merchants had been denied more lucrative access to the primary caravan and sea routes to the East because of the all but impenetrable barrier of the Islamic world. Hostile to the Christian states that continually made war against them during the Crusades (1095–c.1291), and enjoying the monopoly that their enemies coveted, the Islamic empires effectively prevented even the most commercially advanced among the Mediterranean powers from doing much to explore beyond the Middle East. The Crusades themselves, despite some success in establishing mercantile outposts in the eastern Mediterranean, were of limited effect in securing Western interests in the larger trade, though they did help open up the trade itself, Crusaders having brought back to their native lands tastes for eastern commodities that would increasingly have to be supplied. What did open up the East in the thirteenth century to subsequent merchants, diplomats and missionaries, including Marco Polo, came from another quarter, raising new problems and opportunities for the Christian states of medieval Europe.

This challenge came from a force of tremendous military power that took both Europe and the Islamic world by surprise: the Mongols. From their nomadic origins at the edges of the Gobi desert in central Asia, the Mongols built an amazingly organised social, political, and above all imperial structure in a matter of decades. Around 1206, the Mongol nobleman Temujin was elected emperor or Grand Khan, and assumed the new name of Chingis-khan. Before his death in 1227, Chingis had begun the conquest of China, taking Beijing in 1215, and had entered Persia and Russia. Combining superb horsemanship with ruthless suppression of resistance, the Mongol conquerors appeared unstoppable, and the successes of Chingis were advanced by his successors. By the time his famous grandson, Kublai-khan, died in 1294, the Mongol empire included most of the Eurasian continent. The juggernaut was checked only by determined Egyptian resistance in Palestine, and the Mongols' inability to accommodate their military tactics to jungle warfare in India, Burma and the Annam peninsula (Vietnam). In 1240 the Mongols met no such resistance in Poland and Hungary, easily defeating a Polish-Silesian army the following year at the brink of a disunited Europe. Inexplicably, the Mongols did not prosecute their advantage, but turned back, perhaps recalled upon the death of the Grand Khan in 1241.

In his chapters on the history of the Tartars, Marco Polo himself eulogises the Mongols' first imperial ruler, Chingis-khan, as a man of 'approved integrity, great wisdom, commanding eloquence' who reigned with 'justice and moderation' (p. 67), and who forged the nucleus of the empire as much through the force of his personality as the force of arms. However, Polo's nineteenth-century translator, William Marsden, regards Chingis as 'one of those scourges of mankind, which, like plague, pestilence, or famine, is sent from time to time to visit and desolate the world'. The two positions, though separated by centuries, capture something of the complexity of reaction to the Mongols in Polo's day. On the one hand, Marsden's rhetoric recalls the defensive horror of Christian consciousness under threat; the Mongols were associated with the apocalyptic armies of Gog and Magog which, according to Revelations 20: 7-8, were to accompany Satan 'loosed out from his prison' (see Map 2), and they earned the appellation of 'Tartars' after the classical hell, Tartarus. On the other hand, Marco Polo's more generous attitude towards the Mongols recognises them as a civilised people with whom one can do business, and even Christian leaders were quick to recognise that a Mongol alliance against the Muslims could achieve the ends of the Crusades in a blow. Mongol religious tolerance, coupled with the popular legend of a Christian potentate called Prester John exerting influence within the regions of the East, helped promote a sense in which Christianity might establish inroads into the burgeoning empire in ways never possible among the Muslims.[2]

2 In Book 1, Chapter 44–45 of this text, Marco Polo identifies Prester John with a 'prince of the North' to whom the Mongols or Tartars owed allegiance before the rise of Chingis-khan. Chingis defeats Prester John in battle, but marries his daughter. See also Chapter 55.

By mid-century, when the immediate threat to Europe itself was subsiding, diplomats and missionaries began testing the waters of such a Christian-Mongol alliance. On a diplomatic mission at the behest of Pope Innocent IV, John of Plano Carpini reached the Mongol capital of Kara-korum in 1245, and became the first European to proceed east of Baghdad and return to tell the tale with his *History of the Mongols*. In 1253, the year of Marco Polo's birth, a second mission under the Franciscan friar William of Rubruck established contact with the Grand Khan in the name of Louis IX of France, resulting among other achievements in a travel narrative that one modern commentator has praised more highly than Polo's own.[3] Meanwhile the relative stability of the Mongol empire and its guarantee of safety for travellers opened up the possibility of another kind of contact: commerce. In 1260 Marco Polo's father, Niccolo, and uncle, Maffeo, took advantage of this opening by undertaking a trading mission that took them from Venice as far as Bukhara, where they then joined a Mongolian embassy to the court of Kublai-khan. Much pleased with these merchants and intrigued by their accounts of the Latin world, Kublai bade them journey back to their country as *his* emissaries, and instructed them to return to his court at Kanbalu (Beijing) bearing oil from the lamp of the Holy Sepulchre in Jerusalem, as well as a hundred Christian scholars. Niccolo and Maffeo arrived back in Europe in 1269, a year after the death of Pope Clement IV. Unable to gather the scholars without papal orders, the Polo brothers returned to Venice where they awaited the election of a successor. Two years later, the election was not forthcoming, and fearing the Grand Khan's displeasure over their delay, the brothers set out on their travels. Having obtained a letter of explanation from the papal legate at the eastern Mediterranean port of Acre, the Polos departed, only to be recalled soon after by the same legate, who had since been himself elected Pope Gregory X. The new Pope, however, ap-pointed only two missionaries to accompany the expedition, both of whom abandoned the cause after rumours of war reached them in Armenia. The Polos were left with only letters, gifts, and the holy oil for the Grand Khan, but in the event the Mongol emperor proved

3 See Mary B. Campbell, *The Witness and the Other World: Exotic European Travel Writing, 400-1600*, Cornell U P, Ithaca and London 1988 (p. 112)

equally pleased with a new member of the delegation, Maffeo's son Marco, who had accompanied them since Venice.

The Polos would not return to Venice until 1295. In the meantime, Marco came of age and reached his middle years gathering notes and memories from travels whose scope few of his most well-travelled contemporaries could have equalled. By Polo's own account, he became Kublai's trusted envoy, travelling the breadth of the empire on semi-official business, compiling notes for the entertainment of his patron back in Kanbalu. The Travels is in fact a compendium of these journeys as well as of knowledge gathered from other sources, although it is structured around loose itineraries that also sum up Polo's major movements over the twenty-four year period of his life abroad (see Map 3).[4] After a preliminary chapter which provides an overview of the travels, the text details the outward trans-Asian journey from Armenia to the Khan's summer palace at Shandu, the magical description of which concludes the first Book.[5] Book 2 opens with an extended discussion of Kublai's capital at Kanbalu, focusing on the Khan himself, his court, the history of his rule, Mongol customs and religious practices (Ch. 1–26). The rest of the Book relates two separate itineraries radiating from the capital. The first (Ch. 27–49) follows Polo's south-westerly route on an official journey to the outposts of the empire in northern Burma. The second (Ch. 50–77) traces the first leg of Polo's homeward path from Kanbalu south through the Manji province of China, and ends with a beautiful description of Kin-sai, among the finest in the text. In the final Book, Polo recounts his sea route from Zai-tun (Amoy) to the Persian Gulf (Ch. 1-44). Having brought his description to Ormus, however, Polo 'step[s] back, in order to notice some regions lying towards the north' (p. 260), especially Russia, and the polar 'Region of Darkness'. At this point until its conclusion, the text is no longer structured by travel but instead attempts to fill in some of the spaces left in Polo's cosmography.

4 Polo reveals his own artifice in Chapter 28 when he notes that he describes 'not only the countries through which the route immediately lies, but also those in its vicinity, to the right and left' (p. 50).
5 The description of Shandu or 'Xanadu' inspired the poet Coleridge to compose his famous 'Kubla Khan' ('In Xanadu did Kubla Khan/A stately pleasure dome decree . . .').

As this outline might suggest, the figure of Kublai and the empire he embodies knit together the narrative. Kublai's court was the young Polo's first goal; his patronage provided Polo with the means of travel within the empire. Even Polo's homeward voyage becomes a tribute to the mutual esteem between emperor and resourceful traveller, for Polo embarks as the appointed chaperone to the Mongol princess picked by the Grand Khan as the bride for the Khan of Persia. As Polo travels to and from the imperial centre, the presence or absence of the Grand Khan's influence becomes almost a measure of the degree of civilisation achieved by a people and of their integration into a progressive mercantile order. To be sure, this becomes more obvious on the outward journey only beyond Kashcar (p. 51), but even when discussing the former Saracen strongholds of Persia, Polo balances the Tartars' reputation for ruthless depredation against their role as the defenders of free trade; while acknowledging that the 'noble province' (p. 28) of ancient Persia had been overrun by the Mongol hordes, Polo goes on to mention a class of 'savage and bloodthirsty' Persians who 'would not refrain from doing injury to the merchants and travellers, were they not in terror of the eastern Tartars' (p. 30). But for Polo, the Tartars are as much a moral as a coercive force, as his anecdote on the fate of the avaricious khalif of Baldach (Baghdad) illustrates. When his Tartar conquerors realise that the khalif has hoarded his wealth rather than using it to bolster his defences, they immure him in a tower filled with gold but no sustenance: 'I judge,' writes Polo, 'that our Lord Jesus Christ herein thought proper to avenge the wrongs of his faithful Christians, so abhorred by this khalif (p. 24). Closer to the centre of power in the district of Kamul, Polo relates another historical anecdote of men 'addicted to pleasure' who by custom offer their wives, daughters and other female relations 'to accidental guests, who assume the same privileges and meet with the same indulgences as if they were their own wives'. Again the Khan intervenes by banning the practice, relenting only after the gravest protestations of the people of Kamul, with a ringing moral pronouncement: ' "Go, live according to your base customs and manners, and let your wives continue to receive the beggarly wages of their prostitution" '(p. 60–1). It seems that for Polo the Mongols are a good substitute for the civilising work of Christian missionaries (an opinion not shared by the missionaries who preceded him).

Yet for Polo the lesson of Kamul is not that pleasure is a sin, but that excessive pleasure weakens the faculties. The moralising tone of the prose changes to one of wonder and admiration when Polo describes the Khan's own pleasure gardens at Shandu with their 'rich and beautiful meadows, watered by many rivulets' (p. 84), not least one suspects because the Khan has *earned* his respite by ruling well. Indeed, the entire account of Shandu emphasises the control which the Khan exercises over his surroundings: the royal pavilion 'constructed with so much ingenuity of contrivance' lay at 'the centre of these grounds' and all the forests and game that radiate from it seem tributes to 'his majesty's pleasure'. Another cautionary tale towards the end of Book 2 forms an effective contrast. There Polo explores the ruins of the court of King Facfur, former ruler of Kin-sai, and recreates the splendour of its heyday in terms that would recall Shandu, but for the emasculated presence of King Facfur himself. The king surrounds himself with 'a thousand young women' who entertain him with their company, their feats of hunting and their alluring displays:

> No male person was allowed to be of these parties, but on the other hand, the females were practised in the art of coursing with dogs, and pursuing the animals . . . When fatigued with these exercises, they retired into the groves on the banks of the lake, and there quitting their dresses, rushed into the water in a state of nudity, sportively swimming about, some in one direction and some in another, whilst the king remained a spectator of the exhibition . . . Thus was his time consumed amidst the enervating charms of his women, and in profound ignorance of whatever related to martial concerns, the consequence of which was, that his depraved habits and his pusillanimity enabled the grand khan to deprive him of his splendid possessions . . . (p. 196)

Polo himself takes vicarious enjoyment in spectacle – the most satisfying passages in the *Travels* are those in which he describes natural abundance, architectural ornament or curious cultural practices. But the Shandu and Kin-sai tableaux affirm that pleasure is subordinate to power, and that the active life alone, be it of traveller, merchant or ruler, can ensure the permanence of either.

Polo's approach to the city of Kin-sai itself begins with an economic shorthand more typical of his observations throughout his travels than what follows. The outlying districts are 'well-inhabited and opulent', while 'the people are idolaters, and the subjects of the grand khan, and they use paper money and have abundance of provisions'. But Kin-sai promises something different:

> At the end of three days you reach the noble and magnificent city of Kin-sai, a name that signifies 'the celestial city', and which merits its pre-eminence to all others in the world, in point of grandeur and beauty, as well as from its abundant delights, which might lead an inhabitant to imagine himself in paradise. (p. 185)

Kin-sai, the jewel in the crown wrested from King Facfur, becomes for Polo the showpiece of the Mongol empire, more so than even Kanbalu, which features so large at the beginning of Book 2. At Kin-sai, the Khan has achieved the balance between business and pleasure that eluded Facfur, and Polo takes great delight in listing its features: the twelve thousand bridges, the provisions at market ('common fowls, capons, and such numbers of ducks and geese as can scarcely be expressed'), the 'multitudes of people passing and repassing', including courtesans, physicians and astrologers (p. 186–90). This 'celestial city', this paradise, is also a centre of international trade, as Polo applies his Augustinian rhetoric to a city of the world. Kin-sai is Venice transposed, and we realise that all along Polo has been celebrating his own city as much as the Khan's.

Polo found himself defending the values he exemplified in Kin-sai soon after his return to Venice in 1295, for in 1298 the Genoese fleet set out against their Venetian rivals. The defending fleet was crushed and among the commanders taken prisoner was Polo himself. Only then, with time on his hands, did Polo commit his eastern travels to writing, with the help of a scribe, one Rusticello of Pisa, a writer of Alexander and Arthurian romances at the court of Edward I of England. It is difficult to gauge the extent to which Rusticello's mediation colours the text that comes down to us, since romance writing includes stylised descriptions of travelling protagonists.

What is certain is that the *Travels* rather quickly became as much the stuff of legend as of fact. Even as Polo's voice became supplanted by Rusticello's manuscript and that manuscript by subsequent transcriptions and retranscriptions, history was doing its part to distance the text from travel experience. The Mongol empire was in decline and would not survive the coming century. Kublai's death in

1294 left no successor of equal merit. By 1347 the great plague all but finished Europe's contact with the East, and a xenophobic Ming dynasty rose up from the ashes of the Mongol empire. So distant had the East become again that an armchair traveller by the name of Sir John Mandeville captured Europe's imagination with a fantastic travel book pieced together from writers like Polo and William of Rubruck. For contemporaries, Mandeville's work had the air of authenticity, Polo's of fiction. But Polo's story did have its influence on perceptions of the world; the first surviving map incorporating his geographical discoveries dates from 1351, and the Catalan Map of 1371 confirms that picture (see Map 2). And as the riches of Asia that Polo so lovingly described became a distant dream again, a new generation of explorers looked to him for evidence that their goals were worthy. In 1492, one such reader set off to discover a new sea-route to the marvellous East. But another world intervened.

BENJAMIN COLBERT
University of Wolverhampton

FURTHER READING

Mary B. Campbell, *The Witness and the Other World: Exotic European Travel Writing, 400–1600*, Cornell University Press, Ithaca and London 1988

Richard Humble, *Marco Polo*, George Weidenfeld and Nicolson, London 1975

Donald F. Lach, *Asia in the Making of Europe*, Vol. 1, Book 1: *The Century of Discovery*, University of Chicago Press, Chicago and London 1965.

Leonardo Olschki (tr. John A. Scott), *Marco Polo's Asia: An Introduction to His Description of the World Called "Il Milione"*, University of California Press, Berkeley 1960

Eugene O'Neill, "Marco Millions". *Nine Plays*, The Modern Library, New York 1932

J. R. S. Phillips, *The Medieval Expansion of Europe*, Oxford University Press, Oxford 1988

William D. Phillips and Carla Rahn Phillips, *The Worlds of Christopher Columbus*, Cambridge University Press, Cambridge 1992

Eileen Power, *Medieval People*, Methuen, London 1924

Scott D. Westrem, (ed.), *Discovering New Worlds: Essays on Medieval Exploration and Imagination*, Garland, New York and London 1991

Frances Wood, *Did Marco Polo Go to China?* Secker and Warburg, London 1995

NOTES ON THE TEXT

The Travels of Marco Polo exists in numerous early versions, none of which may be said to represent a definitive text, let alone the original manuscript of Rusticello, Marco Polo's copyist. The present text reprints the translation of William Marsden (1754–1836) from the Italian of Giambattista Ramusio's printed edition, dated 1553. First published in 1818, Marsden's is the first major modern English translation of the *Travels* and it remained the authoritative text throughout the nineteenth century. In this century, scholars attempting to piece together Rusticello's (and Polo's) original words have produced new translations that better reflect the complexities of the case, but Ramusio's edition remains a key text and Marsden's translation one of the most readable English renderings for the common reader.

For the purposes of this edition, Marsden's lengthy footnotes (over one third of the 1818 text) have been deemed sufficiently archaic or arcane to be removed altogether. Where confusing, the spelling of names and places has been standardised, although there are enough inconsistencies remaining to give readers a flavour of the quirkiness in the original. Finally, the well-known general prologue that heads this text was omitted from Marsden's edition.

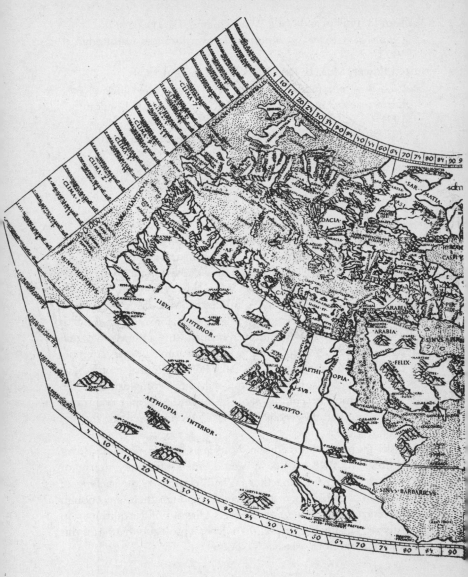

Map 1   Asia from Ptolemy's *Geographia*

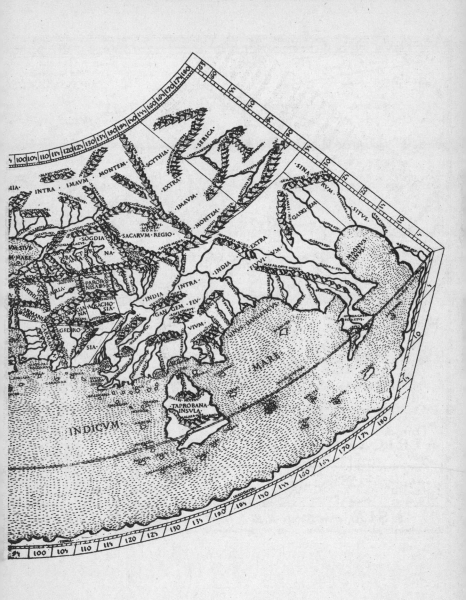

Map 2   The Catalan map of 1375

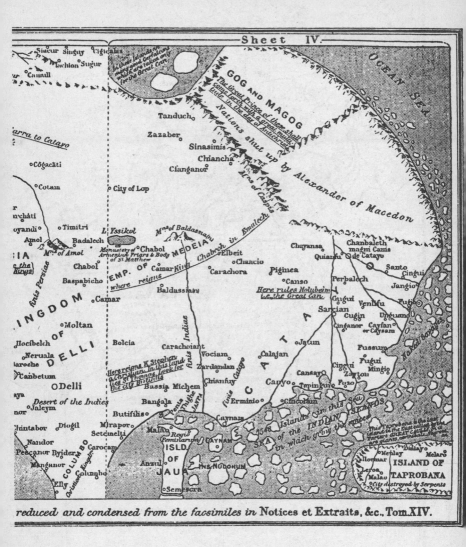

reduced and condensed from the facsimiles in Notices et Extraits, &c., Tom. XIV.

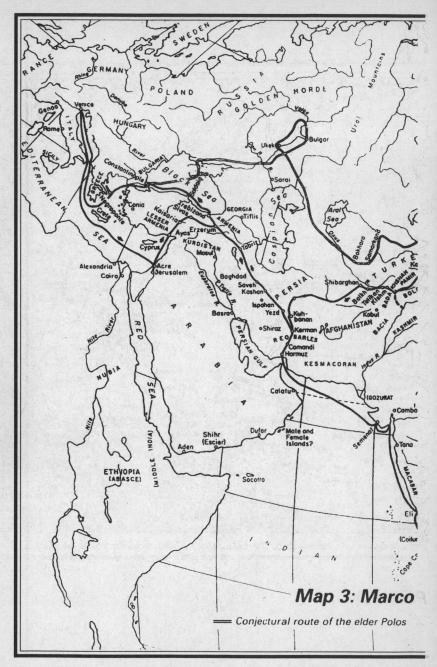

Map 3: Marco

—— Conjectural route of the elder Polos

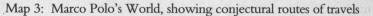

Map 3: Marco Polo's World, showing conjectural routes of travels

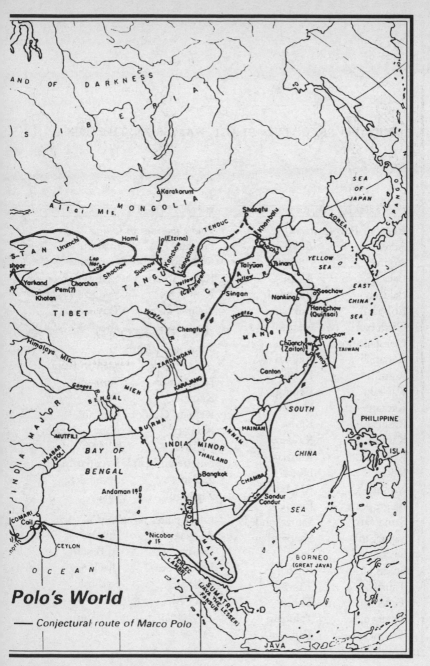

Polo's World

—— Conjectural route of Marco Polo

mentioned in *The Travels of Marco Polo*.

KEY TO SELECTED PLACE NAMES IN THE TEXT

TEXT REFERENCES	MODERN NAME
Route of Polo (outward)	
Acre	Akko
Argiron	Erzurum
Balach	Balkh
Baldach	Baghdad
Bokhara	Bukhara
Charchan	Oiemo
Constantinople	Istanbul
Kaisariah	Kayseri
Kamul	Hami
Kanbalu	Beijing
Karkan	Shache
Kashcar	Kashi
Kasibin	Kashan
Kierman	Kerman
Kotan	Hotan
Mosul	Al Mawsil
Negropont	Evvoia
Samarcan	Samarkand
Sapurgan	Sheberghan
Sevasta	Sivas
Spaan	Esfahan
Tauris	Tabriz
Teflis	Tbilisi
Thaikan	Taloqan
Trebisond	Trabzon

TEXT REFERENCES	MODERN NAME
Polo's journies in China	
Fu-giu	Fuzhou
Kan-giu	Canton
Kara-Moran	Yellow River
Kian River	Yangtze River
Ta-in-fu	Taiyuan
Polo's homeward voyage	
Angaman Island	Andaman Island
Java Minor	Sumatra
Kanan	Thane
Keinan, Gulf of	Hainan
Komari	Cape Comorin
Malaiur	Malaya
Nocueran Island	Nicobar Island
Zeilan	Sri Lanka
Zipangu	Japan
Other places mentioned in map	
Abascia	Ethiopia
Balsara	Al Basrah
Euxine Sea	Black Sea
Kesmur	Kashmir
Thebeth	Tibet
Tholoman	Thailand
Zorzania	Georgia

CONTENTS

BOOK ONE

BOOK TWO

BOOK THREE

BOOK ONE

PROLOGUE

Ye emperors, kings, dukes, marquises, earls, and knights, and all other people desirous of knowing the diversities of the races of mankind, as well as the diversities of kingdoms, provinces, and regions of all parts of the East, read through this book, and ye will find in it the greatest and most marvellous characteristics of the peoples especially of Armenia, Persia, India, and Tartary, as they are severally related in the present work by Marco Polo, a wise and learned citizen of Venice, who states distinctly what things he saw and what things he heard from others. For this book will be a truthful one. It must be known, then, that from the creation of Adam to the present day, no man, whether Pagan, or Saracen, or Christian, or other, of whatever progeny or generation he may have been, ever saw or enquired into so many and such great things as Marco Polo above mentioned. Who, wishing in his secret thoughts that the things he had seen and heard should be made public by the present work, for the benefit of those who could not see them with their own eyes, he himself being in the year of our Lord 1295 in prison at Genoa, caused the things which are contained in the present work to be written by master Rustigielo, a citizen of Pisa, who was with him in the same prison at Genoa; and he divided it into three parts.

§1. It should be known to the reader that, at the time when Baldwin II was emperor of Constantinople, where a magistrate representing the doge of Venice then resided, and in the year of our Lord 1250, Nicolo Polo, the father of the said Marco, and Maffeo, the brother of Nicolo, respectable and well-informed men, embarked in a ship of their own, with a rich and varied cargo of merchandise, and reached Constantinople in safety. After mature deliberation on the subject of their proceedings, it was determined, as the measure most likely to improve their trading capital, that they should prosecute their voyage into the Euxine or Black Sea. With this view they made purchases of many fine and costly jewels, and taking their departure from Constantinople, navigated that sea to a port named Soldaia, from whence they travelled on horseback many days until they reached the court of a powerful chief of the Western Tartars, named Barka, who dwelt in the cities of Bolgara and Assara, and had the reputation of being one of the most liberal and civilised princes hitherto known amongst the tribes of Tartary. He expressed much satisfaction at the arrival of these travellers, and received them with marks of distinction. In return for which courtesy, when they had laid before him the jewels they brought with them, and perceived that their beauty pleased him, they presented them for his acceptance. The liberality of this conduct on the part of the two brothers struck him with admiration; and being unwilling that they should surpass him in generosity, he not only directed double the value of the jewels to be paid to them, but made them in addition several rich presents.

The brothers having resided a year in the dominions of this prince, they became desirous of revisiting their native country, but were impeded by the sudden breaking out of a war between him and another chief, named Alaù, who ruled over the Eastern Tartars. In a fierce and very sanguinary battle that ensued between their respective armies, Alaù was victorious, in consequence of which, the roads being rendered unsafe for travellers, the brothers could not attempt to return by the way they came; and it was recommended to them, as the only practicable mode of reaching Constantinople, to proceed in an easterly direction, by an unfrequented route, so as to skirt the limits of Barka's territories. Accordingly they made their way to a town named Oukaka, situated on the confines of the kingdom of the Western Tartars. Leaving that place, and advancing still farther, they crossed the Tigris, one of the four rivers of Paradise, and came to a desert, the extent of which was seventeen days' journey, wherein they found neither town, castle, nor any substantial building, but only Tartars with their herds, dwelling in tents on the plain. Having passed this tract they arrived at length at a well-built city called Bokhara, in a province of that name, belonging to the dominions of Persia, and the noblest city of that kingdom, but governed by a prince whose name was Barak. Here, from inability to proceed farther, they remained three years.

It happened while these brothers were in Bokhara, that a person of consequence and gifted with eminent talents made his appearance there. He was proceeding as ambassador from Alaù before mentioned, to the Grand Khan, supreme chief of all the Tartars, named Kublai, whose residence was at the extremity of the continent, in a direction between north-east and east. Not having ever before had an opportunity, although he wished it, of seeing any natives of Italy, he was gratified in a high degree at meeting and conversing with these brothers, who had now become proficients in the Tartar language; and after associating with them for several days, and finding their manners agreeable to him, he proposed to them that they should accompany him to the presence of the great khan, who would be pleased by their appearance at his court, which had not hitherto been visited by any person from their country; adding assurances that they would be honourably received, and recompensed with many gifts. Convinced as they were that their endeavours to return homeward would expose them to the most imminent risks, they agreed to this proposal, and recommending themselves to the protection of the Almighty, they set out on their journey in the suite of the ambassador, attended by several Christian servants whom they had brought with them from Venice. The course they took at first was between the north-east and north, and an entire year was consumed before they were enabled to reach the imperial residence, in consequence of the extraordinary delays occasioned by the snows and the swelling of the rivers, which obliged them to halt until the former had melted and the floods had subsided. Many things worthy of admiration were observed by them in the progress of their journey, but which are here omitted, as they will be described by Marco Polo, in the sequel of the book.

§2. Being introduced to the presence of the Grand Khan, Kublai, the travellers were received by him with the condescension and affability that belonged to his character, and as they were the first Latins who had made their appearance in that country, they were entertained with feasts and honoured with other marks of distinction. Entering graciously into conversation with them, he made earnest enquiries on the subject of the western parts of the world, of the emperor of the Romans, and of other Christian kings and princes. He wished to be informed of their relative consequence, the extent of their possessions, the manner in which justice was administered in their several kingdoms and principalities, how they conducted themselves in warfare, and above all he questioned them particularly respecting the Pope, the affairs of the Church, and the religious worship and doctrine of the Christians. Being well instructed and discreet men, they gave appropriate answers upon all these points, and as they were perfectly acquainted with the Tartar (Moghul) language, they expressed themselves always in becoming terms; insomuch that the Grand Khan, holding them in high estimation, frequently commanded their attendance.

When he had obtained all the information that the two brothers communicated with so much good sense, he expressed himself well satisfied, and having formed in his mind the design of employing them as his ambassadors to the Pope, after consulting with his ministers on the subject, he proposed to them, with many kind entreaties, that they should accompany one of his officers, named Khogatal, on a mission to the see of Rome. His object, he told them, was to make a request to his holiness that he would send to him a hundred men of learning, thoroughly acquainted with the principles of the Christian religion, as well as with the seven arts, and qualified to prove to the learned of his dominions by just and fair argument, that the faith professed by Christians is superior to, and founded upon more evident truth than, any other; that the gods of the Tartars and the idols worshipped in their houses were only evil spirits, and that they and the people of the East in general were under an error in reverencing them as divinities. He moreover signified his pleasure that upon their return they should bring with them, from Jerusalem, some of the holy oil from the lamp which is kept burning over the sepulchre of our Lord Jesus Christ, whom he professed to hold in veneration and to consider as the true God. Having heard these commands addressed to them by the Grand Khan they humbly prostrated themselves before him, declaring their willingness and instant readiness to perform, to the utmost of their ability, whatever might be the royal will. Upon which he caused letters, in the Tartarian language, to be written in his name to the Pope of Rome, and these he delivered into their hands. He likewise gave orders that they should be furnished with a golden tablet displaying the imperial cipher, according to the usage established by his majesty; in virtue of which the person bearing it, together with his whole suite, are safely conveyed and escorted from station to station by the governors of all places within the imperial dominions, and are entitled, during the time of their residing in any city, castle, town, or village, to a supply of provisions and everything necessary for their accommodation.

Being thus honourably commissioned they took their leave of the Grand Khan, and set out on their journey, but had not proceeded more than twenty days when the officer, named Khogatal, their companion, fell dangerously ill, in the city named Alau. In this dilemma it was determined, upon consulting all who were present, and with the approbation of the man himself, that they should leave him behind. In the prosecution of their journey they derived essential benefit from being provided with the royal tablet, which procured them attention in every place through which they passed. Their expenses were defrayed, and escorts were furnished. But notwithstanding these advantages, so great were the natural difficulties they had to encounter, from the extreme cold, the snow, the ice, and the flooding of the rivers, that their progress was unavoidably tedious, and three years elapsed before they were enabled to reach a sea-port town in the lesser Armenia, named Laiassus. Departing from thence by sea, they arrived at Acre in the month of April, 1269, and there learned, with extreme concern, that Pope Clement the Fourth was recently dead. A legate whom he had appointed, named M. Tebaldo de' Vesconti di Piacenza, was at this time resident in Acre, and to him they gave an account of what they had in command from the Grand Khan of Tartary. He advised them by all means to wait the election of another pope, and when that should take place, to proceed with the object of their embassy. Approving of this counsel, they determined upon employing the interval in a visit to their families in Venice. They accordingly embarked at Acre in a ship bound to Negropont, and from thence went on to Venice, where Nicolo Polo found that his wife, whom he had left with child at his departure, was dead, after having been delivered of a son, who received the name of Marco, and was now of the age of nineteen years. This is the Marco by whom the present work is composed, and who will give therein a relation of all those matters of which he has been an eye-witness.

§3. In the meantime the election of a pope was retarded by so many obstacles, that they remained two years in Venice, continually expecting its accomplishment; when at length, becoming apprehensive that the Grand Khan might be displeased at their delay, or might suppose it was not their intention to revisit his country, they judged it expedient to return to Acre; and on this occasion they took with them young Marco Polo. Under the sanction of the legate they made a visit to Jerusalem, and there provided themselves with some of the oil belonging to the lamp of the holy sepulchre, conformably to the directions of the Grand Khan. As soon as they were furnished with his letters addressed to that prince bearing testimony to the fidelity with which they had endeavoured to execute his commission, and explaining to him that the Pope of the Christian Church had not as yet been chosen, they proceeded to the before-mentioned port of Laiassus. Scarcely however had they taken their departure, when the legate received messengers from Italy, despatched by the college of cardinals, announcing his own elevation to the papal chair; and he thereupon assumed the name of Gregory the Tenth. Considering that he was now in a situation that enabled him fully to satisfy the wishes of the Tartar sovereign, he hastened to transmit letters to the king of Armenia, communicating to him the event of his election, and requesting, in case the two ambassadors who were on their way to the court of the Grand Khan should not have already quitted his dominions, that he would give directions for their immediate return. These letters found them still in Armenia, and with great alacrity they obeyed the summons to repair once more to Acre; for which purpose the king furnished them with an armed galley; sending at the same time an ambassador from himself, to offer his congratulations to the sovereign pontiff.

Upon their arrival, his holiness received them in a distinguished manner, and immediately despatched them with letters papal, accompanied by two friars of the Order of Preachers, who happened to be on the spot; men of letters and of science, as well as profound theologians. One of them was named Fra Nicolo da Vicenza, and the other, Fra Guielmo da Tripoli. To them he gave licence and authority to ordain priests, to consecrate bishops, and to grant absolution as fully as he could do in his own person. He also charged them with valuable presents, and among these, several handsome vases of crystal, to be delivered to the Grand Khan in his name, and along with his benediction. Having taken leave, they again steered their course to the port of Laiassus, where they landed, and from thence proceeded into the country of Armenia. Here they received intelligence that the soldan of Babylonia, named Bundokdari, had invaded the Armenian territory with a numerous army, and had overrun and laid waste the country to a great extent. Terrified at these accounts, and apprehensive for their lives, the two friars determined not to proceed further, and delivering over to the Venetians the letters and presents entrusted to them by the Pope, they placed themselves under the protection of the master of the knights templars, and with him returned directly to the coast. Nicolo, Maffeo, and Marco, however, undismayed by perils or difficulties (to which they had long been inured), passed the borders of Armenia, and prosecuted their journey. After crossing deserts of several days' march, and passing many dangerous defiles, they advanced so far, in a direction between north-east and north, that at length they gained information of the Grand Khan, who then had his residence in a large and magnificent city named Cle-men-fu. Their whole journey to this place occupied no less than three years and a half; but, during the winter months, their progress had been inconsiderable. The Grand Khan having notice of their approach whilst still remote, and being aware how much they must have suffered from fatigue, sent forward to meet them at the distance of forty days' journey, and gave orders to prepare in every place through which they were to pass, whatever might be requisite to their comfort. By these means, and through the blessing of God, they were conveyed in safety to the royal court.

§4. Upon their arrival they were honourably and graciously received by the Grand Khan, in a full assembly of his principal officers. When they drew nigh to his person, they paid their respects by prostrating themselves on the floor. He immediately commanded them to rise, and to relate to him the circumstances of their travels, with all that had taken place in their negotiation with his holiness the Pope. To their narrative, which they gave in the regular order of events, and delivered in perspicuous language, he listened with attentive silence. The letters and the presents from Pope Gregory were then laid before him, and, upon hearing the former read, he bestowed much commendation on the fidelity, the zeal, and the diligence of his ambassadors; and receiving with due reverence the oil from the holy sepulchre, he gave directions that it should be preserved with religious care. Upon his observing Marco Polo, and enquiring who he was, Nicolo made answer, 'That is your servant, and my son'; upon which the Grand Khan replied, 'He is welcome, and it pleases me much,' and he caused him to be enrolled amongst his attendants of honour. And on account of their return he made a great feast and rejoicing; and as long as the said brothers and Marco remained in the court of the Grand Khan, they were honoured even above his own courtiers. Marco was held in high estimation and respect by all belonging to the court. He learnt in a short time and adopted the manners of the Tartars, and acquired a proficiency in four different languages, which he became qualified to read and write. Finding him thus accomplished, his master was desirous of putting his talents for business to the proof, and sent him on an important concern of state to a city named Karazan, situated at the distance of six months' journey from the imperial residence; on which occasion he conducted himself with so much wisdom and prudence in the management of the affairs entrusted to him, that his services became highly acceptable. On his part, perceiving that the Grand Khan took a pleasure in hearing accounts of whatever was new to him respecting the customs and manners of people, and the peculiar circumstances of distant countries, he endeavoured, wherever he went, to obtain correct information on these subjects, and made notes of all he saw and heard, in order to gratify the curiosity of his master. In short, during seventeen years that he continued in his service, he rendered himself so useful, that he was employed on confidential missions to every part of the empire and its dependencies; and sometimes also he travelled on his own private account, but always with the consent, and sanctioned by the authority, of the Grand Khan. Under such circumstances it was that Marco Polo had the opportunity of acquiring a knowledge, either by his own observation, or what he collected from others, of so many things, until his time unknown, respecting the eastern parts of the world, and which he diligently and regularly committed to writing, as in the sequel will appear. And by this means he obtained so much honour, that he provoked the jealousy of the other officers of the court.

§5. Our Venetians having now resided many years at the imperial court, and in that time having realised considerable wealth, in jewels of value and in gold, felt a strong desire to revisit their native country, and, however honoured and caressed by the sovereign, this sentiment was ever predominant in their minds. It became the more decidedly their object, when they reflected on the very advanced age of the Grand Khan, whose death, if it should happen previously to their departure, might deprive them of that public assistance by which alone they could expect to surmount the innumerable difficulties of so long a journey, and reach their homes in safety; which on the contrary, in his lifetime, and through his favour, they might reasonably hope to accomplish. Nicolo Polo accordingly took an opportunity one day, when he observed him to be more than usually cheerful, of throwing himself at his feet, and soliciting on behalf of himself and his family to be indulged with his majesty's gracious permission for their departure. But far from showing himself disposed to comply with the request, he appeared hurt at the application, and asked what motive they could have for wishing to expose themselves to all the inconveniences and hazards of a journey in which they might probably lose their lives. If gain, he said, was their object, he was ready to give them the double of whatever they possessed, and to gratify them with honours to the extent of their desires; but that, from the regard he bore to them, he must positively refuse their petition.

It happened, about this period, that a queen named Bolgana, the wife of Arghun, sovereign of India, died, and as her last request (which she likewise left in a testamentary writing) conjured her husband that no one might succeed to her place on his throne and in his affections, who was not a descendant of her own family, now settled under the dominion of the Grand Khan, in the country of Kathay. Desirous of complying with this solemn entreaty, Arghun deputed three of his nobles, discreet men, whose names were Ulatai, Apusca, and Goza, attended by a numerous retinue, as his ambassadors to the Grand Khan, with a request that he might receive at his hands a maiden to wife, from among the relatives of his deceased queen. The application was taken in good part, and under the directions of his majesty, choice was made of a damsel aged seventeen, extremely handsome and accomplished, whose name was Kogatin, and of whom the ambassadors, upon her being shown to them, highly approved. When everything was arranged for their departure, and a numerous suite of attendants appointed, to do honour to the future consort of King Arghun, they received from the Grand Khan a gracious dismissal, and set out on their return by the way they came. Having travelled for eight months, their further progress was obstructed and the roads shut up against them, by fresh wars that had broken out amongst the Tartar princes. Much against their inclinations, therefore, they were constrained to adopt the measure of returning to the court of the Grand Khan, to whom they stated the interruption they had met with.

About the time of their reappearance, Marco Polo happened to arrive from a voyage he had made, with a few vessels under his orders, to some parts of the East Indies, and reported to the Grand Khan the intelligence he brought respecting the countries he had visited, with the circumstances of his own navigation, which, he said, was performed in those seas with the utmost safety. This latter observation having reached the ears of the three ambassadors, who were extremely anxious to return to their own country, from whence they had now been absent three years, they presently sought a conference with our Venetians, whom they found equally desirous of revisiting their home; and it was settled between them that the former, accompanied by their young queen, should obtain an audience of the Grand Khan, and represent to him with what convenience and security they might effect their return by sea, to the dominions of their master; whilst the voyage would be attended with less expense than the journey by land, and be performed in a shorter time; according to the experience of Marco Polo, who had lately sailed in those parts. Should his majesty incline to give his consent to their adopting that mode of conveyance, they were then to urge him to suffer the three Europeans, as being persons well skilled in the practice of navigation, to accompany them until they should reach the territory of King Arghun. The Grand Khan upon receiving this application showed by his countenance that it was exceedingly displeasing to him, averse as he was to parting with the Venetians.

Feeling nevertheless that he could not with propriety do otherwise than consent, he yielded to their entreaty. Had it not been that he found himself constrained by the importance and urgency of this peculiar case, they would never otherwise have obtained permission to withdraw themselves from his service. He sent for them, however, and addressed them with much kindness and condescension, assuring them of his regard, and requiring from them a promise that when they should have resided some time in Europe and with their own family, they would return to him once more. With this object in view he caused them to be furnished with the golden tablet (or royal *chop*), which contained his order for their having free and safe conduct through every part of his dominions, with the needful supplies for themselves and their attendants. He likewise gave them authority to act in the capacity of his ambassadors to the Pope, the kings of France and Spain, and the other Christian princes.

At the same time preparations were made for the equipment of fourteen ships, each having four masts, and capable of being navigated with nine sails, the construction and rigging of which would admit of ample description; but, to avoid prolixity, it is for the present omitted. Among these vessels there were at least four or five that had crews of two hundred and fifty or two hundred and sixty men. On them were embarked the ambassadors, having the queen under their protection, together with Nicolo, Maffeo, and Marco Polo, when they had first taken their leave of the Grand Khan, who presented them with many rubies and other handsome jewels of great value. He also gave directions that the ships should be furnished with stores and provisions for two years.

§6. After a navigation of about three months, they arrived at an island which lay in a southerly direction, named Java, where they saw various objects worthy of attention, of which notice shall be taken in the sequel of the work. Taking their departure from thence, they employed eighteen months in the Indian seas before they were enabled to reach the place of their destination in the territory of King Arghun; and during this part of their voyage also they had an opportunity of observing many things, which shall, in like manner, be related hereafter. But here it may be proper to mention, that between the day of their sailing and that of their arrival, they lost by deaths, of the crews of the vessels and others who were embarked, about six hundred persons; and of the three ambassadors, only one, whose name was Goza, survived the voyage; whilst of all the ladies and female attendants one only died.

Upon landing they were informed that King Arghun had died some time before, and that the government of the country was then administered, on behalf of his son, who was still a youth, by a person of the name of Ki-akato. From him they desired to receive instructions as to the manner in which they were to dispose of the princess, whom, by the orders of the late king, they had conducted thither. His answer was, that they ought to present the lady to Kasan, the son of Arghun, who was then at a place on the borders of Persia, which has its denomination from the Arbor Secco, where an army of sixty thousand men was assembled for the purpose of guarding certain passes against the irruption of the enemy. This they proceeded to carry into execution, and having effected it, they returned to the residence of Ki-akato, because the road they were afterwards to take lay in that direction. Here, however, they reposed themselves for the space of nine months. When they took their leave he furnished them with four golden tablets, each of them a cubit in length, five inches wide, and weighing three or four marks of gold. Their inscription began with invoking the blessing of the Almighty upon the Grand Khan, that his name might be held in reverence for many years, and denouncing the punishment of death and confiscation of goods to all who should refuse obedience to the mandate. It then proceeded to direct that the three ambassadors, as his representatives, should be treated throughout his dominions with due honour, that their expenses should be defrayed, and that they should be provided with the necessary escorts. All this was fully complied with, and from many places they were protected by bodies of two hundred horse; nor could this have been dispensed with as the government of Ki-akato was unpopular, and the people were disposed to commit insults and proceed to outrages, which they would not have dared to attempt under the rule of their proper sovereign. In the course of their journey our travellers received intelligence of the Grand Khan (Kublai) having departed this life; which entirely put an end to all prospect of their revisiting those regions. Pursuing, therefore, their intended route, they at length reached the city of Trebizond, from whence they proceeded to Constantinople, then to Negropont, and finally to Venice, at which place, in the enjoyment of health and abundant riches, they safely arrived in the year 1295. On this occasion they offered up their thanks to God, who had now been pleased to relieve them from such great fatigues, after having preserved them from innumerable perils. The foregoing narrative may be considered as a preliminary chapter, the object of which is to make the reader acquainted with the opportunities Marco Polo had of acquiring a knowledge of the things he describes, during a residence of so many years in the eastern parts of the world.

CHAPTER II

*Of Armenia Minor – Of the Port of Laiassus – And of the
Boundaries of the Province*

In commencing the description of the countries which Marco Polo visited in Asia, and of things worthy of notice which he observed therein, it is proper to mention that we are to distinguish two Armenias, the Lesser and the Greater. The king of the Lesser Armenia dwells in a city called Sebastoz, and rules his dominions with strict regard to justice. The towns, fortified places, and castles are numerous. There is abundance of all necessaries of life, as well as of those things which contribute to its comfort. Game, both of beasts and birds, is in plenty. It must be said, however, that the air of the country is not remarkably healthy. In former times its gentry were esteemed expert and brave soldiers; but at the present day they are great drinkers, pusillanimous, and worthless. On the sea-coast there is a city named Laiassus, a place of considerable traffic. Its port is frequented by merchants from Venice, Genoa, and many other places, who trade in spiceries and drugs of different sorts, manufactures of silk and of wool, and other rich commodities. Those persons who design to travel into the interior of the Levant, usually proceed in the first instance to this port of Laiassus. The boundaries of the Lesser Armenia are, on the south, the Land of Promise, now occupied by the Saracens; on the north, Karamania, inhabited by Turkomans; towards the north-east lie the cities of Kaisariah, Sevasta, and many others subject to the Tartars; and on the western side it is bounded by the sea, which extends to the shores of Christendom.

CHAPTER III

Of the Province called Turkomania, where are the Cities of Kogni, Kaisariah, and Sevasta, and of its Commerce

The inhabitants of Turkomania may be distinguished into three classes. The Turkomans, who reverence Mahomet and follow his law, are a rude people, and dull of intellect. They dwell amongst the mountains and in places difficult of access, where their object is to find good pasture for their cattle, as they live entirely upon animal food. There is here an excellent breed of horses which has the appellation of Turki, and fine mules which are sold at high prices. The other classes are Greeks and Armenians, who reside in the cities and fortified places, and gain their living by commerce and manufacture. The best and handsomest carpets in the world are wrought here, and also silks of crimson and other rich colours. Amongst its cities are those of Kogni, Kaisariah, and Sevasta, in which last Saint Blaise obtained the glorious crown of martyrdom. They are all subject to the great khan, emperor of the Oriental Tartars, who appoints governors to them. We shall now speak of the Greater Armenia.

CHAPTER IV

Of Armenia Major, in which are the Cities of Arzingan, Argiron, and Darziz – Of the Castle of Paipurth – Of the Mountain where the Ark of Noah rested – Of the Boundaries of the Province – And of a Remarkable Fountain of Oil

Armenia Major is an extensive province, at the entrance of which is a city named Arzingan, where there is a manufacture of very fine cotton cloth called bombazines, as well as of many other curious fabrics, which it would be tedious to enumerate. It possesses the handsomest and most excellent baths of warm water, issuing from the earth, that are anywhere to be found. Its inhabitants are for the most part native Armenians, but under the dominion of the Tartars. In this province there are many cities, but Arzingan is the principal, and the seat of an archbishop; and the next in consequence are Argiron and Darziz. It is very extensive, and, in the summer season, the station of a part of the army of the Eastern Tartars, on account of the good pasture it affords for their cattle; but on the approach of winter they are obliged to change their quarters, the fall of snow being so very deep that the horses could not find subsistence, and for the sake of warmth and fodder they proceed to the southward. Within a castle named Paipurth, which you meet with in going from Trebisond to Tauris, there is a rich mine of silver. In the central part of Armenia stands an exceedingly large and high mountain, upon which, it is said, the ark of Noah rested, and for this reason it is termed the mountain of the ark. The circuit of its base cannot be compassed in less than two days. The ascent is impracticable on account of the snow towards the summit, which never melts, but goes on increasing by each successive fall. In the lower region, however, near the plain, the melting of the snow fertilises the ground, and occasions such an abundant vegetation, that all the cattle which collect there in summer from the neighbouring country, meet with a never-failing supply. Bordering upon Armenia, to the south-west, are the districts of Mosul and Maredin, which shall be described hereafter, and many others too numerous to particularise. To the north lies Zorzania, near the confines of which there is a fountain of oil which discharges so great a quantity as to furnish loading for many camels. The use made of it is not for the purpose of food, but as an unguent for the cure of cutaneous distempers in men and cattle, as well as other complaints; and it is also good for burning. In the neighbouring country no other is used in their lamps, and people come from distant parts to procure it.

CHAPTER V

Of the Province of Zorzania and its Boundaries — Of the
Pass where Alexander the Great constructed the Gate of
Iron — And of the miraculous Circumstances attending a
Fountain at Teflis

In Zorzania the king is usually styled David Melik, which in our
language signifies David the king. One part of the country is subject
to the Tartars, and the other part, in consequence of the strength of
its fortresses, has remained in the possession of its native princes. It is
situated between two seas, of which that on the northern (western)
side is called the Greater sea (Euxine), and the other, on the eastern
side, is called the sea of Abakù (Caspian). This latter is in circuit two
thousand eight hundred miles, and partakes of the nature of a lake,
not communicating with any other sea. It has several islands, with
handsome towns and castles, some of which are inhabited by people
who fled before the grand Tartar, when he laid waste the kingdom or
province of Persia, and took shelter in these islands or in the fastnesses
of the mountains, where they hoped to find security. Some of the
islands are uncultivated. This sea produces abundance of fish,
particularly sturgeon and salmon at the mouths of the rivers, as well as
others of a large sort. The general wood of the country is the box
tree. I was told that in ancient times the kings of the country were
born with the mark of an eagle on the right shoulder. The people are
well made, bold sailors, expert archers, and fair combatants in battle.
They are Christians, observing the ritual of the Greek Church, and
wear their hair short, in the manner of the Western clergy. This is the
province into which, when Alexander the Great attempted to
advance northwards, he was unable to penetrate, by reason of the
narrowness and difficulty of a certain pass, which on one side is
washed by the sea, and is confined on the other by high mountains
and woods, for the length of four miles; so that a very few men were
capable of defending it against the whole world. Disappointed in this
attempt, Alexander caused a great wall to be constructed at the

entrance of the pass, and fortified it with towers, in order to restrain those who dwelt beyond it from giving him molestation. From its uncommon strength the pass obtained the name of the Gate of Iron, and Alexander is commonly said to have enclosed the Tartars between two mountains. It is not correct, however, to call the people Tartars, which in those days they were not, but of a race named Cumani, with a mixture of other nations. In this province there are many towns and castles, the necessaries of life are in abundance; the country produces a great quantity of silk, and a manufacture is carried on of silk interwoven with gold. Here are found vultures of a large size, of a species named *avigi*. The inhabitants in general gain their livelihood by trade and manual labour. The mountainous nature of the country, with its narrow and strong defiles, have prevented the Tartars from effecting the entire conquest of it. At a convent of monks dedicated to Saint Lunardo, the following miraculous circumstances are said to take place. In a saltwater lake, four days' journey in circuit, upon the border of which the church is situated, the fish never make their appearance until the first day of Lent, and from that time to Easter Eve they are found in vast abundance; but on Easter Day they are no longer to be seen, nor during the remainder of the year. It is called the lake of Geluchalat. Into the before-mentioned sea of Abakù, which is encompassed with mountains, the great rivers Herdil, Geihon, Kur, and Araz, with many others, disembogue. The Genoese merchants have recently begun to navigate it, and they bring from thence the kind of silk called *ghellie*. In this province there is a handsome city named Teflis, around which are suburbs and many fortified posts. It is inhabited by Armenian and Georgian Christians, as well as by some Mahometans and Jews; but these last are in no great numbers. Manufactures of silks and of many other articles are carried on there. Its inhabitants are subjects of the great king of the Tartars. Although we speak only of a few of the principal cities in each province, it is to be understood that there are many others, which it is unnecessary to particularise, unless they happened to contain something remarkable; but should the occasion present itself, these will be hereafter described. Having spoken of the countries bordering on Armenia to the north, we shall now mention those which lie to the south and to the east.

CHAPTER VI

*Of the Province of Mosul and its different Inhabitants – Of
the People named Kurds – And of the Trade of this Country*

Mosul is a large province inhabited by various descriptions of people,
one class of whom pay reverence to Mahomet, and are called
Arabians. The others profess the Christian faith, but not according to
the canons of the Church, which they depart from in many instances,
and are denominated Nestorians, Jacobites, and Armenians. They
have a patriarch whom they call Jacolit, and by him archbishops,
bishops, and abbots are consecrated and sent to all parts of India, to
Cairo, to Baldach (Baghdad), and to all places inhabited by Christians;
in the same manner as by the Pope of the Romish Church. All those
cloths of gold and of silk which we call muslins are of the
manufacture of Mosul, and all the great merchants termed Mossulini,
who convey spices and drugs, in large quantities, from one country to
another, are from this province. In the mountainous parts there is a
race of people named Kurds, some of whom are Christians of the
Nestorian and Jacobite sects, and others Mahometans. They are all an
unprincipled people, whose occupation it is to rob the merchants. In
the vicinity of this province there are places named Mus and
Maredin, where cotton is produced in great abundance, of which
they prepare the cloths called boccasini, and many other fabrics. The
inhabitants are manufacturers and traders, and are all subjects of the
king of the Tartars. We shall now speak of the city of Baldach.

CHAPTER VII

*Of the great City of Baldach or Bagadet, anciently called
Babylon — Of the Navigation from thence to Balsara,
situated in what is termed the Sea of India, but properly the
Persian Gulf — And of the various Sciences studied in that
City*

Baldach is a large city, heretofore the residence of the khalif or pontiff
of all the Saracens, as the Pope is of all Christians. A great river flows
through the midst of it, by means of which the merchants transport
their goods to and from the sea of India; the distance being computed
at seventeen days' navigation, in consequence of the windings of its
course. Those who undertake the voyage, after leaving the river,
touch at a place named Kisi, from whence they proceed to sea: but
previously to their reaching this anchorage they pass a city named
Balsara, in the vicinity of which are groves of palm trees producing
the best dates in the world. In Baldach there is a manufacture of silks
wrought with gold, and also of damasks, as well as of velvets
ornamented with the figures of birds and beasts. Almost all the pearls
brought to Europe from India have undergone the process of boring,
at this place. The Mahometan law is here regularly studied, as are also
magic, physics, astronomy, geomancy, and physiognomy. It is the
noblest and most extensive city to be found in this part of the world.

CHAPTER VIII

Concerning the Capture and Death of the Khalif of Baldach,
and the miraculous Removal of a Mountain

The above-mentioned khalif, who is understood to have amassed greater treasures than had ever been possessed by any other sovereign, perished miserably under the following circumstances. At the period when the Tartar princes began to extend their dominion, there were amongst them four brothers, of whom the eldest, named Mangu, reigned in the royal seat of the family. Having subdued the country of Cathay, and other districts in that quarter, they were not satisfied, but coveting further territory, they conceived the idea of universal empire, and proposed that they should divide the world amongst them. With this object in view, it was agreed that one of them should proceed to the east, that another should make conquests in the south, and that the other two should direct their operations against the remaining quarters. The southern portion fell to the lot of Ulaù, who assembled a vast army, and having subdued the provinces through which his route lay, proceeded in the year 1255 to the attack of this city of Baldach. Being aware, however, of its great strength and the prodigious number of its inhabitants, he trusted rather to stratagem than to force for its reduction, and in order to deceive the enemy with regard to the number of his troops, which consisted of a hundred thousand horse, besides foot soldiers, he posted one division of his army on the one side, another division on the other side of the approach to the city, in such a manner as to be concealed by a wood, and placing himself at the head of the third, advanced boldly to within a short distance of the gate. The khalif made light of a force apparently so inconsiderable, and confident in the efficacy of the usual Mahometan ejaculation, thought of nothing less than its entire destruction, and for that purpose marched out of the city with his guards; but as soon as Ulaù perceived his approach, he feigned to retreat before him, until by this means he had drawn him beyond the wood where the other divisions were posted. By the closing of these from both sides, the army of the khalif was surrounded and broken, himself was made prisoner, and the city surrendered to the conqueror. Upon entering it, Ulaù discovered, to his great astonishment, a tower filled with gold. He called the khalif before him, and after reproaching him with his avarice, that prevented him from employing his treasures in the formation of an army for the defence of his capital against the powerful invasion with which it had long been threatened, gave orders for his being shut up in this same tower, without sustenance; and there, in the midst of his wealth, he soon finished a miserable existence.

I judge that our Lord Jesus Christ herein thought proper to avenge the wrongs of his faithful Christians, so abhorred by this khalif. From the time of his accession in 1225, his daily thoughts were employed on the means of converting to his religion those who resided within his dominions, or, upon their refusal, in forming pretences for putting them to death. Consulting with his learned men for this purpose, they discovered a passage in the Gospel where it is said: 'If ye have faith as a grain of mustard seed, ye shall say unto this mountain, Remove hence to yonder place, and it shall remove,' (upon prayer to that effect addressed to the Divine Majesty); and being rejoiced at the discovery, persuaded as he was that the thing was utterly impossible, he gave orders for assembling all the Nestorian and Jacobite Christians who dwelt in Baghdad, and who were very numerous. To these the question was propounded, whether they believed all that is asserted in the text of their Gospel to be true, or not. They made answer that it was true. 'Then,' said the khalif, 'if it be true, let us see which of you will give the proof of his faith; for certainly if there is not to be found one amongst you who possesses even so small a portion of faith in his Lord, as to be equal to a grain of mustard, I shall be justified in regarding you, henceforth, as a wicked, reprobate, and faithless people. I allow you therefore ten days, before the expiration of which you must either, through the power of Him whom you worship, remove the mountain now before you, or embrace the law of our prophet; in either of which cases you will be safe; but otherwise you must all expect to suffer the most cruel deaths.' The Christians, acquainted as they were with his merciless disposition, as well as his eagerness to despoil them of their property, upon hearing these words, trembled for their lives; but nevertheless, having confidence in their Redeemer, that He would deliver them from their peril, they held an assembly and deliberated on the course they ought to take. None other presented itself than that of imploring the Divine Being to grant them the aid of His mercy. To obtain this, every individual, great and small, prostrated himself night and day upon the earth, shedding tears profusely, and attending to no other occupation than that of prayer to the Lord. When they had thus persevered during eight days, a divine revelation came at length, in a dream, to a bishop of exemplary life, directing him to proceed in search of a certain shoemaker (whose name is not known) having only one eye, whom he should summon to the mountain, as a person capable of effecting its removal, through the divine grace. Having found the shoemaker and made him acquainted with the revelation, he replied that he did not feel himself worthy of the undertaking, his merits not being such as to entitle him to the reward of such abundant grace. Importuned, however, by the poor terrified Christians, he at length assented. It should be understood that he was a man of strict morals and pious conversation, having his mind pure and faithful to his God, regularly attending the celebration of the mass and other divine offices, fervent in works of charity, and rigid in the observance of fasts. It once happened to him, that a handsome young woman who came to his shop in order to be fitted with a pair of slippers, in presenting her foot, accidentally exposed a part of her leg, the beauty of which excited in him a momentary concupiscence; but recollecting himself, he presently dismissed her, and calling to mind the words of the Gospel, where it is said, 'If thine eye offend thee, pluck it out and cast it from thee; for it is better to enter the kingdom of God with one eye, than having two eyes, to be cast into hell fire,' he immediately, with an instrument of his trade, scooped out his right eye; evincing by that act, beyond all doubt, the excellence of his faith.

The appointed day being arrived, divine service was performed at an early hour, and a solemn procession was made to the plain where the mountain stood, the holy cross being borne in front. The khalif likewise, in the conviction of its proving a vain ceremony on the part of the Christians, chose to be present, accompanied by a number of his guards, for the purposing of destroying them in the event of failure. Here the pious artisan, kneeling before the cross, and lifting up his hands to heaven, humbly besought his Creator that he would compassionately look down upon earth, and for the glory and excellence of his name, as well as for the support and confirmation of the Christian faith, would lend assistance to his people in the accomplishment of the task imposed upon them, and thus manifest his power to the revilers of his law. Having concluded his prayer, he cried with a loud voice: 'In the name of the Father, Son, and Holy Ghost, I command thee, O mountain, to remove thyself!' Upon these words being uttered, the mountain moved, and the earth at the same time trembled in a wonderful and alarming manner. The khalif and all those by whom he was surrounded, were struck with terror, and remained in a state of stupefaction. Many of the latter became Christians, and even the khalif secretly embraced Christianity, always wearing a cross concealed under his garment, which after his death was found upon him; and on this account it was that they did not entomb him in the shrine of his predecessors. In commemoration of this singular grace bestowed upon them by God, all the Christians, Nestorians, and Jacobites, from that time forth have continued to celebrate in a solemn manner the return of the day on which the miracle took place; keeping a fast also on the vigil.

CHAPTER IX

Of the noble City of Tauris, in Irak, and of its Commercial and other Inhabitants

Tauris is a large and very noble city belonging to the province of Irak, which contains many other cities and fortified places, but this is the most eminent and most populous. The inhabitants support themselves principally by commerce and manufactures, which latter consist of various kinds of silk, some of them interwoven with gold, and of high price. It is so advantageously situated for trade, that merchants from India, from Baldach, Mosul, Cremessor, as well as from different parts of Europe, resort thither to purchase and to sell a number of articles. Precious stones and pearls in abundance may be procured at this place. The merchants concerned in foreign commerce acquire considerable wealth, but the inhabitants in general are poor. They consist of a mixture of various nations and sects, Nestorians, Armenians, Jacobites, Georgians, Persians, and the followers of

Mahomet, who form the bulk of the population, and are those properly called Taurisians. Each description of people have their peculiar language. The city is surrounded with delightful gardens, producing the finest fruits. The Mahometan inhabitants are treacherous and unprincipled. According to their doctrine, whatever is stolen or plundered from others of a different faith, is properly taken, and the theft is no crime; whilst those who suffer death or injury by the hands of Christians, are considered as martyrs. If, therefore, they were not prohibited and restrained by the powers who now govern them, they would commit many outrages. These principles are common to all the Saracens. When they are at the point of death, their priest attends upon them, and asks whether they believe that Mahomet was the true apostle of God. If their answer be that they do believe, their salvation is assured to them; and in consequence of this facility of absolution, which gives free scope to the perpetration of everything flagitious, they have succeeded in converting to their faith a great proportion of the Tartars, who consider it as relieving them from restraint in the commission of crimes. From Tauris to Persia is twelve days' journey.

CHAPTER X

Of the Monastery of Saint Barsamo, in the Neighbourhood of Tauris

Not far from Tauris is a monastery that takes its name from the holy saint Barsamo, and is eminent for devotion. There is here an abbot and many monks, who resemble the order of Carmelites in the fashion of their dress. That they may not lead a life of idleness, they employ themselves continually in the weaving of woollen girdles, which they place upon the altar of their saint during the celebration of divine service, and when they make the circuit of the provinces, soliciting alms (in the same manner as do the brethren of the order of the Holy Ghost), they present these girdles to their friends and to persons of distinction; being esteemed good for rheumatic pains, on which account they are devoutly sought for by all ranks.

CHAPTER XI

Of the Province of Persia

Persia was anciently a large and noble province, but it is now a great part destroyed by the Tartars. In Persia there is a city which is called Saba, from whence were the three magi who came to adore Christ in Bethlehem; and the three are buried in that city in a fair sepulchre, and they are all three entire with their beards and hair. One was called Baldasar, the second Gaspar, and the third Melchior. Marco enquired often in that city concerning the three magi, and nobody could tell him anything about them, except that the three magi were buried there in ancient times. After three days' journey you come to a castle which is called Palasata, which means the castle of the fire-worshippers; and it is true that the inhabitants of that castle worship fire, and this is given as the reason. The men of that castle say, that anciently three kings of that country went to adore a certain king who was newly born, and carried with them three offerings, namely, gold, frankincense, and myrrh: gold, that they might know if he were an earthly king; frankincense, that they might know if he were God; and myrrh, that they might know if he were a mortal man. When these magi were presented to Christ, the youngest of the three adored him first, and it appeared to him that Christ was of his stature and age. The middle one came next, and then the eldest, and to each he seemed to be of their own stature and age. Having compared their observations together, they agreed to go all to worship at once, and then he appeared to them all of his true age. When they went away, the infant gave them a closed box, which they carried with them for several days, and then becoming curious to see what he had given them, they opened the box and found in it a stone, which was intended for a sign that they should remain as firm as a stone in the faith they had received from him. When, however, they saw the stone, they marvelled, and thinking themselves deluded, they threw the stone into a certain pit, and instantly fire burst forth in the pit. When they saw this, they repented bitterly of what they had done, and taking some of the fire with them they carried it home. And having placed it in one of their churches, they keep it continually burning, and adore that fire as a god, and make all their sacrifices with it; and if it happen to be extinguished, they go for more to the original fire in the pit where they threw the stone, which is never extinguished, and they take of none other fire. And therefore the people of that country worship fire. Marco was told all this by the people of the country; and it is true that one of those kings was of Saba, and the second was of Dyava, and the third was of the castle. Now we will treat of the people of Persia and of their customs.

CHAPTER XII

Of the Names of the Eight Kingdoms that constitute the Province of Persia and of the Breed of Horses and of Asses found therein

In Persia, which is a large province, there are eight kingdoms, the names of which are as follows: the first which you meet with upon entering the country is Kasibin; the second, lying towards the south (west), is Kurdistan; the third is Lor; towards the north, the fourth is Suolistan; the fifth, Spaan; the sixth, Siras; the seventh, Soncara; the eighth, Timocain, which is at the extremity of Persia. All these kingdoms lie to the south, excepting Timocain, and this is to the north, near the place called Arbor Secco. The country is distinguished for its excellent breed of horses, many of which are carried for sale to India, and bring high prices, not less in general than two hundred livres tournois. It produces also the largest and handsomest breed of asses in the world, which sell (on the spot) at higher prices than the horses, because they are more easily fed, are capable of carrying heavier burthens, and travel further in the day than either horses or mules, which cannot support an equal degree of fatigue. The merchants, therefore, who in travelling from one province to another are obliged to pass extensive deserts and tracts of sand, where no kind of herbage is to be met with, and where, on account of the distance between the wells or other watering places, it is necessary to make long journeys in the course of the day, are desirous of providing themselves with asses in preference, as they get sooner over the ground and require a smaller allowance of food. Camels also are employed here, and these in like manner carry great weights and are maintained at little cost, but they are not so swift as the asses. The traders of these parts convey the horses to Kisi, to Ormus, and to other places on the coast of the Indian sea, where they are purchased by those who carry them to India. In consequence, however, of the greater heat of that country, they do not last many years, being natives of a temperate climate. In some of these districts, the people are savage and bloodthirsty, making a common practice of wounding and murdering each other. They would not refrain from doing injury to the merchants and travellers, were they not in terror of the eastern Tartars, who cause them to be severely punished. A regulation is also established, that in all roads where danger is apprehended, the inhabitants shall be obliged, upon the requisition of the merchants, to provide active and trusty conductors for their guidance and security, between one district and another; who are to be paid at the rate of two or three groats for each loaded beast, according to the distance. They are all followers of the Mahometan religion. In the cities, however, there are merchants and numerous artisans, who manufacture a variety of stuffs of silk and gold. Cotton grows abundantly in this country, as do wheat, barley, millet, and several other sorts of grain; together with grapes and every species of fruit. Should anyone assert that the Saracens do not drink wine, being forbidden by their law, it may be answered that they quiet their consciences on this point by persuading themselves that if they take the precaution of boiling it over the fire, by which it is partly consumed and becomes sweet, they may drink it without infringing the commandment; for having changed its taste, they change its name, and no longer call it wine, although it is such in fact.

CHAPTER XIII

Of the City of Yasdi and its Manufactures, and of the Animals found in the Country between that place and Kierman

Yasdi is a considerable city on the confines of Persia, where there is much traffic. A species of cloth of silk and gold manufactured there is known by the appellation of Yasdi, and is carried from thence by the merchants to all parts of the world. Its inhabitants are of the Mahometan religion. Those who travel from that city, employ eight days in passing over a plain, in the course of which they meet with only three places that afford accommodation. The road lies through extensive groves of the date-bearing palm, in which there is abundance of game, as well beasts as partridges and quails; and those travellers who are fond of the amusements of the chase, may here enjoy excellent sport. Wild asses are likewise to be met with, very numerous and handsome. At the end of eight days you arrive at a kingdom named Kierman.

CHAPTER XIV

Of the Kingdom of Kierman, by the Ancients named Karmania – Of its Fossil and Mineral Productions – Its Manufactures – Its Falcons – And of a great Descent observed upon passing out of that Country

Kierman is a kingdom on the eastern confines of Persia, which was formerly governed by its own monarchs, in hereditary succession; but since the Tartars have brought it under their dominion, they appoint governors to it at their pleasure. In the mountains of this country are found the precious stones that we call turquoises. There are also veins of steel and of antimony in large quantities. They manufacture here in great perfection all the articles necessary for warlike equipment, such as saddles, bridles, spurs, swords, bows, quivers, and every kind of arms in use amongst these people. The women and young persons work with the needle, in embroideries of silk and gold, in a variety of colours and patterns, representing birds and beasts, with other ornamental devices. These are designed for the curtains, coverlets, and cushions of the sleeping places of the rich; and the work is executed with so much taste and skill as to be an object of admiration. In the mountainous parts are bred the best falcons that anywhere take wing. They are smaller than the peregrine falcon; reddish about the breast, belly, and under the tail; and their flight is so swift that no bird can escape them. Upon leaving Kierman, you travel for seven days along a plain, by a pleasant road, and rendered still more delightful by the abundance of partridges and other game. You also meet frequently with towns and castles, as well as scattered habitations; until at length you arrive at a mountain whence there is a considerable descent, which occupies two days. Fruit trees are found there in great numbers; the district having formerly been peopled, though at present without inhabitants, except herdsmen alone, who are seen attending the pasturing of their cattle. In that part of the country which you pass before you reach the descent, the cold is so severe that a man can with difficulty defend himself against it by wearing many garments and pelisses.

CHAPTER XV

Of the City of Kamandu, and District of Reobarle – Of certain Birds found there – Of a peculiar kind of Oxen – And of the Karaunas, a Tribe of Robbers

At the end of the descent of this mountain, you arrive at a plain that extends, in a southern direction, to the distance of five days' journey; at the commencement of which there is a town named Kamandu, formerly a very large place and of much consequence, but not so at this day, having been repeatedly laid waste by the Tartars. The neighbouring district is called Reobarle. The temperature of the plain is very warm. It produces wheat, rice, and other grains. On that part of it which lies nearest to the hills, dates, pomegranates, quinces, and a variety of other fruits, grow, amongst which is one called Adam's apple, not known in our cool climate. Turtle-doves are found here in vast numbers, occasioned by the plenty of small fruits which supply them with food, and their not being eaten by the Mahometans, who hold them in abomination. There are likewise many pheasants and francolins, which latter do not resemble those of other countries, their colour being a mixture of white and black with red legs and beak. Among the cattle also there are some of an uncommon kind, particularly a species of large white oxen, with short, smooth coats (the effect of a hot climate), horns short, thick, and obtuse, and having between the shoulders a gibbous rising or hump, about the height of two palms. They are beautiful animals, and being very strong are made to carry great weights. Whilst loading, they are accustomed to kneel down like the camel, and then to rise up with the burthen. We find here also sheep that are equal to the ass in size, with long and thick tails, weighing thirty pounds and upwards, which are fat and excellent to eat. In this province there are many towns encompassed with lofty and thick walls of earth, for the purpose of defending the inhabitants against the incursions of the Karaunas, who scour the country and plunder everything within their reach. In order that the reader may understand what people these are, it is necessary to mention that there was a prince named Nugodar, the nephew of Zagataï, who was brother of the Grand Khan (Oktaï), and reigned in Turkestan. This Nugodar, whilst living at Zagataï's court, became ambitious of being himself a sovereign, and having heard that in India there was a province called Malabar, governed at that time by a king named As-idin Sultan, which had not yet been brought under the dominion of the Tartars, he secretly collected a body of about ten thousand men, the most profligate and desperate he could find, and separating himself from his uncle without giving him any intimation of his designs, proceeded through Balashan to the kingdom of Kesmur, where he lost many of his people and cattle, from the difficulty and badness of the roads, and at length entered the province of Malabar. Coming thus upon As-idin by surprise, he took from him by force a city called Dely, as well as many others in its vicinity, and there began to reign. The Tartars whom he carried thither, and who were men of a light complexion, mixing with the dark Indian women, produced the race to whom the appellation of Karaunas is given, signifying, in the language of the country, a mixed breed; and these are the people who have since been in the practice of committing depredations, not only in the country of Reobarle, but in every other to which they have access. In India they acquired the knowledge of magical and diabolical arts, by means of which they are enabled to produce darkness, obscuring the light of day to such a degree, that persons are invisible to each other, unless within a very small distance. Whenever they go on their predatory excursions, they put this art in practice, and their approach is consequently not perceived. Most frequently this district is the scene of their operations; because when the merchants from various parts assemble at Ormus, and wait for those who are on their way from India, they send, in the winter season, their horses and mules, which are out of condition from the length of their journey, to the plain of Reobarle, where they find abundance of pasture and become fat. The Karaunas, aware that this will take place, seize the opportunity of effecting a general pillage, and make slaves of the people who attend the cattle, if they have not the means of ransom. Marco Polo himself was once enveloped in a factitious obscurity of this kind, but escaped from it to the castle of Konsalmi. Many of his companions, however, were taken and sold, and others were put to death. These people have a king named Corobar.

CHAPTER XVI

Of the City of Ormus, situated on an Island not far from the Main, in the Sea of India – Of its Commercial Importance – And of the Hot Wind that blows there

At the extremity of the plain before mentioned as extending in a southern direction to the distance of five days' journey, there is a descent for about twenty miles, by a road that is extremely dangerous, from the multitude of robbers, by whom travellers are continually assaulted and plundered. This declivity conducts you to another plain, very beautiful in its appearance, two days' journey in extent, which is called the plain of Ormus. Here you cross a number of fine streams, and see a country covered with date-palms, amongst which are found the francoline partridge, birds of the parrot kind, and a variety of others unknown to our climate. At length you reach the border of the ocean, where, upon an island, at no great distance from the shore, stands a city named Ormus, whose port is frequented by traders from all parts of India, who bring spices and drugs, precious stones, pearls, gold tissues, elephants' teeth, and various other articles of merchandise. These they dispose of to a different set of traders, by whom they are dispersed throughout the world. This city, indeed, is eminently commercial, has towns and castles dependent upon it, and is esteemed the principal place in the kingdom of Kierman. Its ruler is named Rukmedin Achomak, who governs with absolute authority, but at the same time acknowledges the King of Kierman as his liege lord. When any foreign merchant happens to die within his jurisdiction, he confiscates the property, and deposits the amount in his treasury. During the summer season, the inhabitants do not remain in the city, on account of the excessive heat, which renders the air unwholesome, but retire to their gardens along the shore or on the banks of the river, where with a kind of ozier-work they construct huts over the water. These they enclose with stakes, driven in the water on the one side, and on the other upon the shore, making a covering of leaves to shelter them from the sun. Here they reside during the period in which there blows, every day, from about the hour of nine until noon, a land-wind so intensely hot as to impede respiration, and to occasion death by suffocating the person exposed to it. None can escape from its effects who are overtaken by it on the sandy plain. As soon as the approach of this wind is perceived by the inhabitants, they emerge themselves to the chin in water, and continue in that situation until it ceases to blow. In proof of the extraordinary degree of this heat, Marco Polo says that he happened to be in these parts when the following circumstance occurred. The ruler of Ormus having neglected to pay his tribute to the King of Kierman, the latter took the resolution of enforcing it at the season when the principal inhabitants reside out of the city, upon the main land, and for this purpose despatched a body of troops, consisting of sixteen hundred horse and five thousand foot, through the country of Reobarle, in order to seize them by surprise. In consequence, however, of their being misled by the guides, they failed to arrive at the place intended before the approach of night, and halted to take repose in a grove not far distant from Ormus; but upon recommencing their march in the morning, they were assailed by this hot wind, and were all suffocated; not one escaping to carry the fatal intelligence to his master. When the people of Ormus became acquainted with the event, and proceeded to bury the carcases, in order that their stench might not infect the air, they found them so baked by the intenseness of the heat, that the limbs, upon being handled, separated from the trunks, and it became necessary to dig the graves close to the spot where the bodies lay.

CHAPTER XVII

Of the Shipping employed at Ormus — Of the Season in which the Fruits are produced — And of the Manner of Living and Customs of the Inhabitants

The vessels built at Ormus are of the worst kind, and dangerous for navigation, exposing the merchants and others who make use of them to great hazards. Their defects proceed from the circumstance of nails not being employed in the construction; the wood being of too hard a quality, and liable to split or to crack like earthenware. When an attempt is made to drive a nail, it rebounds, and is frequently broken. The planks are bored, as carefully as possible, with an iron auger, near the extremities; and wooden pins or trenails being driven into them, they are in this manner fastened (to the stem and stern). After this they are bound, or rather sewed together, with a kind of rope-yarn stripped from the husk of the Indian (cocoa) nuts, which are of a large size, and covered with a fibrous stuff like horsehair. This being steeped in water until the softer parts putrefy, the threads or strings remain clean, and of these they make twine for sewing the planks, which lasts a long time under water. Pitch is not used for preserving the bottoms of vessels, but they are smeared with an oil made from the fat of fish, and then caulked with oakum. The vessel has no more than one mast, one helm, and one deck. When she has taken in her lading it is covered over with hides, and upon these hides they place the horses which they carry to India. They have no iron anchors, but in their stead employ another kind of ground-tackle; the consequence of which is, that in bad weather, (and these seas are very tempestuous,) they are frequently driven on shore and lost.

The inhabitants of the place are of a dark colour, and are Mahometans. They sow their wheat, rice, and other grain in the month of November, and reap their harvest in March. The fruits also they gather in that month, with the exception of the dates, which are collected in May. Of these, with other ingredients, they make a good kind of wine. When it is drunk, however, by persons not accustomed to the beverage, it occasions an immediate flux; but upon their recovering from its first effects, it proves beneficial to them, and contributes to render them fat. The food of the natives is different from ours; for were they to eat wheaten bread and flesh meat their health would be injured. They live chiefly upon dates and salted fish, such as the thunnus, cepole (*cepola tania*), and others which from experience they know to be wholesome. Excepting in marshy places, the soil of this country is not covered with grass, in consequence of the extreme heat, which burns up everything. Upon the death of men of rank, their wives loudly bewail them, once in the course of each day, during four successive weeks; and there are also people to be found here who make such lamentations a profession, and are paid for uttering them over the corpses of persons to whom they are not related.

CHAPTER XVIII

Of the Country travelled over upon leaving Ormus, and returning to Kierman by a different Route; and of a Bitterness in the Bread occasioned by the Quality of the Water

Having spoken of Ormus, I shall for the present defer treating of India, intending to make it the subject of a separate Book, and now return to Kierman in a northerly direction. Leaving Ormus, therefore, and taking a different road to that place, you enter upon a beautiful plain, producing in abundance every article of food; and birds are numerous, especially partridges: but the bread, which is made from wheat grown in the country, cannot be eaten by those who have not learned to accommodate their palates to it, having a bitter taste derived from the quality of the waters, which are all bitter and salsuginous. On every side you perceive warm, sanative streams, applicable to the cure of cutaneous and other bodily complaints. Dates and other fruits are in great plenty.

CHAPTER IX

Of the Desert Country between Kierman and Kobiam, and of the Bitter Quality of the Water

Upon leaving Kierman and travelling three days, you reach the borders of a desert extending to the distance of seven days' journey, at the end of which you arrive at Kobiam. During the first three days (of these seven) but little water is to be met with, and that little is impregnated with salt, green as grass, and so nauseous that none can use it as drink. Should even a drop be swallowed, frequent calls of nature will be occasioned; and the effect is the same from eating a grain of the salt made from this water. In consequence of this, persons who travel over the desert are obliged to carry a provision of water along with them. The cattle, however, are compelled by thirst to drink such as they find, and a flux immediately ensues. In the course of these three days not one habitation is to be seen. The whole is arid and desolate. Cattle are not found there, because there is no subsistence for them. On the fourth day you come to a river of fresh water, but which has its channel for the most part under ground. In some parts, however, there are abrupt openings, caused by the force of the current, through which the stream becomes visible for a short space, and water is to be had in abundance. Here the wearied traveller stops to refresh himself and his cattle after the fatigues of the preceding journey. The circumstances of the latter three days resemble those of the former, and conduct him at length to the town of Kobiam.

CHAPTER XX

Of the Town of Kobiam, and its Manufactures

Kobiam is a large town, the inhabitants of which observe the law of Mahomet. They have plenty of iron, *accarum*, and *andanicum*. Here they make mirrors of highly polished steel, of a large size and very handsome. Much antimony or zinc is found in the country, and they procure tutty which makes an excellent collyrium, together with spodium, by the following process. They take the crude ore from a vein that is known to yield such as is fit for the purpose, and put it into a heated furnace. Over the furnace they place an iron grating formed of small bars set close together. The smoke or vapour ascending from the ore in burning attaches itself to the bars, and as it cools becomes hard. This is the tutty; whilst the gross and heavy part, which does not ascend, but remains as a cinder in the furnace, becomes the spodium.

CHAPTER XXI

Of the Journey from Kobiam to the Province of Timochain on the Northern Confines of Persia – And of a Particular Species of Tree

Leaving Kobiam you proceed over a desert of eight days' journey exposed to great drought; neither fruits nor any kind of trees are met with, and what water is found has a bitter taste. Travellers are therefore obliged to carry with them so much as may be necessary for their sustenance. Their cattle are constrained by thirst to drink such as the desert affords, which their owners endeavour to render palatable to them by mixing it with flour. At the end of eight days you reach the province of Timochain, situated towards the north, on the borders of Persia, in which are many towns and strong places. There is here an extensive plain remarkable for the production of a species of tree called the tree of the sun, and by Christians *arbor secco*, the dry or fruitless tree. Its nature and qualities are these: it is lofty, with a large stem, having its leaves green on the upper surface, but white or glaucous on the under. It produces husks or capsules like those in which the chestnut is enclosed, but these contain no fruit. The wood is solid and strong, and of a yellow colour resembling the box. There is no other species of tree near it for the space of a hundred miles, excepting in one quarter, where trees are found within the distance of about ten miles. It is reported by the inhabitants of this district that a battle was fought there between Alexander, King of Macedonia, and Darius. The towns are well supplied with every necessary and convenience of life, the climate being temperate and not subject to extremes either of heat or cold. The people are of the Mahometan religion. They are in general a handsome race, especially the women, who, in my opinion, are the most beautiful in the world.

CHAPTER XXII

Of the Old Man of the Mountain – Of his Palace and Gardens – Of his Capture and his Death

Having spoken of this country, mention shall now be made of the old man of the mountain. The district in which his residence lay obtained the name of Mulehet, signifying in the language of the Saracens, the place of heretics, and his people that of Mulehetites, or holders of heretical tenets; as we apply the term of Patharini to certain heretics amongst Christians. The following account of this chief, Marco Polo testifies to having heard from sundry persons. He was named Aloeddin, and his religion was that of Mahomet. In a beautiful valley enclosed between two lofty mountains, he had formed a luxurious garden, stored with every delicious fruit and every fragrant shrub that could be procured. Palaces of various sizes and forms were erected in different parts of the grounds, ornamented with works in gold, with paintings, and with furniture of rich silks. By means of small conduits contrived in these buildings, streams of wine, milk, honey, and some of pure water, were seen to flow in every direction. The inhabitants of these palaces were elegant and beautiful damsels, accomplished in the arts of singing, playing upon all sorts of musical instruments, dancing, and especially those of dalliance and amorous allurement. Clothed in rich dresses they were seen continually sporting and amusing themselves in the garden and pavilions, their female guardians being confined within doors and never suffered to appear. The object which the chief had in view in forming a garden of this fascinating kind, was this: that Mahomet having promised to those who should obey his will the enjoyments of Paradise, where every species of sensual gratification should be found, in the society of beautiful nymphs, he was desirous of its being understood by his followers that he also was a prophet and the compeer of Mahomet, and had the power of admitting to Paradise such as he should choose to favour. In order that none without his licence might find their way into this delicious valley, he caused a strong and inexpugnable castle to be erected at the opening of it, through which the entry was by a secret passage. At his court, likewise, this chief entertained a number of youths, from the age of twelve to twenty years, selected from the inhabitants of the surrounding mountains, who showed a disposition for martial exercises, and appeared to possess the quality of daring courage. To them he was in the daily practice of discoursing on the subject of the Paradise announced by the prophet, and of his own power of granting admission; and at certain times he caused opium to be administered to ten or a dozen of the youths; and when half dead with sleep he had them conveyed to the several apartments of the palaces in the garden. Upon awakening from the state of lethargy, their senses were struck with all the delightful objects that have been described, and each perceived himself surrounded by lovely damsels, singing, playing, and attracting his regards by the most fascinating caresses, serving him also with delicate viands and exquisite wines; until intoxicated with excess of enjoyment amidst actual rivulets of milk and wine, he believed himself assuredly in Paradise, and felt an unwillingness to relinquish its delights. When four or five days had thus been passed, they were thrown once more into a state of somnolency, and carried out of the garden. Upon their being introduced to his presence, and questioned by him as to where they had been, their answer was, 'In Paradise, through the favour of your highness': and then before the whole court, who listened to them with eager curiosity and astonishment, they gave a circumstantial account of the scenes to which they had been witnesses. The chief thereupon addressing them, said: 'We have the assurances of our prophet that he who defends his lord shall inherit Paradise, and if you show yourselves devoted to the obedience of my orders, that happy lot awaits you.' Animated to enthusiasm by words of this nature, all deemed themselves happy to receive the commands of their master, and were forward to die in his service. The consequence of this system was, that when any of the neighbouring princes, or others, gave umbrage to this chief, they were put to death by these his disciplined assassins; none of whom felt terror at the risk of losing their own lives, which they held in little estimation, provided they could execute their master's will. On this account his tyranny became the subject of dread in all the surrounding countries. He had also constituted two deputies or representatives of himself, of whom one had his residence in the vicinity of Damascus, and the other in Kurdistan; and these pursued the plan he had established for training their young dependants. Thus there was no person, however powerful, who, having become exposed to the enmity of the old man of the mountain, could escape assassination. His territory being situated within the dominions of Ulaù (Hulagu), the brother of the Grand Khan (Mangu), that prince had information of his atrocious practices, as above related, as well as of his employing people to rob travellers in their passage through his country, and in the year 1262 sent one of his armies to besiege this chief in his castle. It proved, however, so capable of defence, that for three years no impression could be made upon it; until at length he was forced to surrender from the want of provisions, and being made prisoner was put to death. His castle was dismantled, and his garden of Paradise destroyed. And from that time there has been no old man of the mountain.

CHAPTER XXIII

Of a fertile Plain of six Days' Journey, succeeded by a Desert of eight, to be passed in the Way to the City of Sapurgan — Of the Excellent Melons produced there — And of the City of Balach

Leaving this castle, the road leads over a spacious plain, and then through a country diversified with hill and dale, where there is herbage and pasture, as well as fruits in great abundance, by which the army of Ulaù was enabled to remain so long upon the ground. This country extends to the distance of full six days' journey. It contains many cities and fortified places, and the inhabitants are of the Mahometan religion. A desert then commences, extending forty or fifty miles, where there is no water; and it is necessary that the traveller should make provision of this article at his outset. As the cattle find no drink until this desert is passed, the greatest expedition is necessary, that they may reach a watering place. At the end of the sixth days' journey, he arrives at a town named Sapurgan, which is plentifully supplied with every kind of provision, and is particularly celebrated for producing the best melons in the world. These are preserved in the following manner. They are cut spirally, in thin slices, as the pumpkin with us, and after they have been dried in the sun, are sent, in large quantities, for sale, to the neighbouring countries; where they are eagerly sought for, being sweet as honey. Game is also in plenty there, both of beasts and birds.

Leaving this place, we shall now speak of another named Balach; a large and magnificent city. It was formerly still more considerable, but has sustained much injury from the Tartars, who in their frequent attacks have partly demolished its buildings. It contained many palaces constructed of marble, and spacious squares, still visible, although in a ruinous state. It was in this city, according to the report of the inhabitants, that Alexander took to wife the daughter of King Darius. The Mahometan religion prevails here also. The dominion of the lord of the Eastern Tartars extends to this place; and to it the limits of the Persian empire extend, in a north-eastern direction. Upon leaving Balach and holding the same course for two days, you traverse a country that is destitute of every sign of habitation, the people having all fled to strong places in the mountains, in order to secure themselves against the predatory attack of lawless marauders, by whom these districts are overrun. Here are extensive waters, and game of various kinds. Lions are also found in these parts, very large and numerous. Provisions, however, are scarce in the hilly tract passed during these two days, and the traveller must carry with him food sufficient both for himself and his cattle.

<h2 style="text-align:center">CHAPTER XXIV</h2>

Of the Castle named Thaikan — Of the Manners of the Inhabitants — And of Salt-Hills

At the end of these two days' journey you reach a castle named Thaikan, where a great market for corn is held, it being situated in a fine and fruitful country. The hills that lie to the south of it are large and lofty. They all consist of white salt, extremely hard, with which the people, to the distance of thirty days' journey round, come to provide themselves, for it is esteemed the purest that is found in the world; but it is at the same time so hard that it cannot be detached otherwise than with iron instruments. The quantity is so great that all the countries of the earth might be supplied from thence. Other hills produce almonds and pistachio nuts, in which articles the natives carry on a considerable trade. Leaving Thaikan and travelling three days still in a north-east direction, you pass through a well inhabited country, very beautiful, and abounding in fruit, corn, and vines. The people are Mahometans, and are bloodthirsty and treacherous. They are given also to debauchery, and to excess in drink, to which the excellence of their sweet wine encourages them. On their heads they wear nothing but a cord, about ten spans in length, with which they bind them round. They are keen sportsmen, and take many wild animals, wearing no other clothing than the skins of the beasts they kill, of which materials their shoes also are made. They are all taught to prepare the skins.

CHAPTER XXV

Of the Town of Scassem, and of the Porcupines found there

During a journey of three days there are cities and many castles, and at the end of that distance you reach a town named Scassem, governed by a chief whose title is equivalent to that of our barons or counts; and amongst the mountains he possesses other towns and strong places. Through the midst of this town runs a river of tolerable size. Here are found porcupines, which roll themselves up when the hunters set their dogs at them, and with great fury shoot out the quills or spines with which their skins are furnished, wounding both men and dogs. The people of this country have their peculiar language. The herdsmen who attend the cattle have their habitations amongst the hills, in caverns they form for themselves; nor is this a difficult operation, the hills consisting, not of stone, but only of clay. Upon departing from this place you travel for three days without seeing any kind of building, or meeting with any of the necessaries required by a traveller, excepting water; but for the horses there is sufficient pasture. You are therefore obliged to carry with you every article for which there may be occasion on the road. At the end of the third day you arrive at the province of Balashan.

CHAPTER XXVI

Of the Province of Balashan — Of the Precious Stones found there and which become the Property of the King — Of the Horses and the Falcons of the Country — Of the Salubrious Air of the Mountains — And of the Dress with which the Women adorn their Persons

In the province of Balashan, the people are Mahometans, and have their peculiar language. It is an extensive kingdom, being in length full twelve days' journey, and is governed by princes in hereditary succession, who are all descended from Alexander, by the daughter of Darius, King of the Persians. All these have borne the title in the Saracenic tongue of Zulkarnen, being equivalent to Alexander. In this country are found the precious stones called balass rubies, of fine quality and great value, so called from the name of the province. They are embedded in the high mountains, but are searched for only in one, named Sikinan. In this the king causes mines to be worked, in the same manner as for gold or silver; and through this channel alone they are obtained; no person daring under pain of death, to make an excavation for the purpose, unless as a special favour he obtains his majesty's licence. Occasionally the king gives them as presents to strangers who pass through his dominions, as they are not procurable by purchase from others, and cannot be exported without his permission. His object in these restrictions is, that the rubies of his country, with which he thinks his credit connected, should preserve their estimation and maintain their high price; for if they could be dug for indiscriminately, and everyone could purchase and carry them out of the kingdom, so great is their abundance, that they would soon be of little value. Some he sends as complimentary gifts to other kings and princes; some he delivers as tribute (to his superior lord); and some also he exchanges for gold and silver. These he allows to be exported. There are mountains likewise in which are found veins of lapis lazuli, the stone which yields the azure colour (ultramarine), here the finest in the world. The mines of silver, copper, and lead, are likewise very productive. It is a cold country. The horses bred here are of a superior quality, and have great speed. Their hoofs are so hard that they do not require shoeing. The natives are in the practice of galloping them on declivities where other cattle could not or would not venture to run. They asserted that not long since there were still found in this province horses of the breed of Alexander's celebrated Bucephalus, which were all foaled with a particular mark in the forehead. The whole of the breed was in the possession of one of the king's uncles, who, upon his refusal to yield them to his nephew, was put to death; whereupon his widow, exasperated at the murder, caused them all to be destroyed; and thus the race was lost to the world. In the mountains there are falcons of the species called saker (*falco sacer*), which are excellent birds, and of strong flight; as well as of that called laner (*falco lanarius*). There are also goshawks of a perfect kind (*falco astur*, or *palumbarius*), and sparrow hawks (*falco nisus*). The people of the country are expert at the chase both of beasts and birds. Good wheat is grown there, and a species of barley without the husk. There is no oil of olives, but they express it from certain nuts, and from the grain called sesame, which resembles the seed of flax, excepting that it is light-coloured; and the oil this yields is better, and has more flavour than any other. It is used by the Tartars and other inhabitants of these parts.

In this kingdom there are many narrow defiles, and strong situations, which diminish the apprehension of any foreign power entering it with a hostile intention. The men are good archers and excellent sportsmen; generally clothing themselves with the skins of wild animals; other materials for the purpose being scarce. The mountains afford pasture for an innumerable quantity of sheep, which ramble about in flocks of four, five, and six hundred, all wild; and although many are taken and killed, there does not appear to be any diminution. These mountains are exceedingly lofty, insomuch that it employs a man from morning till night to ascend to the top of them. Between them there are wide plains clothed with grass and with trees, and large streams of the purest water precipitating themselves through the fissures of the rocks. In these streams are trout and many other delicate sorts of fish. On the summits of the mountains the air is so pure and so salubrious, that when those who dwell in the towns, and in the plains and valleys below, find themselves attacked with fevers or other inflammatory complaints, they immediately remove thither, and remaining for three or four days in that situation, recover their health. Marco Polo affirms that he had experience in his own person of its excellent effects; for having been confined by sickness, in this country, for nearly a year, he was advised to change the air by ascending the hills; when he presently became convalescent. A peculiar fashion of dress prevails amongst the women of the superior class, who wear below their waists, in the manner of drawers, a kind of garment, in the making of which they employ, according to their means, an hundred, eighty, or sixty ells of fine cotton cloth; which they also gather or plait, in order to increase the apparent size of their hips; those being accounted the most handsome who are the most bulky in that part.

CHAPTER XXVII

Of the Province of Bascià lying South of the former — Of the Golden Ornaments worn by the Inhabitants in their Ears — And of their Manners

Leaving Balashan and travelling in a southerly direction for ten days, you reach the province of Bascià, the people of which have a peculiar language. They worship idols; are of a dark complexion, and of evil disposition; and are skilled in the art of magic, and the invocations of demons, a study to which they continually apply themselves. They wear in their ears pendent rings of gold and silver, adorned with pearls and precious stones. The climate of the province is in some parts extremely hot. The food of the inhabitants is meat and rice.

CHAPTER XXVIII

Of the Province of Kesmur situated towards the South-East —
Of its Inhabitants who are skilled in Magic — Of their
Communication with the Indian Sea — And of a Class of
Hermits, their Mode of Life, and Extraordinary Abstinence

Kesmur is a province distant from Bascià seven days' journey. Its inhabitants also have their peculiar language. They are adepts beyond all others in the art of magic; insomuch that they can compel their idols, although by nature dumb and deaf, to speak; they can likewise obscure the day, and perform many other miracles. They are pre-eminent amongst the idolatrous nations, and from them the idols, worshipped in other parts, proceed. From this country there is a communication by water with the Indian Sea. The natives are of a dark complexion, but by no means black; and the women, although dark, are very comely. Their food is flesh, with rice and other grains; yet they are in general of a spare habit. The climate is moderately warm. In this province, besides the capital, there are many other towns and strong places. There are also woods, desert tracts, and difficult passes in the mountains, which give security to the inhabitants against invasion. Their king is not tributary to any power. They have amongst them a particular class of devotees, who live in communities, observe strict abstinence in regard to eating, drinking, and the intercourse of the sexes, and refrain from every kind of sensual indulgence, in order that they may not give offence to the idols whom they worship. These persons live to a considerable age. They have several monasteries, in which certain superiors exercise the functions of our abbots, and by the mass of the people they are held in great reverence. The natives of this country do not deprive any creature of life, nor shed blood, and if they are inclined to eat flesh-meat, it is necessary that the Mahometans who reside amongst them should slay the animal. The article of coral carried thither from Europe is sold at a higher price than in any other part of the world.

If I were to proceed in the same direction, it would lead me to

India; but I have judged it proper to reserve the description of that country for a third book; and shall therefore return to Balashan, intending to pursue from thence the straight road to Cathay, and to describe, as has been done from the commencement of the work, not only the countries through which the route immediately lies, but also those in its vicinity, to the right and left.

CHAPTER XXIX

Of the Province of Vokhan — Of an Ascent for three Days, leading to the Summit of a High Mountain — Of a peculiar Breed of Sheep found there — Of the Effect of the great Elevation upon Fires — And of the Savage Life of the Inhabitants

Leaving the province of Balashan, and travelling in a direction between north-east and east, you pass many castles and habitations on the banks of the river, belonging to the brother of the king of that place, and after three days' journey, reach a province named Vokhan; which itself extends in length and width to the distance of three days' journey. The people are Mahometans, have a distinct language, are civilised in their manners, and accounted valiant in war. Their chief holds his territory as a fief dependent upon Balashan. They practise various modes of taking wild animals. Upon leaving this country, and proceeding for three days still in an east-north-east course, ascending mountain after mountain, you at length arrive at a point of the road, where you might suppose the surrounding summits to be the highest lands in the world. Here, between two ranges, you perceive a large lake, from which flows a handsome river, that pursues its course along an extensive plain, covered with the richest verdure. Such indeed is its quality that the leanest cattle turned upon it would become fat in the course of ten days. In this plain there are wild animals in great numbers, particularly sheep of a large size, having horns, three, four, and even six palms in length. Of these the shepherds form ladles and vessels for holding their victuals; and with the same materials they construct fences for enclosing their cattle, and securing them against the wolves, with which, they say, the country is infested, and which likewise destroy many of these wild sheep or goats. Their horns and bones being found in large quantities, heaps are made of them at the sides of the road, for the purpose of guiding travellers at the season when it is covered with snow. For twelve days the course is along this elevated plain, which is named Pamer; and as during all that time you do not meet with any habitations, it is necessary to make provision at the outset accordingly. So great is the height of the mountains, that no birds are to be seen near their summits; and however extraordinary it may be thought, it was affirmed, that from the keenness of the air, fires when lighted do not give the same heat as in lower situations, nor produce the same effect in dressing victuals.

After having performed this journey of twelve days, you have still forty days to travel in the same direction, over mountains, and through valleys, in perpetual succession, passing many rivers and desert tracts, without seeing any habitations or the appearance of verdure. Every article of provision must therefore be carried along with you. This region is called Beloro. Even amidst the highest of these mountains, there live a tribe of savage, ill-disposed, and idolatrous people, who subsist upon the animals they can destroy, and clothe themselves with the skins.

CHAPTER XXX

Of the City of Kashcar, and of the Commerce of its Inhabitants

At length you reach a place called Kashcar, which, it is said, was formerly an independent kingdom, but is now subject to the dominion of the Grand Khan. Its inhabitants are of the Mahometan religion. The province is extensive, and contains many towns and castles, of which Kashcar is the largest and most important. The language of the people is peculiar to themselves. They subsist by commerce and manufacture, particularly works of cotton. They have handsome gardens, orchards, and vineyards. Abundance of cotton is produced there, as well as flax and hemp. Merchants from this country travel to all parts of the world; but in truth they are a covetous, sordid race, eating badly and drinking worse. Besides the Mahometans there are amongst the inhabitants several Nestorian Christians, who are permitted to live under their own laws, and to have their churches. The extent of the province is five days' journey.

CHAPTER XXXI

Of the City of Samarcan, and of the Miraculous Column in the Church of St John the Baptist

Samarcan is a noble city, adorned with beautiful gardens, and surrounded by a plain, in which are produced all the fruits that man can desire. The inhabitants, who are partly Christians and partly Mahometans, are subject to the dominion of a nephew of the Grand Khan, with whom, however, he is not upon amicable terms, but on the contrary there is perpetual strife and frequent wars between them. This city lies in the direction of north-west. A miracle is said to have taken place there, under the following circumstances. Not long ago, a prince named Zagatai, who was own brother to the (then reigning) Grand Khan, became a convert to Christianity; greatly to the delight of the Christian inhabitants of the place, who under the favour and protection of the prince, proceeded to build a church, and dedicated it to St John the Baptist. It was so constructed that all the weight of the roof (being circular) should rest upon a column in the centre, and beneath this, as a base, they fixed a square stone, which, with the permission of the prince, they had taken from a temple belonging to the Mahometans, who dared not to prevent them from so doing. But upon the death of Zagatai, his son who succeeded him showing no disposition to become a Christian, the Mussulmans had influence enough to obtain from him an order that their opponents should restore to them the stone they had appropriated; and although the latter offered to pay them a compensation in money, they refused to listen to the proposal, because they hoped that its removal would occasion the church to tumble down. In this difficulty the afflicted

Christians had no other resource than with tears and humility to recommend themselves to the protection of the glorious St John the Baptist. When the day arrived on which they were to make restitution of the stone, it came to pass that through the intercession of the Saint, the pillar raised itself from its base to the height of three palms, in order to facilitate the removal of the stone, and in that situation, without any kind of support, it remains to the present day. Enough being said of this, we shall now proceed to the province of Karkan.

CHAPTER XXXII

Of the Province of Karkan, the Inhabitants of which are troubled with Swollen Legs and with Goitres

Departing from thence you enter the province of Karkan, which continues to the distance of five days' journey. Its inhabitants, for the most part Mahometans, with some Nestorian Christians, are subjects of the Grand Khan. Provisions are here in abundance, as is also cotton. The people are expert artisans. They are in general afflicted with swellings in the legs, and tumours in the throat, occasioned by the quality of the water they drink. In this country there is not anything further that is worthy of observation.

CHAPTER XXXIII

Of the City of Kotan, which is abundantly supplied with all the Necessaries of Life

Following a course between north-east and east, you next come to the province of Kotan, the extent of which is eight days' journey. It is under the dominion of the Grand Khan, and the people are Mahometans. It contains many cities and fortified places, but the principal city, and which gives its name to the province, is Kotan. Everything necessary for human life is here in the greatest plenty. It yields likewise cotton, flax, hemp, grain, wine, and other articles. The inhabitants cultivate farms and vineyards, and have numerous gardens. They support themselves also by trade and manufactures, but they are not good soldiers. We shall now speak of a province named Peyn.

CHAPTER XXXIV

Of the Province of Peyn — Of the Chalcedonies and Jasper found in its River — and of a Peculiar Custom with regard to Marriages

Peyn is a province of five days' journey in extent, in the direction of east-north-east. It is under the dominion of the Grand Khan, and contains many cities and strong places, the principal one of which is likewise named Peyn. Through this flows a river, and in its bed are found many of those stones called chalcedonies and jasper. All kinds of provision are obtained here. Cotton also is produced in the country. The inhabitants live by manufacture and trade. They have this custom, that if a married man goes to a distance from home to be absent twenty days, his wife has a right, if she is inclined, to take another husband; and the men, on the same principle, marry wherever they happen to reside. All the before-mentioned provinces, that is to say, Kashcar, Kotan, Peyn, and as far as the desert of Lop, are within the limits of Turkistan. Next follows the province of Charchan.

CHAPTER XXXV

Of the Province of Charchan — Of the kinds of Stone found in its Rivers — And of the Necessity the Inhabitants are under, of flying to the Desert on the approach of the Armies of the Tartars

Charchan is also a province of Turkistan, lying in an east-north-east direction (from Peyn). In former times it was flourishing and productive, but has been laid waste by the Tartars. The people are Mahometans. Its chief city is likewise named Charchan. Through this province run several large streams, in which also are found chalcedonies and jaspers, which are carried for sale to Cathay, and such is their abundance that they form a considerable article of commerce. The country from Peyn to this district, as well as throughout its whole extent, is an entire sand, in which the water is for the most part bitter and unpalatable, although in particular places it is sweet and good. When an army of Tartars passes through these places, if they are enemies the inhabitants are plundered of their goods, and if friends their cattle are killed and devoured. For this reason, when they are aware of the approach of any body of troops, they flee, with their families and cattle, into the sandy desert, to the distance of two days' journey, towards some spot where they can find fresh water, and are by that means enabled to subsist. From the same apprehension, when they collect their harvest, they deposit the grain in caverns amongst the sands; taking monthly from the store so much as may be wanted for their consumption; nor can any person besides themselves know the places to which they resort for this purpose, because the tracks of their feet are presently effaced by the wind. Upon leaving Charchan the road lies for five days over sands, where the water is generally, but not in all places, bad. Nothing else occurs here that is worthy of remark. At the end of these five days you arrive at the city of Lop, on the borders of the great desert.

CHAPTER XXXVI

Of the Town of Lop – Of the Desert in its Vicinity – And
of the Strange Noises heard by those who pass over the latter

The town of Lop is situated towards the north-east, near the
commencement of the great desert, which is called the Desert of Lop.
It belongs to the dominions of the Grand Khan, and its inhabitants
are of the Mahometan religion. Travellers who intend to cross the
desert usually halt for a considerable time at this place, as well to
repose from their fatigues as to make the necessary preparations for
their further journey. For this purpose they load a number of stout
asses and camels with provisions and with their merchandise. Should
the former be consumed before they have completed the passage,
they kill and eat the cattle of both kinds; but camels are commonly
here employed in preference to asses, because they carry heavy
burthens and are fed with a small quantity of provender. The stock of
provisions should be laid in for a month, that time being required for
crossing the desert in the narrowest part. To travel it in the direction
of its length would prove a vain attempt, as little less than a year must
be consumed, and to convey stores for such a period would be found
impracticable. During these thirty days the journey is invariably over
either sandy plains or barren mountains; but at the end of each day's
march you stop at a place where water is procurable; not indeed in
sufficient quantity for large numbers, but enough to supply a hundred
persons, together with their beasts of burthen. At three or four of
these halting-places the water is salt and bitter, but at the others,
amounting to about twenty, it is sweet and good. In this tract neither
beasts nor birds are met with, because there is no kind of food for
them.
It is asserted as a well-known fact that this desert is the abode of many
evil spirits, which amuse travellers to their destruction with most
extraordinary illusions. If, during the daytime, any persons remain
behind on the road, either when overtaken by sleep or detained by
their natural occasions, until the caravan has passed a hill and is no

longer in sight, they unexpectedly hear themselves called to by their names, and in a tone of voice to which they are accustomed. Supposing the call to proceed from their companions, they are led away by it from the direct road, and not knowing in what direction to advance, are left to perish. In the night-time they are persuaded they hear the march of a large cavalcade on one side or the other of the road, and concluding the noise to be that of the footsteps of their party, they direct theirs to the quarter from whence it seems to proceed; but upon the breaking of day, find they have been misled and drawn into a situation of danger. Sometimes likewise during the day these spirits assume the appearance of their travelling companions, who address them by name and endeavour to conduct them out of the proper road. It is said also that some persons, in their course across the desert, have seen what appeared to them to be a body of armed men advancing towards them, and apprehensive of being attacked and plundered have taken to flight. Losing by this means the right path, and ignorant of the direction they should take to regain it, they have perished miserably of hunger. Marvellous indeed and almost passing belief are the stories related of these spirits of the desert, which are said at times to fill the air with the sounds of all kinds of musical instruments, and also of drums and the clash of arms; obliging the travellers to close their line of march and to proceed in more compact order. They find it necessary also to take the precaution before they repose for the night, to fix an advanced signal, pointing out the course they are afterwards to hold, as well as to attach a bell to each of the beasts of burthen for the purpose of their being more easily kept from straggling. Such are the excessive troubles and dangers that must unavoidably be encountered in the passage of this desert.

CHAPTER XXXVII

Of the Province of Tanguth — Of the City of Sachion — Of the Custom observed there upon the Birth of a Male Child — And of the Ceremony of Burning the Bodies of the Dead

When the journey of thirty days across the desert has been completed, you arrive at a city called Sachion, which belongs to the Grand Khan. The province is named Tanguth. The people are worshippers of idols. There are Turkomans among them, with a few Nestorian Christians and Mahometans. Those who are idolaters have a language distinct from the others. This city lies towards the east-north-east. They are not a commercial, but an agricultural people, having much wheat. There are in this country a number of monasteries and abbeys, which are filled with idols of various descriptions. To these, which they regard with the profoundest reverence, they also offer sacrifices; and upon the birth of a son, they recommend him to the protection of some one of their idols. In honour of this deity the father rears a sheep in his house until the expiration of a year, when, upon the day of the idol's peculiar festival, they conduct their son, together with the sheep, into its presence, and there sacrifice the animal. The flesh they seethe, and then they carry it and lay it before the idol, and stand there until they have finished a long prayer, the subject of which is to entreat the idol to preserve the health of their child; and they believe that during this interval it has sucked in all the savoury juices of the meat. The remaining substance they then carry home, and, assembling all their relations and friends, eat it with much devout festivity. They collect the bones, and preserve them in handsome urns. The priests of the idol have for their portion the head, the feet, the intestines, and the skin, together with some parts of the flesh. In respect to the dead, likewise, these idolaters have particular ceremonies. Upon the decease of a person of rank, whose body it is intended to burn, the relations call together the astrologers, and make them acquainted with the year, the day, and the hour in which he was born; whereupon these proceed to examine the horoscope, and having ascertained the constellation or sign, and the planet therein presiding, declare the day on which the funeral ceremony shall take place. If it should happen that the same planet be not then in the ascendant, they order the body to be kept a week or more, and sometimes even for the space of six months, before they allow the ceremony to be performed. In the hope of a propitious aspect, and dreading the effects of a contrary influence, the relations do not presume to burn the corpse until the astrologers have fixed the proper time. It being necessary on this account that, in many cases, the body should remain long in the house, in order to guard against the consequences of putrefaction, they prepare a coffin made of boards a palm in thickness, well fitted together and painted, in which they deposit the corpse, and along with it a quantity of sweet-scented gums, camphor, and other drugs; the joints or seams they smear with a mixture of pitch and lime, and the whole is then covered with silk. During this period the table is spread every day with bread, wine, and other provisions, which remain so long as is necessary for a convenient meal, as well as for the spirit of the deceased, which they suppose to be present on the occasion, to satisfy itself with the fumes of the victuals. Sometimes the astrologers signify to the relations that the body must not be conveyed from the house through the principal door, in consequence of their having discovered from the aspect of the heavens, or otherwise, that such a course would be unlucky, and it must therefore be taken out from a different side of the house. In some instances, indeed, they oblige them to break through the wall that happens to stand opposite to the propitious and beneficent planet, and to convey the corpse through that aperture; persuading them that if they should refuse to do so, the spirit of the defunct would be incensed against the family and cause them some injury. Accordingly, when any misfortune befalls a house, or any person belonging to it meets with an accident or loss, or with an untimely death, the astrologers do not fail to attribute the event to a funeral not having taken place during the ascendency of the planet under which the deceased relative was born, but, on the contrary, when it was exposed to a malign influence, or to its not having been conducted through the proper door. As the ceremony of burning the body must be performed without the city, they erect from space to space in the road by which the procession is to pass, small wooden buildings, with a portico which they cover with silk; and under these, as it arrives at each, the body is set down. They place before it meats and liquors, and this is repeated until they reach the appointed spot, believing, as they do, that the spirit is thereby refreshed and acquires energy to attend the funeral pile. Another ceremony also is practised on these occasions. They provide a number of pieces of paper, made of the bark of a certain tree, upon which are painted the figures of men, women, horses, camels, pieces of money, and dresses, and these they burn along with the corpse, under the persuasion that in the next world the deceased will enjoy the services and use of the domestics, cattle, and all the articles depicted on the paper. During the whole of these proceedings, all the musical instruments belonging to the place are sounded with an incessant din. Having now spoken of this city, others lying towards the north-west, near the head of the desert, shall next be mentioned.

CHAPTER XXXVIII

Of the District of Kamul, and of some peculiar Customs respecting the Entertainment of Strangers

Kamul is a district situated within the great province of Tanguth, subject to the Grand Khan, and contains many towns and castles, of which the principal city is also named Kamul. This district lies in the intermediate space between two deserts; that is to say, the great desert already described, and another of smaller extent, being only about three days' journey across. The inhabitants are worshippers of idols, and have their peculiar language. They subsist on the fruits of the earth, which they possess in abundance, and are enabled to supply the wants of travellers. The men are addicted to pleasure, and attend to little else than playing upon instruments, singing, dancing, reading, writing, according to the practice of the country, and the pursuit, in short, of every kind of amusement. When strangers arrive, and desire to have lodging and accommodation at their houses, it affords them the highest gratification. They give positive orders to their wives, daughters, sisters, and other female relations, to indulge their guests in every wish, whilst they themselves leave their homes, and retire into the city, and the stranger lives in the house with the females as if they were his own wives, and they send whatever necessaries may be wanted; but for which, it is to be understood, they expect payment: nor do they return to their houses so long as the strangers remain in them. This abandonment of the females of their family to accidental guests, who assume the same privileges and meet with the same indulgences as if they were their own wives, is regarded by these people as doing them honour and adding to their reputation; considering the hospitable reception of strangers, who (after the perils and fatigues of a long journey) stand in need of relaxation, as an action agreeable to their deities, calculated to draw down the blessing of increase upon their families, to augment their substance, and to procure them safety from all dangers, as well as a successful issue to all their undertakings. The women are in truth very handsome, very sensual, and fully disposed to conform in this respect to the injunction of their husbands. It happened at the time when Mangu Khan held his court in this province, that the above scandalous custom coming to his knowledge, he issued an edict strictly commanding the people of Kamul to relinquish a practice so disgraceful to them, and forbidding individuals to furnish lodging to strangers, who should be obliged to accommodate themselves at a house of public resort or *caravanserai*. In grief and sadness the inhabitants obeyed for about three years the command of their master; but finding at length that the earth ceased to yield the accustomed fruits, and that many unfortunate events occurred in their families, they resolved to despatch a deputation to the Grand Khan, in their names, to beseech him that he should be pleased to suffer them to resume the observance of a custom that had been solemnly handed down to them by their fathers, from their ancestors in the remotest times; and especially as since they had failed in the exercise of these offices of hospitality and gratification to strangers, the interest of their families had gone progressively to ruin. The Grand Khan, having listened to this application, replied: 'Since you appear so anxious to persist in your own shame and ignominy, let it be granted as you desire. Go, live according to your base customs and manners, and let your wives continue to receive the beggarly wages of their prostitution.' With this answer the deputies returned home, to the great delight of all the people, who, to the present day, observe their ancient practice.

CHAPTER XXXIX

Of the City of Chinchitalas

Next to the district of Kamul follows that of Chinchitalas, which in its northern part borders on the desert, and is in length sixteen days' journey. It is subject to the Grand Khan, and contains cities and several strong places. Its inhabitants consist of three religious sects. A few of them confess Christ, according to the Nestorian doctrine; others are followers of Mahomet; and a third class worship idols. There is in this district a mountain where the mines produce steel, and also zinc or antimony. A substance is likewise found of the nature of the salamander, for when woven into cloth, and thrown into the fire, it remains incombustible. The following mode of preparing it I learned from one of my travelling companions, named Curficar, a very intelligent Turkoman, who had the direction of the mining operations of the province for three years. The fossil substance procured from the mountain consists of fibres not unlike those of wool. This, after being exposed to the sun to dry, is pounded in a brass mortar, and is then washed until all the earthy particles are separated. The fibres thus cleansed and detached from each other, they then spin into thread and weave into cloth. In order to render the texture white, they put it into the fire, and suffer it to remain there about an hour, when they draw it out uninjured by the flame, and become white as snow. By the same process they afterwards cleanse it, when it happens to contract spots, no other abstergent lotion than an igneous one being ever applied to it. Of the salamander under the form of a serpent, supposed to exist in fire, I could never discover any traces in the eastern regions. It is said that they preserve at Rome a napkin woven from this material, in which was wrapped the *sudarium* of our Lord, sent as a gift from one of the Tartar princes to the Roman Pontiff.

CHAPTER XL

*Of the District of Succuir, where the Rhubarb is produced,
and from whence it is carried to all parts of the World*

Upon leaving the district last mentioned, and proceeding for ten days
in the direction of east-north-east, through a country where there are
few habitations, and little of any kind worthy of remark, you arrive at
a district named Succuir, in which are many towns and castles, the
principal one being likewise named Succuir. The inhabitants are in
general idolaters, with some Christians. They are subject to the
dominion of the Grand Khan. The extensive province, which
contains these and the two districts which shall be next mentioned, is
called Tanguth, and throughout all the mountainous parts of it the
most excellent kind of rhubarb is produced, in large quantities, and
the merchants who procure loadings of it on the spot convey it to all
parts of the world. It is a fact that when they take that road, they
cannot venture amongst the mountains with any beasts of burthen
excepting those accustomed to the country, on account of a
poisonous plant growing there, which, if eaten by them, has the effect
of causing the hoofs of the animal to drop off; but those of the
country, being aware of its dangerous quality, take care to avoid it.
The people of Succuir depend for subsistence upon the fruits of the
earth and the flesh of their cattle, and do not engage in trade. The
district is perfectly healthy, and the complexion of the natives is
brown.

CHAPTER XLI

Of the City of Kampion, the principal one of the Province of Tanguth — Of the nature of their Idols, and of the Mode of Life of those amongst the Idolaters who are devoted to the services of Religion — Of the Almanac they make use of — And the Customs of the other Inhabitants with regard to Marriage

Kampion, the chief city of the province of Tanguth, is large and magnificent, and has jurisdiction over all the province. The bulk of the people worship idols, but there are some who follow the religion of Mahomet, and some Christians. The latter have three large and handsome churches in the city. The idolaters have many religious houses, or monasteries and abbeys, built after the manner of the country, and in these a multitude of idols, some of which are of wood, some of stone, and some of clay, are covered with gilding. They are carved in a masterly style. Among these are some of very large size, and others are small. The former are full ten paces in length, and lie in a recumbent posture; the small figures stand behind them, and have the appearance of disciples in the act of reverential salutation. Both great and small are held in extreme veneration. Those persons amongst the idolaters who are devoted to the services of religion lead more correct lives, according to their ideas of morality, than the other classes, abstaining from the indulgence of carnal and sensual appetites. The unlicensed intercourse of the sexes is not in general considered by these people as a serious offence; and their maxim is, that if the advances are made by the female, the connection does not constitute an offence, but it is held to be such when the proposal comes from the man. They employ an almanac, in many respects like our own, according to the rules of which, during five, four, or three days in the month, they do not shed blood, nor eat flesh or fowl; as is our usage in regard to Friday, the Sabbath, and the vigils of the saints. The laity take to themselves as many as thirty wives, some more, some fewer, according to their ability to maintain them; for they do not receive any dowry with them, but, on the contrary, settle dowers upon their wives, in cattle, slaves, and money. The wife who is first married always maintains the superior rank in the family; but if the husband observes that anyone amongst them does not conduct herself well to the rest, or if she becomes otherwise disagreeable to him, he can send her away. They take to their beds those who are nearly related to them by blood, and even espouse their mothers-in-law. Many other mortal sins are regarded by them with indifference, and they live in this respect like the beasts of the field. In this city Marco Polo remained, along with his father and uncle, about the space of one year, which the state of their concerns rendered necessary.

CHAPTER XLII

Of the City of Ezina — Of the kinds of Cattle and Birds found there — And of a Desert extending Forty Days' Journey towards the North

Leaving this city of Kampion, and travelling for twelve days in a northerly direction, you come to a city named Ezina, at the commencement of the sandy desert, and within the province of Tanguth. The inhabitants are idolaters. They have camels, and much cattle of various sorts. Here you find lanner-falcons and many excellent sakers. The fruits of the soil and the flesh of the cattle supply the wants of the people, and they do not concern themselves with trade. Travellers passing through this city lay in a store of provisions for forty days, because, upon their leaving it to proceed northwards, that space of time is employed in traversing a desert, where there is not any appearance of dwelling, nor are there any inhabitants excepting a few during the summer, among the mountains and in some of the valleys. In these situations, frequented by wild asses and other animals equally wild, they find water and woods of pine trees. Having passed this desert, you arrive at a city on the northern side of it, named Kara-korum. All the districts and cities previously mentioned, that is to say, Sakion, Kamul, Chinchitalas, Succuir, Kampion, and Ezina, belong to the great province of Tanguth.

CHAPTER XLIII

*Of the City of Kara-korum, the first in which the Tartars
fixed their Residence*

The city of Kara-korum is about three miles in circuit, and is the first
place in which the Tartars established their residence in remote times.
It is surrounded with a strong rampart of earth, there not being any
good supply of stone in that part of the country. On the outside of
the rampart, but near to it, stands a castle of great size, in which is a
handsome palace occupied by the governor of the place.

CHAPTER XLIV

*Of the Origin of the Kingdom of the Tartars — Of the
Quarter from whence they came — And of their former
Subjection to Un-khan, a Prince of the North, called also
Prester John*

The circumstances under which these Tartars first began to exercise
dominion shall now be related. They dwelt in the northern countries
of Jorza and Bargu, but without fixed habitations, that is, without
towns or fortified places; where there were extensive plains, good
pasture, large rivers, and plenty of water. They had no sovereign of
their own, and were tributary to a powerful prince, who (as I have
been informed) was named in their language, Un-khan, by some
thought to have the same signification as Prester John in ours. To him
these Tartars paid yearly the tenth part of (the increase of) their cattle.
In process of time the tribe multiplied so exceedingly that Un-khan,
that is to say, Prester John, becoming apprehensive of their strength,
conceived the plan of separating them into different bodies, who
should take up their abode in distinct tracts of country. With this

view also, whenever the occasion presented itself, such as a rebellion in any of the provinces subject to him, he drafted three or four in the hundred of these people, to be employed on the service of quelling it; and thus their power was gradually diminished. He in like manner despatched them upon other expeditions, and sent among them some of his principal officers to see that his intentions were carried into effect. At length the Tartars, becoming sensible of the slavery to which he attempted to reduce them, resolved to maintain a strict union amongst themselves, and seeing that nothing short of their final ruin was in contemplation, they adopted the measure of removing from the places which they then inhabited, and proceeded in a northerly direction across a wide desert, until they felt assured that the distance afforded them security, when they refused any longer to pay to Un-khan the accustomed tribute.

CHAPTER XLV

Concerning Chingis-khan, first Emperor of the Tartars, and his Warfare with Un-khan, whom he overthrew, and of whose Kingdom he possessed himself

Some time after the migration of the Tartars to this place, and about the year of our Lord 1162, they proceeded to elect for their king a man who was named Chingis-khan, one of approved integrity, great wisdom, commanding eloquence, and eminent for his valour. He began his reign with so much justice and moderation, that he was beloved and revered as their deity rather than their sovereign; and the fame of his great and good qualities spreading over that part of the world, all the Tartars, however dispersed, placed themselves under his command. Finding himself thus at the head of so many brave men, he became ambitious of emerging from the deserts and wildernesses by which he was surrounded, and gave them orders to equip themselves with bows, and such other weapons as they were expert at using, from the habits of their pastoral life. He then proceeded to render himself master of cities and provinces; and such was the effect produced by his character for justice and other virtues, that wherever he went, he found the people disposed to submit to him, and to esteem themselves happy when admitted to his protection and favour. In this manner he acquired the possession of about nine provinces. Nor is his success surprising, when we consider that at this period each town and district was either governed by the people themselves, or had its petty king or lord; and as there existed amongst them no general confederacy, it was impossible for them to resist, separately, so formidable a power. Upon the subjugation of these places, he appointed governors to them, who were so exemplary in their conduct that the inhabitants did not suffer, either in their persons or their properties; and he likewise adopted the policy of taking along with him, into other provinces, the principal people, on whom he bestowed allowances and gratuities. Seeing how prosperously his enterprises succeeded, he resolved upon attempting still greater things. With this view he sent ambassadors to Prester John, charged with a specious message, which he knew at the same time would not be listened to by that prince, demanding his daughter in marriage. Upon receiving the application, the monarch indignantly exclaimed: 'Whence arises this presumption in Chingis-khan, who, knowing himself to be my servant, dares to ask for the hand of my child? Depart instantly,' he said, 'and let him know from me, that upon the repetition of such a demand, I shall put him to an ignominious death.' Enraged at this reply, Chingis-khan collected a very large army, at the head of which he entered the territory of Prester John, and encamping on a great plain called Tenduk, sent a message desiring him to defend himself. The latter advanced likewise to the plain with a vast army, and took his position at the distance of about ten miles from the other. In this conjuncture Chingis-khan commanded his astrologers and magicians to declare to him which of the two armies, in the approaching conflict, should obtain the victory. Upon this they took a green reed, and dividing it lengthways into two parts, they wrote upon one the name of their master, and upon the other the name of Un-khan. They then placed them on the ground, at some distance from each other, and gave notice to the king that during the time of their pronouncing their incantations, the two pieces of reed, through the power of their idols, would advance towards each other, and that the victory would fall to the lot of that monarch whose piece should be seen to mount upon the other. The whole army was assembled to be spectators of this ceremony, and whilst the astrologers were employed in reading their books of necromancy, they perceived the two pieces begin to move and to approach, and after some small interval of time, that inscribed with the name of Chingis-khan to place itself upon the top of its adversary. Upon witnessing this, the king and his band of Tartars marched with exultation to the attack of the army of Un-khan, broke through its ranks and entirely routed it. Un-khan himself was killed, his kingdom fell to the conqueror, and Chingis-khan espoused his daughter. After this battle he continued during six years to render himself master of additional kingdoms and cities; until at length, in the siege of a castle named Thaigin, he was struck by an arrow in the knee, and dying of the wound, was buried in the mountain of Altaï.

CHAPTER XLVI

Of six successive Emperors of the Tartars, and of the Ceremonies that take place when they are carried for Interment to the Mountain of Altaï

To Chingis-khan succeeded Cyhn-khan; the third was Bathyn-khan, the fourth Esu-khan, the fifth Mongù-khan, the sixth Kublai-khan, who became greater and more powerful than all the others, inasmuch as he inherited what his predecessors possessed, and afterwards, during a reign of nearly sixty years, acquired, it may be said, the remainder of the world. The title of khan or kaan, is equivalent to emperor in our language. It has been an invariable custom, that all the Grand Khans, and chiefs of the race of Chingis-khan, should be carried for interment to a certain lofty mountain named Altaï, and in whatever place they may happen to die, although it should be at the distance of a hundred days' journey, they are nevertheless conveyed thither. It is likewise the custom, during the progress of removing the bodies of these princes, for those who form the escort to sacrifice such persons as they chance to meet on the road, saying to them, 'Depart for the next world, and there attend upon your deceased master,' being impressed with the belief that all whom they thus slay do actually become his servants in the next life. They do the same also with

respect to horses, killing the best of the stud, in order that he may
have the use of them. When the corpse of Mongù was transported to
this mountain, the horsemen who accompanied it, having this blind
and horrible persuasion, slew upwards of twenty thousand persons
who fell in their way.

CHAPTER XLVII

*Of the Wandering Life of the Tartars — Of their Domestic
Manners, their Food, and the Virtue and Useful Qualities of
their Women*

Now that I have begun speaking of the Tartars, I will tell you more
about them. The Tartars never remain fixed, but as the winter
approaches remove to the plains of a warmer region, in order to find
sufficient pasture for their cattle; and in summer they frequent cold
situations in the mountains, where there is water and verdure, and
their cattle are free from the annoyance of horse-flies and other biting
insects. During two or three months they progressively ascend higher
ground, and seek fresh pasture, the grass not being adequate in any
one place to feed the multitudes of which their herds and flocks
consist. Their huts or tents are formed of rods covered with felt, and
being exactly round, and nicely put together, they can gather them
into one bundle, and make them up as packages, which they carry
along with them in their migrations, upon a sort of car with four
wheels. When they have occasion to set them up again, they always
make the entrance front to the south. Besides these cars they have a
superior kind of vehicle upon two wheels, covered likewise with
black felt, and so effectually as to protect those within it from wet,
during a whole day of rain. These are drawn by oxen and camels, and
serve to convey their wives and children, their utensils, and such
provisions as they require. The women it is who attend to their
trading concerns, who buy and sell, and provide everything necessary
for their husbands and their families; the time of the men being
entirely devoted to hunting and hawking, and matters that relate to

the military life. They have the best falcons in the world, and also the best dogs. They subsist entirely upon flesh and milk, eating the produce of their sport, and a certain small animal, not unlike a rabbit, called by our people Pharaoh's mice, which, during the summer season are found in great abundance in the plains. But they likewise eat flesh of every description, horses, camels, and even dogs, provided they are fat. They drink mares' milk, which they prepare in such a manner that it has the qualities and flavour of white wine. They term it in their language *kemurs*. Their women are not excelled in the world for chastity and decency of conduct, nor for love and duty to their husbands. Infidelity to the marriage bed is regarded by them as a vice not merely dishonourable, but of the most infamous nature; whilst on the other hand it is admirable to observe the loyalty of the husbands towards their wives, amongst whom, although there are perhaps ten or twenty, there prevails a degree of quiet and union that is highly laudable. No offensive language is ever heard, their attention being fully occupied with their traffic (as already mentioned) and their several domestic employments, such as the provision of necessary food for the family, the management of the servants, and the care of the children, which are amongst them a common concern. And the more praiseworthy are the virtues of modesty and chastity in the wives, because the men are allowed the indulgence of taking as many as they choose. Their expense to the husband is not great, and on the other hand the benefit he derives from their trading, and from the occupations in which they are constantly engaged, is considerable; on which account it is, that when he receives a young woman in marriage, he pays a dower to her parent. The wife who is the first espoused has the privilege of superior attention, and is held to be the most legitimate, which extends also to the children borne by her. In consequence of this unlimited number of wives, the offspring is more numerous than amongst any other people. Upon the death of the father, the son may take to himself the wives he leaves behind, with the exception of his own mother. They cannot take their sisters to wife, but upon the death of their brothers they can marry their sisters-in-law. Every marriage is solemnised with great ceremony.

CHAPTER XLVIII

Of the Celestial and Terrestrial Deities of the Tartars, and of their Modes of Worship — Of their Dress, Arms, Courage in Battle, Patience under Privations, and Obedience to their Leaders

The doctrine and faith of the Tartars are these: They believe in a deity whose nature is sublime and heavenly. To him they burn incense in censers, and offer up prayers for the enjoyment of intellectual and bodily health. They worship another likewise, named Natigay, whose image, covered with felt or other cloth, every individual preserves in his house. To this deity they associate a wife and children, placing the former on his left side, and the latter before him, in a posture of reverential salutation. Him they consider as the divinity who presides over their terrestrial concerns, protects their children, and guards their cattle and their grain. They show him great respect, and at their meals they never omit to take a fat morsel of the flesh, and with it to grease the mouth of the idol, and at the same time the mouths of its wife and children. They then throw out of the door some of the liquor in which the meat has been dressed, as an offering to the other spirits. This being done, they consider that their deity and his family have had their proper share, and proceed to eat and drink without further ceremony. The rich amongst these people dress in cloth of gold and silks with skins of the sable, the ermine, and other animals. All their accoutrements are of an expensive kind. Their arms are bows, iron maces, and in some instances, spears; but the first is the weapon at which they are the most expert, being accustomed, from children, to employ it in their sports. They wear defensive armour made of the thick hides of buffaloes and other beasts, dried by the fire, and thus rendered extremely hard and strong. They are brave in battle, almost to desperation, setting little value upon their lives, and exposing themselves without hesitation to all manner of danger. Their disposition is cruel. They are capable of supporting every kind of privation, and when there is a necessity for it, can live for a month on the milk of their mares, and upon such wild animals as they may chance to catch. Their horses are fed upon grass alone, and do not require barley, or other grain. The men are habituated to remain on horseback during two days and two nights, without dismounting; sleeping in that situation whilst their horses graze. No people upon earth can surpass them in fortitude under difficulties, nor show greater patience under wants of every kind. They are perfectly obedient to their chiefs, and are maintained at small expense. From these qualities, so essential to the formation of soldiers, it is, that they are fitted to subdue the world, as in fact they have done in regard to a considerable portion of it.

CHAPTER XLIX

Of the Tartar Armies, and the manner in which they are constituted — Of their Order of Marching — Of their Provisions — And of their Mode of Attacking the Enemy

When one of the great Tartar chiefs proceeds on an expedition, he puts himself at the head of an army of an hundred thousand horse, and organises them in the following manner. He appoints an officer to the command of every ten men, and others to command an hundred, a thousand, and ten thousand men, respectively. Thus ten of the officers commanding ten men take their orders from him who commands a hundred; of these, each ten, from him who commands a thousand; and each ten of these latter, from him who commands ten thousand. By this arrangement each officer has only to attend to the management of ten men or ten bodies of men; and when the commander of these hundred thousand men has occasion to make a detachment for any particular service, he issues his orders to the commanders of ten thousand to furnish him with a thousand men each; and these, in like manner, to the commanders of a thousand, who give their orders to those commanding a hundred, until the order reaches those commanding ten, by whom the number required is immediately supplied to their superior officers. A hundred men are in this manner delivered to every officer commanding a thousand,

and a thousand men to every officer commanding ten thousand. The drafting takes place without delay, and all are implicitly obedient to their respective superiors. Every company of a hundred men is denominated a *tuc*, and ten of these constitute a *toman*. When the army proceeds on service, a body of men is sent two days' march in advance, and parties are stationed upon each flank and in the rear, in order to prevent its being attacked by surprise. When the service is distant, they carry but little with them, and that, chiefly what is requisite for their encampment, and utensils for cooking. They subsist for the most part upon milk, as has been said. Each man has, on an average, eighteen horses and mares, and when that which they ride is fatigued, they change it for another. They are provided with small tents made of felt, under which they shelter themselves against rain. Should circumstances render it necessary, in the execution of a duty that requires despatch, they can march for ten days together without dressing victuals, during which time they subsist upon the blood drawn from their horses, each man opening a vein and drinking from his own cattle. They make provision also of milk, thickened and dried to the state of a hard paste (or curd), which is prepared in the following manner. They boil the milk, and skimming off the rich or creamy part as it rises to the top, put it into a separate vessel as butter; for so long as that remains in the milk, it will not become hard. The latter is then exposed to the sun until it dries. Upon going on service they carry with them about ten pounds for each man, and of this, half a pound is put, every morning, into a leathern bottle, or small *outre*, with as much water as is thought necessary. By their motion in riding the contents are violently shaken, and a thin porridge is produced, upon which they make their dinner. When these Tartars come to engage in battle, they never mix with the enemy, but keep hovering about him, discharging their arrows first from one side and then from the other, occasionally pretending to fly, and during their flight shooting arrows backwards at their pursuers, killing men and horses, as if they were combating face to face. In this sort of warfare the adversary imagines he has gained a victory, when in fact he has lost the battle; for the Tartars, observing the mischief they have done him, wheel about, and renewing the fight, overpower his remaining troops, and make them prisoners in spite of their utmost exertions. Their horses are so well broken-in to quick changes of movement, that upon the signal given, they instantly turn in every direction; and by these rapid manoeuvres many victories have been obtained. All that has been here related is spoken of the original manners of the Tartar chiefs; but at the present day they are much corrupted. Those who dwell at Ukaka, forsaking their own laws, have adopted the customs of the people who worship idols, and those who inhabit the eastern provinces have adopted the manners of the Saracens.

CHAPTER L

Of the Rules of Justice observed by these People – And of an Imaginary Kind of Marriage contracted between the Deceased Children of Different Families

Justice is administered by them in the following manner. When a person is convicted of a robbery not meriting the punishment of death, he is condemned to receive a certain number of strokes with a cane – seven, seventeen, twenty-seven, thirty-seven, forty-seven, or as far as one hundred and seven, according to the value of the article stolen, and circumstances of the theft; and many die under this chastisement. When for stealing a horse or other article that subjects the offender to capital punishment, he is condemned to suffer death, the sentence is executed by cutting his body in two with a sword. But if the thief has the means of paying nine times the value of the property stolen, he escapes all further punishment. It is usual for every chief of a tribe or other person possessing large cattle, such as horses, mares, camels, oxen, or cows, to distinguish them by his mark, and then to suffer them to graze at large, in any part of the plains or mountains, without employing herdsmen to look after them; and if any of them should happen to mix with the cattle of other proprietors, they are restored to the person whose mark they bear. Sheep and goats, on the contrary, have people to attend them. Their cattle of every kind are well-sized, fat, and exceedingly handsome. When one man has had a son, and another man a daughter, although both may have been dead for some years, they have a practice of contracting a marriage between their deceased children, and of bestowing the girl upon the youth. They at the same time paint upon pieces of paper human figures to represent attendants with horses and other animals, dresses of all kinds, money, and every article of furniture; and all these, together with the marriage contract, which is regularly drawn up, they commit to the flames, in order that through the medium of the smoke (as they believe) these things may be conveyed to their children in the other world, and that they may become husband and wife in due form. After this ceremony, the fathers and mothers consider themselves as mutually related, in the same manner as if a real connection had taken place between their living children. Having thus given an account of the manners and customs of the Tartars, although not yet of the brilliant acts and enterprises of their Grand Khan, who is lord of all the Tartars, we shall now return to our former subject, that is, to the extensive plain which we were traversing when we stopped to relate the history of this people.

CHAPTER LI

Of the Plain of Bargu near Kara-korum − Of the Customs of its Inhabitants − Of the Ocean, at the Distance of Forty Days' Journey from thence − Of the Falcons produced in the Country on its Borders − And of the Bearings of the Northern Constellation to an Observer in those Parts

Upon leaving Kara-korum and the mountains of Altaï, the burial-place, as has been said, of the imperial Tartar family, you proceed, in a northern direction, through a country termed the plain of Bargu, extending to the distance of about forty days' journey. The people who dwell there are called Mekriti, a rude tribe, who live upon the flesh of animals, the largest of which are of the nature of stags; and these they also make use of for the purposes of travelling. They feed likewise upon the birds that frequent their numerous lakes and marshes, as well as upon fish. It is at the moulting season, or during summer, that the birds seek these waters. And being then, from want of their feathers, incapable of flight, they are taken by the natives without difficulty. This plain borders on the ocean at its northern extremity. The customs and manners of the people resemble those of the Tartars that have been described, and they are subjects of the Grand Khan. They have neither corn nor wine; and although in summer they derive subsistence from the chase, yet in winter the cold is so excessive that neither birds nor beasts can remain there. Upon travelling forty days, as it is said, you reach the (northern) ocean. Near to this is a mountain, in which, as well as in the neighbouring plain, vultures and peregrine falcons have their nests. Neither men nor cattle are found there, and of birds there is only a species called bargelak, and the falcons to which they serve for food. The former are about the size of a partridge, with tails like the swallow, claws like those of the parrot kind, and are swift of flight. When the Grand Khan is desirous of having a brood of peregrine falcons, he sends to procure them at this place; and in an island lying off the coast, gerfalcons are found in such numbers that his majesty may be supplied with as many of them as he pleases. It must not be supposed that the gerfalcons sent from Europe for the use of the Tartars are conveyed to the court of the Grand Khan. They go only to some of the Tartar or other chiefs of the Levant, bordering on the countries of the Comanians and Armenians. This island is situated so far to the north that the polar constellation appears to be behind you, and to have in part a southerly bearing. Having thus spoken of the regions in the vicinity of the northern ocean, we shall now describe the provinces lying nearer to the residence of the Grand Khan, and shall return to that of Kampion, of which mention has already been made.

CHAPTER LII

Of the Kingdom of Erginul, adjoining to that of Kampion, and of the City of Singui — Of a Species of Oxen covered with extremely fine Hair — Of the Form of the Animal that yields the Musk, and the Mode of taking it — And of the Customs of the Inhabitants of that Country, and the Beauty of the Women

Upon leaving Kampion, and proceeding five days' journey towards the east, in the course of which travellers are frequently terrified in the night-time by the voices of spirits, they reach a kingdom named Erginul, subject to the Grand Khan, and included in the province of Tangut. Within the limits of this kingdom are several principalities, the inhabitants of which are, in general, idolaters, with some few Nestorian Christians and worshippers of Mahomet. Amongst many cities and strong places the principal one is Erginul. Proceeding from thence in a south-eastern direction, the road takes you to Cathay, and in that route you find a city called Singui, in a district of the same name, where are many towns and castles, in like manner belonging to Tangut, and under the dominion of the Grand Khan. The population of this country consists chiefly of idolaters; but there are also some Mahometans and Christians. Here are found many wild cattle that, in point of size, may be compared to elephants. Their colour is a mixture of white and black, and they are very beautiful to the sight. The hair upon every part of their bodies lies down smooth, excepting upon the shoulder, where it stands up to the height of about three palms. This hair, or rather wool, is white, and more soft and delicate than silk. Marco Polo carried some of it to Venice, as a singular curiosity, and such it was esteemed by all who saw it. Many of these cattle taken wild have become domesticated, and the breed produced between them and the common cow are noble animals, and better qualified to undergo fatigue than any other kind. They are accustomed to carry heavier burthens and to perform twice the labour in husbandry that could be derived from the ordinary sort, being both active and powerful. In this country it is that the finest and most valuable musk is procured. The animal which yields it is not larger than the female goat, but in form resembles the antelope. It is called in the Tartar language, *gudderi*. Its coat is like that of the larger kind of deer: its feet and tail are those of the antelope, but it has not the horns. It is provided with four projecting teeth or tusks, three inches in length, two in the upper jaw pointing downwards, and two in the lower jaw pointing upwards; small in proportion to their length, and white as ivory. Upon the whole it is a handsome creature. The musk is obtained in the following manner. At the time when the moon is at the full, a bag or imposthume of coagulated blood forms itself about the umbilical region, and those whose occupation it is to take the animal avail themselves of the moonlight for that purpose, when they cut off the membrane, and afterwards dry it, with its contents, in the sun. It proves the finest musk that is known. Great numbers are caught, and the flesh is esteemed good to eat. Marco Polo brought with him to Venice the head and the feet of one of them dried. The inhabitants of this country employ themselves in trade and manufactures. They have grain in abundance. The extent of the province is twenty-five days' journey. Pheasants are found in it that are twice the size of ours, but something smaller than the peacock. The tail feathers are eight or ten palms in length. There are other pheasants also, in size and appearance like our own, as well as a great variety of other birds, some of which have beautiful plumage. The inhabitants are idolaters. In person they are inclined to corpulency, and their noses are small. Their hair is black, and they have scarcely any beard, or only a few scattered hairs on the chin. The women of the superior class are in like manner free from superfluous hairs; their skins are fair, and they are well formed; but in their manners they are dissolute. The men are much devoted to female society; and, according to their laws and customs, they may have as many wives as they please, provided they are able to maintain them. If a young woman, although poor, be handsome, the rich are induced to take her to wife, and in order to obtain her, make valuable presents to her parents and relations, beauty alone being the quality held in estimation. We shall now take our leave of this district, and proceed to speak of another, situated further to the eastward.

CHAPTER LIII

*Of the Province of Egrigaia, and of the City of Kalacha − Of
the Manners of its Inhabitants − And of the Camelots
manufactured there*

Departing from Erginul, and proceeding easterly for eight days, you
come to a country named Egrigaia, still belonging to the great
province of Tangut, and subject to the Grand Khan, in which there
are many cities and castles, the principal one of which is called
Kalacha. The inhabitants are in general idolaters; but there are three
churches of Nestorian Christians. In this city they manufacture
beautiful camelots, the finest known in the world, of the hair of
camels and likewise of white wool. These are of a beautiful white.
They are purchased by the merchants in considerable quantities, and
carried to many other countries, especially to Cathay. Leaving this
province, we shall now speak of another situated towards the (north-)
east, named Tenduk, and shall thus enter upon the territory of Prester
John.

CHAPTER LIV

*Of the Province of Tenduk, governed by Princes of the Race
of Prester John, and chiefly inhabited by Christians − Of the
Ordination of their Priests − And of a Tribe of People called
Argon, the most personable and the best-informed of any in
these Countries*

Tenduk, belonging to the territory of Prester John, is an eastern
province, in which there are many cities and castles, subject to the
rule of the Grand Khan; all the princes of that family having remained
dependent, since Chingis, the first emperor, subdued the country.
The capital is likewise named Tenduk. The king now reigning is a

descendant of Prester John, and is still Prester John, and named George. He is both a Christian and a priest; the greater part of the inhabitants being also Christians. This King George holds his country as a fief of the Grand Khan; not, indeed, the entire possessions of the original Prester John, but a certain portion of them; and the khan always bestows upon him, as well as upon the other princes of his house, his daughters, and other females of the royal family, in marriage. In this province, the stone of which the azure colour is made is found in abundance, and of fine quality. Here likewise they manufacture stuffs of camels' hair. The people gain their subsistence by agriculture, trade, and mechanical labours. Although subject to the dominion of the Grand Khan, the king being a Christian, as has been said, the government of the country is in the hands of Christians. Amongst the inhabitants, however, there are both worshippers of idols and followers of the law of Mahomet. There is likewise a class of people known by the appellation of Argon, because they are produced from a mixture of two races, namely, those natives of Tenduk who are idolaters, and the Mahometans. The men of this country are fairer complexioned and better looking than those in the other countries of which we have been speaking, and also better instructed, and more skilful traders.

CHAPTER LV

Of the Seat of Government of the Princes of the Family of Prester John, called Gog and Magog — Of the Manners of its Inhabitants — Of their Manufacture of Silk — And of the Mines of Silver worked there

In this province (of Tenduk) was the principal seat of government of the sovereigns styled Prester John, when they ruled over the Tartars of this and the neighbouring countries, and which their successors occupy to the present hour. George, above-mentioned, is the fourth in descent from Prester John, of whose family he is regarded as the head. There are two regions in which they exercise dominion. These in our part of the world are named Gog and Magog, but by the natives Ung and Mongul; in each of which there is a distinct race of people. In Ung they are Gog, and in Mongul they are Tartars. Travelling seven days through this province, in an easterly direction, towards Cathay, you pass many towns inhabited by idolaters, as well as by Mahometans and Nestorian Christians. They gain their living by trade and manufactures, weaving fine-gold tissues, ornamented with mother-of-pearl, named *nasdci*, and silks of different textures and colours, not unlike those of Europe; together with a variety of woollen cloths. These people are all subjects of the Grand Khan. One of the towns, named Sindichin, is celebrated for the manufacture of all kinds of arms, and every article necessary for the equipment of troops. In the mountainous part of the province there is a place called Idifa, in which is a rich mine of silver, from whence large quantities of that metal are obtained. There are also plenty of birds and beasts.

CHAPTER LVI

Of the City of Changa-nor − Of different Species of Cranes − And of Partridges and Quails bred in that Part by the Orders of the Grand Khan

Leaving the city and province last mentioned, and travelling three days, you arrive at a city named Changa-nor, which signifies, the 'white lake'. At this place the Grand Khan has a great palace, which he is fond of visiting, because it is surrounded with pieces of water and streams, the resort of many swans; and there is a fine plain, where are found in great numbers cranes, pheasants, partridges, and other birds. He derives the highest degree of amusement from sporting with gerfalcons and hawks, the game being here in vast abundance. Of the cranes they reckon five species. The first sort are entirely black as coals, and have long wings. The second sort have wings still longer than the first, but are white, and the feathers of the wings are full of eyes, round like those of the peacock, but of a gold colour and very bright; the head is red and black, and well formed; the neck is black and white, and the general appearance of the bird is extremely handsome. The third sort are of the size of ours [in Italy]. The fourth are small cranes, having the feathers prettily streaked with red and azure. The fifth are of a grey colour, with the head red and black, and are of a large size. Nigh to this city is a valley frequented by great numbers of partridges and quails, for whose food the Grand Khan causes millet, panicum, and other grains suitable to such birds, to be sown along the sides of it every season, and gives strict command that no person shall dare to reap the seed; in order that they may not be in want of nourishment. Many keepers, likewise, are stationed there for the preservation of the game, that it may not be taken or destroyed, as well as for the purpose of throwing the millet to the birds during the winter. So accustomed are they to be thus fed, that upon the grain being scattered and the man's whistling, they immediately assemble from every quarter. The Grand Khan also directs that a number of small buildings be prepared for their shelter during the night; and, in consequence of these attentions, he always finds abundant sport when he visits this country; and even in the winter, at which season, on account of the severity of the cold, he does not reside there, he has camel-loads of the birds sent to him, wherever his court may happen to be at the time. Leaving this place, we shall now direct our course three days' journey towards the north-east.

CHAPTER LVII

Of the Grand Khan's beautiful Palace in the City of Shandu — Of his Stud of White Brood-Mares, with whose Milk he performs an Annual Sacrifice — Of the wonderful Operations of the Astrologers on occasions of Bad Weather — Of the Ceremonies practised by them in the Hall of the Royal Palace — And of two Descriptions of Religious Mendicants, with their Modes of Living

Departing from the city last mentioned, and proceeding three days' journey in a north-easterly direction, you arrive at a city called Shandu, built by the Grand Khan Kublai, now reigning. In this he caused a palace to be erected, of marble and other handsome stones, admirable as well for the elegance of its design as for the skill displayed in its execution. The halls and chambers are all gilt, and very handsome. It presents one front towards the interior of the city, and the other towards the wall; and from each extremity of the building runs another wall to such an extent as to enclose sixteen miles in circuit of the adjoining plain, to which there is no access but through the palace. Within the bounds of this royal park there are rich and beautiful meadows, watered by many rivulets, where a variety of animals of the deer and goat kind are pastured, to serve as food for the hawks and other birds employed in the chase, whose mews are also in the grounds. The number of these birds is upwards of two hundred; and the Grand Khan goes in person, at least once in the week, to inspect them. Frequently, when he rides about this enclosed forest, he has one or more small leopards carried on horseback, behind their keepers; and when he pleases to give direction for their being slipped, they instantly seize a stag, or goat, or fallow deer, which he gives to his hawks, and in this manner he amuses himself. In the centre of these grounds, where there is a beautiful grove of trees, he has built a royal pavilion, supported upon a colonnade of handsome pillars, gilt and varnished. Round each pillar a dragon, likewise gilt, entwines its tail, whilst its head sustains the projection of the roof, and its talons or claws are extended to the right and left along the entablature. The roof is of bamboo cane, likewise gilt, and so well varnished that no wet can injure it. The bamboos used for this purpose are three palms in circumference and ten fathoms in length, and being cut at the joints, are split into two equal parts, so as to form gutters, and with these (laid concave and convex) the pavilion is covered; but to secure the roof against the effect of wind, each of the bamboos is tied at the ends to the frame. The building is supported on every side (like a tent) by more than two hundred very strong silken cords, and otherwise, from the lightness of the materials, it would be liable to oversetting by the force of high winds. The whole is constructed with so much ingenuity of contrivance that all the parts may be taken asunder, removed, and again set up, at his majesty's pleasure. This spot he has selected for his recreation on account of the mild temperature and salubrity of the air, and he accordingly makes it his residence during three months of the year, namely, June, July, and August; and every year, on the twenty-eighth day of the moon, in the last of these months, it is his established custom to depart from thence, and proceed to an appointed place, in order to perform certain sacrifices, in the following manner. It is to be understood that his majesty keeps up a stud of about ten thousand horses and mares, which are white as snow; and of the milk of these mares no person can presume to drink who is not of the family descended from Chingis-khan, with the exception only of one other family, named Boriat, to whom that monarch gave the honourable privilege, in reward of valorous achievements in battle, performed in his own presence. So great, indeed, is the respect shown to these horses that, even when they are at pasture in the royal meadows or forests, no one dares to place himself before them, or otherwise to impede their movements. The astrologers whom he entertains in his service, and who are deeply versed in the diabolical art of magic, having pronounced it to be his duty, annually, on the twenty-eighth day of the moon in August, to scatter in the wind the milk taken from these mares, as a libation to all the spirits and idols whom they adore for the purpose of propitiating them and ensuring their protection of the people, male and female, of the cattle, the fowls, the grain and other fruits of the earth; on this account it is that his majesty adheres to the rule that has been mentioned, and on that particular day proceeds to the spot where, with his own hands, he is to make the offering of milk. On such occasions these astrologers, or magicians as they may be termed, sometimes display their skill in a wonderful manner; for if it should happen that the sky becomes cloudy and threatens rain, they ascend the roof of the palace where the Grand Khan resides at the time, and by the force of their incantations they prevent the rain from falling and stay the tempest; so that whilst, in the surrounding country, storms of rain, wind, and thunder are experienced, the palace itself remains unaffected by the elements. Those who operate miracles of this nature are persons of Tebeth and Kesmir, two classes of idolaters more profoundly skilled in the art of magic than the natives of any other country. They persuaded the vulgar that these works are effected through the sanctity of their own lives and the merits of their penances; and presuming upon the reputation thus acquired, they exhibit themselves in a filthy and indecent state, regardless as well of what they owe to their character as of the respect due to those in whose presence they appear. They suffer their faces to continue always uncleansed by washing and their hair uncombed, living altogether in a squalid style. They are addicted, moreover, to this beastly and horrible practice, that when any culprit is condemned to death, they carry off the body, dress it on the fire, and devour it; but of persons who die a natural death they do not eat the bodies. Besides the appellations before mentioned, by which they are distinguished from each other, they are likewise termed *baksi*, which applies to their religious sect or order – as we should say, friars, preachers, or minors. So expert are they in their infernal art, they may be said to perform whatever they will; and one instance shall be given, although it may be thought to exceed the bounds of credibility. When the Grand Khan sits at meals, in his hall of state (as shall be more particularly described in the following book), the table which is placed in the centre is elevated to the height of about eight cubits, and at a distance from it stands a large buffet, where all the drinking vessels are arranged. Now, by means of their supernatural art, they cause the flagons of wine, milk, or any other beverage, to fill the cups spontaneously, without being touched by the attendants, and the cups to move through the air the distance of ten paces until they reach the hand of the Grand Khan. As he empties them, they return to the place from whence they came; and this is done in the presence of such persons as are invited by his majesty to witness the performance. These *baksis*, when the festival days of their idols draw near, go to the palace of the Grand Khan, and thus address him: 'Sire, be it known to your majesty, that if the honours of a holocaust are not paid to our deities, they will in their anger afflict us with bad seasons, with blight to our grain, pestilence to our cattle, and with other plagues. On this account we supplicate your majesty to grant us a certain number of sheep with black heads, together with so many pounds of incense and of lignum aloes, in order that we may be enabled to perform the customary rites with due solemnity.' Their words, however, are not spoken immediately to the Grand Khan, but to certain great officers, by whom the communication is made to him. Upon receiving it he never fails to comply with the whole of their request; and accordingly, when the day arrives, they sacrifice the sheep, and by pouring out the liquor in which the meat has been seethed, in the presence of their idols, perform the ceremony of worship. In this country there are great monasteries and abbeys, so extensive indeed that they might pass for small cities, some of them containing as many as two thousand monks, who are devoted to the service of their divinities, according to the established religious customs of the people. These are clad in a better style of dress than the other inhabitants; they shave their heads and their beards, and celebrate the festivals of their idols with the utmost possible solemnity, having bands of vocal music and burning tapers. Some of this class are allowed to take wives. There is likewise another religious order, the members of which are named *sensim*, who observe strict abstinence and lead very austere lives, having no other food than a kind of pollard, which they steep in warm water until the farinaceous part is separated from the bran, and in that state they eat it. This sect pay adoration to fire, and are considered by the others as schismatics, not worshipping idols as they do. There is a material difference between them in regard to the rules of their orders, and these last described never marry in any instance. They shave their heads and beards like the others, and wear hempen garments of a black or dull colour; but even if the material were silk, the colour would be the same. They sleep upon coarse mats, and suffer greater hardships in their mode of living than any people in the world. We shall now quit this subject, and proceed to speak of the great and wonderful acts of the supreme lord and emperor, Kublai-khan.

BOOK TWO

CHAPTER I

Of the admirable Deeds of Kublai-khan, the Emperor now reigning — Of the Battle he fought with Nayan, his Uncle, and of the Victory he obtained

§ I. In this Book it is our design to treat of all the great and admirable achievements of the Grand Khan now reigning, who is styled Kublai-khan; the latter word implying in our language lord of lords, and with much propriety added to his name; for in respect to number of subjects, extent of territory, and amount of revenue, he surpasses every sovereign that has heretofore been or that now is in the world; nor has any other been served with such implicit obedience by those whom he governs. This will so evidently appear in the course of our work, as to satisfy everyone of the truth of our assertion.

Kublai-khan, it is to be understood, is the lineal and legitimate descendant of Chingis-khan the first emperor, and the rightful sovereign of the Tartars. He is the sixth Grand Khan, and began his reign in the year 1256. He obtained the sovereignty by his consummate valour, his virtues, and his prudence, in opposition to the designs of his brothers, supported by many of the great officers and members of his own family. But the succession appertained to him of right. It is forty-two years since he began to reign to the present year, 1288, and he is fully eighty-five years of age. Previously to his ascending the throne he had served as a volunteer in the army, and endeavoured to take a share in every enterprise. Not only was he brave and daring in action, but in point of judgement and military skill he was considered to be the most able and successful commander that ever led the Tartars to battle. From that period, however, he ceased to take the field in person, and entrusted the conduct of expeditions to his sons and his captains; excepting in one instance, the occasion of which was as follows. A certain chief named Nayan, who, although only thirty years of age, was kinsman to Kublai, had succeeded to the dominion of many cities and provinces, which enabled him to bring into the field an army of four hundred thousand horse. His predecessors, however, had been vassals of the Grand Khan. Actuated by youthful vanity upon finding himself at the head of so great a force, he formed, in the year 1286, the design of throwing off his allegiance, and usurping the sovereignty. With this view he privately despatched messengers to Kaidu, another powerful chief, whose territories lay towards the greater Turkey, and who, although a nephew of the Grand Khan, was in rebellion against him, and bore him determined ill-will, proceeding from the apprehension of punishment for former offences. To Kaidu, therefore, the propositions made by Nayan were highly satisfactory, and he accordingly promised to bring to his assistance an army of a hundred thousand horse. Both princes immediately began to assemble their forces, but it could not be effected so secretly as not to come to the knowledge of Kublai, who upon hearing of their preparations lost no time in occupying all the passes leading to the countries of Nayan and of Kaidu, in order to prevent them from having any information respecting the measures he was himself taking. He then gave orders for collecting, with the utmost celerity, the whole of the troops stationed within ten days' march of the city of Kambalù. These amounted to three hundred and sixty thousand horse, to which was added a body of a hundred thousand foot, consisting of those who were usually about his person, and principally his falconers and domestic servants. In the course of twenty days they were all in readiness. Had he assembled the armies kept up for the constant protection of the different provinces of Cathay, it must necessarily have required thirty or forty days; in which time the enemy would have gained information of his arrangements, and been enabled to effect their junction, and to occupy such strong positions as would best suit with their designs. His object was, by promptitude, which is ever the companion of victory, to anticipate the preparations of Nayan, and by falling upon him whilst single, destroy his power with more certainty and effect than after he should have been joined by Kaidu.

It may be proper here to observe, whilst on the subject of the

armies of the Grand Khan, that in every province of Cathay and of
Manji, as well as in other parts of his dominions, there were many
disloyal and seditious persons, who at all times were disposed to break
out in rebellion against their sovereign, and on this account it became
necessary to keep armies in such of the provinces as contained large
cities and an extensive population, which are stationed at the distance
of four or five miles from those cities, and can enter them at their
pleasure. These armies the Grand Khan makes it a practice to change
every second year, and the same with respect to the officers who
command them. By means of such precautions the people are kept in
quiet subjection, and no movement nor innovation of any kind can
be attempted. The troops are maintained not only from the pay they
receive out of the imperial revenues of the province, but also from
the cattle and their milk, which belong to them individually, and
which they send into the cities for sale, furnishing themselves from
thence, in return, with those articles of which they stand in need. In
this manner they are distributed over the country, in various places,
to the distance of thirty, forty, and even sixty days' journey. If even
the half of these corps were to be collected in one place, the
statement of their number would appear marvellous and scarcely
entitled to belief.

§2. Having formed his army in the manner above described, the
Grand Khan proceeded towards the territory of Nayan, and by forced
marches, continued day and night, he reached it at the expiration of
twenty-five days. So prudently, at the same time, was the expedition
managed, that neither that prince himself nor any of his dependents
were aware of it, all the roads being guarded in such a manner that no
persons who attempted to pass could escape being made prisoners.
Upon arriving at a certain range of hills, on the other side of which
was the plain where Nayan's army lay encamped, Kublai halted his
troops, and allowed them two days of rest. During this interval he
called upon his astrologers to ascertain by virtue of their art, and to
declare in presence of the whole army, to which side the victory
would incline. They pronounced that it would fall to the lot of
Kublai. It has ever been the practice of the Grand Khans to have
recourse to divination for the purpose of inspiriting their men.
Confident therefore of success, they ascended the hill with alacrity
the next morning, and presented themselves before the army of
Nayan, which they found negligently posted, without advance parties

or scouts, whilst the chief himself was asleep in his tent, accompanied by one of his wives. Upon awaking, he hastened to form his troops in the best manner that circumstances would allow, lamenting that his junction with Kaidu had not been sooner effected. Kublai took his station in a large wooden castle, borne on the backs of four elephants, whose bodies were protected with coverings of thick leather hardened by fire, over which were housings of cloth of gold. The castle contained many crossbow-men and archers, and on the top of it was hoisted the imperial standard, adorned with representations of the sun and moon. His army, which consisted of thirty battalions of horse, each battalion containing ten thousand men, armed with bows, he disposed in three grand divisions; and those which formed the left and right wings he extended in such a manner as to outflank the army of Nayan. In front of each battalion of horse were placed five hundred infantry, armed with short lances and swords, who, whenever the cavalry made a show of fight, were practised to mount behind the riders and accompany them, alighting again when they returned to the charge, and killing with their lances the horses of the enemy. As soon as the order of battle was arranged, an infinite number of wind instruments of various kinds were sounded, and these were succeeded by songs, according to the custom of the Tartars before they engage in fight, which commences upon the signal given by the cymbals and drums, and there was such a beating of the cymbals and drums, and such singing, that it was wonderful to hear. This signal, by the orders of the Grand Khan, was first given to the right and left wings; and then a fierce and bloody conflict began. The air was instantly filled with a cloud of arrows that poured down on every side, and vast numbers of men and horses were seen to fall to the ground. The loud cries and shouts of the men, together with the noise of the horses and the weapons, were such as to inspire terror into those who heard them. When their arrows had been discharged, the hostile parties engaged in close combat with their lances, swords, and maces shod with iron; and such was the slaughter, and so large were the heaps of the carcasses of men, and more especially of horses, on the field, that it became impossible for the one party to advance upon the other. Thus the fortune of the day remained for a long time undecided, and victory wavered between the contending parties from morning until noon; for so zealous was the devotion of Nayan's people to the cause of their master, who was most liberal and indulgent towards them, that they were all ready to meet death rather than turn their backs to the enemy. At length, however, Nayan, perceiving that he was nearly surrounded, attempted to save himself by flight, but was presently made prisoner, and conducted to the presence of Kublai, who gave orders for his being put to death. This was carried into execution by enclosing him between two carpets, which were violently shaken until the spirit had departed from the body; the motive for this peculiar sentence being, that the sun and the air should not witness the shedding of the blood of one who belonged to the imperial family. Those of his troops which survived the battle came to make their submission, and swear allegiance to Kublai. They were inhabitants of the four noble provinces of Chorza, Karli, Barskol, and Sitingui.

Nayan, who had privately undergone the ceremony of baptism, but never made open profession of Christianity, thought proper, on this occasion, to bear the sign of the cross in his banners, and he had in his army a vast number of Christians, who were left amongst the slain. When the Jews and the Saracens perceived that the banner of the cross was overthrown, they taunted the Christian inhabitants with it, saying, 'Behold the state to which your (vaunted) banners, and those who followed them, are reduced!' On account of these derisions the Christians were compelled to lay their complaints before the Grand Khan, who ordered the former to appear before him, and sharply rebuked them. 'If the Cross of Christ,' he said, 'has not proved advantageous to the party of Nayan, the effect has been consistent with reason and justice, inasmuch as he was a rebel and a traitor to his lord, and to such wretches it could not afford its protection. Let none therefore presume to charge with injustice the God of the Christians, who is Himself the perfection of goodness and of justice.'

CHAPTER II

*Of the Return of the Grand Khan to the City of Kanbalu
after his Victory — Of the Honour he confers on the
Christians, the Jews, the Mahometans, and the Idolaters, at
their respective Festivals — And the Reason he assigns for his
not becoming a Christian*

The Grand Khan, having obtained this signal victory, returned with
great pomp and triumph to the capital city of Kanbalu. This took
place in the month of November, and he continued to reside there
during the months of February and March, in which latter was our
festival of Easter. Being aware that this was one of our principal
solemnities, he commanded all the Christians to attend him, and to
bring with them their Book, which contains the four Gospels of the
Evangelists. After causing it to be repeatedly perfumed with incense,
in a ceremonious manner, he devoutly kissed it, and directed that the
same should be done by all his nobles who were present. This was his
usual practice upon each of the principal Christian festivals, such as
Easter and Christmas; and he observed the same at the festivals of the
Saracens, Jews, and idolaters. Upon being asked his motive for this
conduct, he said: 'There are four great Prophets who are reverenced
and worshipped by the different classes of mankind. The Christians
regard Jesus Christ as their divinity; the Saracens, Mahomet; the Jews,
Moses; and the idolaters, Sogomombar-kan, the most eminent
amongst their idols. I do honour and show respect to all the four, and
invoke to my aid whichever amongst them is in truth supreme in
heaven.' But from the manner in which his majesty acted towards
them, it is evident that he regarded the faith of the Christians as the
truest and the best; nothing, as he observed, being enjoined to its
professors that was not replete with virtue and holiness. By no means,
however, would he permit them to bear the cross before them in
their processions, because upon it so exalted a personage as Christ had
been scourged and (ignominiously) put to death. It may perhaps be
asked by some, why, if he showed such a preference to the faith of

Christ, he did not conform to it, and become a Christian? His reason for not so doing, he assigned to Nicolo and Maffio Polo, when, upon the occasion of his sending them as his ambassadors to the Pope, they ventured to address a few words to him on the subject of Christianity. 'Wherefore,' he said, 'should I become a Christian? You yourselves must perceive that the Christians of these countries are ignorant, inefficient persons, who do not possess the faculty of performing anything (miraculous); whereas you see that the idolaters can do whatever they will. When I sit at table the cups that were in the middle of the hall come to me filled with wine and other beverage, spontaneously and without being touched by human hand, and I drink from them. They have the power of controlling bad weather and obliging it to retire to any quarter of the heavens, with many other wonderful gifts of that nature. You are witnesses that their idols have the faculty of speech, and predict to them whatever is required. Should I become a convert to the faith of Christ, and profess myself a Christian, the nobles of my court and other persons who do not incline to that religion will ask me what sufficient motives have caused me to receive baptism, and to embrace Christianity. "What extraordinary powers," they will say, "what miracles have been displayed by its ministers? Whereas the idolaters declare that what they exhibit is performed through their own sanctity, and the influence of their idols." To this I shall not know what answer to make, and I shall be considered by them as labouring under a grievous error; whilst the idolaters, who by means of their profound art can effect such wonders, may without difficulty compass my death. But return you to your pontiff, and request of him, in my name, to send hither a hundred persons well skilled in your law, who being confronted with the idolaters shall have power to coerce them, and showing that they themselves are endowed with similar art, but which they refrain from exercising, because it is derived from the agency of evil spirits, shall compel them to desist from practices of such a nature in their presence. When I am witness of this, I shall place them and their religion under an interdict, and shall allow myself to be baptised. Following my example, all my nobility will then in like manner receive baptism, and this will be imitated by my subjects in general; so that the Christians of these parts will exceed in number those who inhabit your own country.' From this discourse it must be evident that if the Pope had sent out persons duly qualified to preach the gospel, the Grand Khan would have embraced Christianity, for which, it is certainly known, he had a strong predilection. But, to return to our subject, we shall now speak of the rewards and honours he bestows on such as distinguish themselves by their valour in battle.

CHAPTER III

Of the kind of Rewards granted to those who conduct themselves well in Fight, and of the Golden Tablets which they receive

The Grand Khan appoints twelve of the most intelligent amongst his nobles, whose duty it is to make themselves acquainted with the conduct of the officers and men of his army, particularly upon expeditions and in battles, and to present their reports to him, and he, upon being apprised of their respective merits, advances them in his service, raising those who commanded an hundred men to the command of a thousand, and presenting many with vessels of silver, as well as the customary tablets or warrants of command and of government. The tablets given to those commanding a hundred men are of silver; to those commanding a thousand, of gold or of silver gilt; and those who command ten thousand receive tablets of gold, bearing the head of a lion; the former being of the weight of a hundred and twenty *saggi*, and those with the lion's head, two hundred and twenty. At the top of the inscription on the tablet is a sentence to this effect: 'By the power and might of the great God, and through the grace which he vouchsafes to our empire, be the name of the kaan blessed; and let all such as disobey (what is herein directed) suffer death and be utterly destroyed.' The officers who hold these tablets have privileges attached to them, and in the inscription is specified what are the duties and the powers of their respective commands. He who is at the head of a hundred thousand men, or the commander in chief of a grand army, has a golden tablet weighing three hundred *saggi*, with the sentence above mentioned, and at the bottom is engraved the figure of a lion, together with representations of the sun and moon. He exercises also the privileges of his high command as set forth in this magnificent tablet. Whenever he rides in public, an umbrella is carried over his head, denoting the rank and authority he holds; and when he is seated, it is always upon a silver chair. The Grand Khan confers likewise upon certain of his nobles tablets on which are represented figures of the gerfalcon, in virtue of which they are authorised to take with them as their guard of honour the whole army of any great prince. They can also make use of the horses of the imperial stud at their pleasure, and can appropriate the horses of any officers inferior to themselves in rank.

CHAPTER IV

Of the Figure and Stature of the Grand Khan — Of his four principal Wives — And of the Annual Selection of Young Women for him in the Province of Ungut

Kublai, who is styled Grand Khan, or lord of lords, is of the middle stature, that is, neither tall nor short; his limbs are well formed, and in his whole figure there is a just proportion. His complexion is fair, and occasionally suffused with red, like the bright tint of the rose, which adds much grace to his countenance. His eyes are black and handsome, his nose is well shaped and prominent. He has four wives of the first rank, who are esteemed legitimate, and the eldest born son of any one of these succeeds to the empire, upon the decease of the Grand Khan. They bear equally the title of empress, and have their separate courts. None of them have fewer than three hundred young female attendants of great beauty, together with a multitude of youths as pages, and other eunuchs, as well as ladies of the bedchamber; so that the number of persons belonging to each of their respective courts amounts to ten thousand. When his majesty is desirous of the company of one of his empresses, he either sends for her, or goes himself to her palace. Besides these, he has many concubines provided for his use, from a province of Tartary named Ungut, having a city of the same name, the inhabitants of which are distinguished for beauty of features and fairness of complexion. Thither the Grand Khan sends his officers every second year, or oftener, as it may happen to be his pleasure, who collect for him, to the number of four or five hundred, or more, of the handsomest of the young women, according to the estimation of beauty communicated to them in their instructions. The mode of their appreciation is as follows. Upon the arrival of these commissioners, they give orders for assembling all the young women of the province, and appoint qualified persons to examine them, who, upon careful inspection of each of them separately, that is to say, of the hair, the countenance, the eyebrows, the mouth, the lips, and other features, as well as the symmetry of these with each other, estimate their value at sixteen, seventeen, eighteen, or twenty, or more carats, according to the greater or less degree of beauty. The number required by the Grand Khan, at the rates, perhaps, of twenty or twenty-one carats, to which their commission was limited, is then selected from the rest, and they are conveyed to his court. Upon their arrival in his presence, he causes a new examination to be made by a different set of inspectors, and from amongst them a further selection takes place, when thirty or forty are retained for his own chamber at a higher valuation. These, in the first instance, are committed separately to the care of the wives of certain of the nobles, whose duty it is to observe them attentively during the course of the night, in order to ascertain that they have not any concealed imperfections, that they sleep tranquilly, do not snore, have sweet breath, and are free from unpleasant scent in any part of the body. Having undergone this rigorous scrutiny, they are divided into parties of five, one of which parties attends during three days and three nights, in his majesty's interior apartment, where they are to perform every service that is required of them, and he does with them as he likes. When this term is completed, they are relieved by another party, and in this manner successively, until the whole number have taken their turn; when the first five recommence their attendance. But whilst the one party officiates in the inner chamber, another is stationed in the outer apartment adjoining; in order that if his majesty should have occasion for anything, such as drink or victuals, the former may signify his commands to the latter, by whom the article required is immediately procured: and thus the duty of waiting upon his majesty's person is exclusively performed by these young females. The remainder of them, whose value had been estimated at an inferior rate, are assigned to the different lords of the household; under whom they are instructed in cookery, in dressmaking, and other suitable works; and upon any person belonging to the court expressing an inclination to take a wife, the Grand Khan bestows upon him one of these damsels, with a handsome portion. In this manner he provides for them all amongst his nobility. It may be asked whether the people of the province do not feel themselves aggrieved in having their daughters thus forcibly taken from them by the sovereign? Certainly not; but, on the contrary, they regard it as a favour and an honour done to them; and those who are the fathers of handsome children feel highly gratified by his condescending to make choice of their daughters. 'If,' say they, 'my daughter is born under an auspicious planet and to good fortune, his majesty can best fulfil her destinies, by matching her nobly; which it would not be in my power to do.' If, on the other hand, the daughter misconducts herself, or any mischance befalls her (by which she becomes disqualified), the father attributes the disappointment to the malign influence of her stars.

CHAPTER V

Of the number of the Grand Khan's Sons by his four Wives, whom he makes Kings of different Provinces, and of Chingis his First-born — Also of the Sons by his Concubines, whom he creates Lords

The Grand Khan has had twenty-two sons by his four legitimate wives, the eldest of whom, named Chingis, was designed to inherit the dignity of Grand Khan, with the government of the empire; and this nomination was confirmed to him during the lifetime of his father. It was not, however, his fate to survive him; but leaving a son, whose name is Themur, he, as the representative of his father, is to succeed to the dominion. The disposition of this prince is good, and he is endowed with wisdom and valour; of the latter he has given proofs in several successful battles. Besides these, his majesty has twenty-five sons by his concubines, all of them brave soldiers, having been continually employed in the military profession. These he has placed in the rank of nobles. Of his legitimate sons, seven are at the

head of extensive provinces and kingdoms, which they govern with
wisdom and prudence, as might be expected of the children of one
whose great qualities have not been surpassed, in the general
estimation, by any person of the Tartar race.

CHAPTER VI

*Of the great and admirable Palace of the Grand Khan, near
to the City of Kanbalu*

The Grand Khan usually resides during three months of the year,
namely, December, January, and February, in the great city of
Kanbalu, situated towards the north-eastern extremity of the province
of Cathay; and here, on the southern side of the new city, is the site of
his vast palace, the form and dimensions of which are as follows. In
the first place is a square enclosed with a wall and deep ditch; each side
of the square being eight miles in length, and having at an equal
distance from each extremity an entrance-gate, for the concourse of
people resorting thither from all quarters. Within this enclosure there
is, on the four sides, an open space one mile in breadth, where the
troops are stationed; and this is bounded by a second wall, enclosing a
square of six miles, having three gates on the south side, and three on
the north, the middle portal of each being larger than the other two,
and always kept shut, excepting on the occasions of the emperor's
entrance or departure. Those on each side always remain open for the
use of common passengers. In the middle of each division of these
walls is a handsome and spacious building, and consequently within
the enclosure there are eight such buildings, in which are deposited
the royal military stores; one building being appropriated to the
reception of each class of stores. Thus, for instance, the bridles, saddles,
stirrups, and other furniture serving for the equipment of cavalry,
occupy one storehouse; the bows, strings, quivers, arrows, and other
articles belonging to archery, occupy another; cuirasses, corselets, and
other armour formed of leather, a third storehouse; and so of the rest.
Within this walled enclosure there is still another, of great thickness,
and its height is full twenty-five feet. The battlements or crenated

parapets are all white. This also forms a square four miles in extent, each side being one mile, and it has six gates, disposed like those of the former enclosure. It contains in like manner eight large buildings, similarly arranged, which are appropriated to the wardrobe of the emperor. The spaces between the one wall and the other are ornamented with many handsome trees, and contain meadows in which are kept various kinds of beasts, such as stags, the animals that yield the musk, roe-bucks, fallow-deer, and others of the same class. Every interval between the walls, not occupied by buildings, is stocked in this manner. The pastures have abundant herbage. The roads across them being raised three feet above their level, and paved, no mud collects upon them, nor rain-water settles, but on the contrary runs off, and contributes to improve the vegetation. Within these walls, which constitute the boundary of four miles, stands the palace of the Grand Khan, the most extensive that has ever yet been known. It reaches from the northern to the southern wall, leaving only a vacant space (or court), where persons of rank and the military guards pass and repass. It has no upper floor, but the roof is very lofty. The paved foundation or platform on which it stands is raised ten spans above the level of the ground, and a wall of marble, two paces wide, is built on all sides, to the level of this pavement, within the line of which the palace is erected; so that the wall, extending beyond the ground plan of the building, and encompassing the whole, serves as a terrace, where those who walk on it are visible from without. Along the exterior edge of the wall is a handsome balustrade, with pillars, which the people are allowed to approach. The sides of the great halls and the apartments are ornamented with dragons in carved work and gilt, figures of warriors, of birds, and of beasts, with representations of battles. The inside of the roof is contrived in such a manner that nothing besides gilding and painting presents itself to the eye. On each of the four sides of the palace there is a grand flight of marble steps, by which you ascend from the level of the ground to the wall of marble which surrounds the building, and which constitute the approach to the palace itself. The grand hall is extremely long and wide, and admits of dinners being there served to great multitudes of people. The palace contains a number of separate chambers, all highly beautiful, and so admirably disposed that it seems impossible to suggest any improvement to the system of their arrangement. The exterior of the roof is adorned with a variety of colours, red, green, azure, and violet, and the sort of covering is so strong as to last for many years. The glazing of the windows is so well wrought and so delicate as to have the transparency of crystal. In the rear of the body of the palace there are large buildings containing several apartments, where is deposited the private property of the monarch, or his treasure in gold and silver bullion, precious stones, and pearls, and also his vessels of gold and silver plate. Here are likewise the apartments of his wives and concubines; and in this retired situation he despatches business with convenience, being free from every kind of interruption. On the other side of the grand palace, and opposite to that in which the emperor resides, is another palace, in every respect similar, appropriated to the residence of Chingis, his eldest son, at whose court are observed all the ceremonials belonging to that of his father, as the prince who is to succeed to the government of the empire. Not far from the palace, on the northern side, and about a bow-shot distance from the surrounding wall, is an artificial mount of earth, the height of which is full a hundred paces, and the circuit at the base about a mile. It is clothed with the most beautiful evergreen trees; for whenever his majesty receives information of a handsome tree growing in any place, he causes it to be dug up, with all its roots and the earth about them, and however large and heavy it may be, he has it transported by means of elephants to this mount, and adds it to the verdant collection. From this perpetual verdure it has acquired the appellation of the Green Mount. On its summit is erected an ornamental pavilion, which is likewise entirely green. The view of this altogether – the mount itself, the trees, and the building, form a delightful and at the same time a wonderful scene. In the northern quarter also, and equally within the precincts of the city, there is a large and deep excavation, judiciously formed, the earth from which supplied the material for raising the mount. It is furnished with water by a small rivulet, and has the appearance of a fish-pond, but its use is for watering the cattle. The stream passing from thence along an aqueduct, at the foot of the Green Mount, proceeds to fill another great and very deep excavation formed between the private palace of the emperor and that of his son Chingis; and the earth from hence equally served to increase the elevation of the mount. In this latter basin there is great store and variety of fish, from which the table of his majesty is supplied with any quantity that may be wanted. The stream discharges itself at the opposite extremity of the piece of water, and precautions are taken to prevent the escape of the fish by placing gratings of copper or iron at the places of its entrance and exit. It is stocked also with swans and other aquatic birds. From the one palace to the other there is a communication by means of a bridge thrown across the water. Such is the description of this great palace. We shall now speak of the situation and circumstances of the city of Tai-du.

CHAPTER VII

Of the new City of Tai-Du, built near to that of Kanbalu –
Of a Rule observed respecting the Entertainment of
Ambassadors – And of the nightly Police of the City

The city of Kanbalu is situated near a large river in the province of Cathay, and was in ancient times eminently magnificent and royal. The name itself implies 'the city of the sovereign'; but his majesty having imbibed an opinion from the astrologers, that it was destined to become rebellious to his authority, resolved upon the measure of building another capital, upon the opposite side of the river, where stand the palaces just described: so that the new and the old cities are separated from each other only by the stream that runs between them. The new-built city received the name of Tai-du, and all the Cathaians, that is, all those of the inhabitants who were natives of the province of Cathay, were compelled to evacuate the ancient city, and to take up their abode in the new. Some of the inhabitants, however, of whose loyalty he did not entertain suspicion, were suffered to remain, especially because the latter, although of the dimensions that shall presently be described, was not capable of containing the same number as the former, which was of vast extent.

This new city is of a form perfectly square, and twenty-four miles in extent, each of its sides being neither more nor less than six miles. It is enclosed with walls of earth, that at the base are about ten paces thick, but gradually diminish to the top, where the thickness is not more than three paces. In all parts the battlements are white. The whole plan of the city was regularly laid out by line, and the streets in general are consequently so straight, that when a person ascends the wall over one of the gates, and looks right forward, he can see the gate opposite to him on the other side of the city. In the public streets there are, on each side, booths and shops of every description. All the allotments of ground upon which the habitations throughout the city were constructed are square, and exactly on a line with each other; each allotment being sufficiently spacious for handsome buildings, with corresponding courts and gardens. One of these was assigned to each head of a family; that is to say, such a person of such a tribe had one square allotted to him, and so of the rest. Afterwards the property passed from hand to hand. In this manner the whole interior of the city is disposed in squares, so as to resemble a chess-board, and planned out with a degree of precision and beauty impossible to describe. The wall of the city has twelve gates, three on each side of the square, and over each gate and compartment of the wall there is a handsome building; so that on each side of the square there are five such buildings, containing large rooms, in which are disposed the arms of those who form the garrison of the city, every gate being guarded by a thousand men. It is not to be understood that such a force is stationed there in consequence of the apprehension of danger from any hostile power whatever, but as a guard suitable to the honour and dignity of the sovereign. Yet it must be allowed that the declaration of the astrologers has excited in his mind a degree of suspicion with regard to the Cathaians. In the centre of the city there is a great bell suspended in a lofty building, which is sounded every night, and after the third stroke no person dares to be found in the streets, unless upon some urgent occasion, such as to call assistance to a woman in labour, or a man attacked with sickness; and even in such necessary cases the person is required to carry a light.

Withoutside of each of the gates is a suburb so wide that it reaches to and unites with those of the other nearest gates on both sides, and in length extends to the distance of three or four miles, so that the number of inhabitants in these suburbs exceeds that of the city itself. Within each suburb there are, at intervals, as far perhaps as a mile from the city, many hotels, or caravanserais, in which the merchants arriving from various parts take up their abode; and to each description of people a separate building is assigned, as we should say, one to the Lombards, another to the Germans, and a third to the French. The number of public women who prostitute themselves for money, reckoning those in the new city as well as those in the suburbs of the old, is twenty-five thousand. To each hundred and to each thousand of these there are superintending officers appointed, who are under the orders of a captain-general. The motive for placing them under such command is this: when ambassadors arrive charged with any business in which the interests of the Grand Khan are concerned, it is customary to maintain them at his majesty's expense, and in order that they may be treated in the most honourable manner, the captain is ordered to furnish nightly to each individual of the embassy one of these courtesans, who is likewise to be changed every night, for which service, as it is considered in the light of a tribute they owe to the sovereign, they do not receive any remuneration. Guards, in parties of thirty or forty, continually patrol the streets during the course of the night, and make diligent search for persons who may be from their homes at an unseasonable hour, that is, after the third stroke of the great bell. When any are met with under such circumstances, they immediately apprehend and confine them, and take them in the morning for examination before officers appointed for that purpose, who, upon the proof of any delinquency, sentence them, according to the nature of the offence, to a severer or lighter infliction of the bastinade, which sometimes, however, occasions their death. It is in this manner that crimes are usually punished amongst these people, from a disinclination to the shedding of blood, which their *baksis* or learned astrologers instruct them to avoid. Having thus described the interior of the city of Tai-du, we shall now speak of the disposition to rebellion shown by its Cathaian inhabitants.

CHAPTER VIII

Of the Treasonable Practices employed to cause the City of Kanbalu to rebel, and of the Apprehension and Punishment of those concerned

Particular mention will hereafter be made of the establishment of a council of twelve persons, who had the power of disposing, at their pleasure, of the lands, the governments, and everything belonging to the state. Amongst these was a Saracen, named Achmac, a crafty and bold man, whose influence with the Grand Khan surpassed that of the other members. To such a degree was his master infatuated with him that he indulged him in every liberty. It was discovered, indeed, after his death, that he had by means of spells so fascinated his majesty as to oblige him to give ear and credit to whatever he represented, and by these means was enabled to act in all matters according to his own arbitrary will. He gave away all the governments and public offices, pronounced judgement upon all offenders, and when he was disposed to sacrifice any man to whom he bore ill-will, he had only to go to the emperor and say to him, 'Such a person has committed an offence against your majesty, and is deserving of death,' when the emperor was accustomed to reply, 'Do as you judge best'; upon which he caused him to be immediately executed. So evident were the proofs of the authority he possessed, and of his majesty's implicit faith in his representations, that none had the hardiness to contradict him in any matter; nor was there a person, however high in rank or office, who did not stand in awe of him. If anyone was accused by him of capital crime, however anxious he might be to exculpate himself, he had not the means of refuting the charge, because he could not procure an advocate, none daring to oppose the will of Achmac. By these means he occasioned many to die unjustly. Besides this, there was no handsome female who became an object of his sensuality that he did not contrive to possess, taking her as a wife if she was unmarried, or otherwise compelling her to yield to his desires. When he obtained information of any man having a beautiful daughter, he despatched his emissaries to the father of the girl, with instructions to say to him: 'What are your views with regard to this handsome daughter of yours? You cannot do better than give her in marriage to the Lord Deputy or Vicegerent' (that is, to Achmac, for so they termed him, as implying that he was his majesty's representative). 'We shall prevail upon him to appoint you to such a government or to such an office for three years.' Thus tempted, he is prevailed upon to part with his child; and the matter being so far arranged, Achmac repairs to the emperor and informs his majesty that a certain government is vacant, or that the period for which it is held will expire on such a day, and recommends the father as a person well qualified to perform the duties. To this his majesty gives his consent, and the appointment is immediately carried into effect. By such means as these, either from the ambition of holding high offices or the apprehension of his power, he obtained the sacrifice of all the most beautiful young women, either under the denomination of wives, or as the slaves of his pleasure. He had sons to the number of twenty-five, who held the highest offices of the state, and some of them, availing themselves of the authority of their father, formed adulterous connections, and committed many other unlawful and atrocious acts. Achmac had likewise accumulated great wealth, for every person who obtained an appointment found it necessary to make him a considerable present.

During a period of twenty-two years he exercised this uncontrolled sway. At length the natives of the country, that is, the Cathaians, no longer able to endure his multiplied acts of injustice or the flagrant wickedness committed against their families, held meetings in order to devise means of putting him to death and raising a rebellion against the government. Amongst the persons principally concerned in this plot was a Cathaian, named Chen-ku, a chief of six thousand men, who, burning with resentment on account of the violation of his mother, his wife, and his daughter, proposed the measure to one of his countrymen, named Van-ku, who was at the head of ten thousand men, and recommended its being carried into execution at the time when the Grand Khan, having completed his three months' residence in Kanbalu, had departed for his palace of Shan-du, and when his son Chingis also had retired to the place he was accustomed to visit at that season; because the charge of the city was then entrusted to Achmac, who communicated to his master whatever matters occurred during his absence, and received in return the signification of his pleasure. Van-ku and Chen-ku, having held this consultation together, imparted their design to some of the leading persons of the Cathaians, and through them to their friends in many other cities. It was accordingly determined amongst them that, on a certain day, immediately upon their perceiving the signal of a fire, they should rise and put to death all those who wore beards; and should extend the signal to other places, in order that the same might be carried into effect throughout the country. The meaning of the distinction with regard to beards was this; that whereas the Cathaians themselves are naturally beardless, the Tartars, the Saracens, and the Christians wear beards. It should be understood that the Grand Khan not having obtained the sovereignty of Cathay by any legal right, but only by force of arms, had no confidence in the inhabitants, and therefore bestowed all the provincial governments and magistracies upon Tartars, Saracens, Christians and other foreigners, who belonged to his household, and in whom he could trust. In consequence of this, his government was universally hated by the natives, who found themselves treated as slaves by these Tartars, and still worse by the Saracens.

Their plans being thus arranged, Van-ku and Chen-ku contrived to enter the palace at night, where the former, taking his place on one of the royal seats, caused the apartment to be lighted up, and sent a messenger to Achmac, who resided in the old city, requiring his immediate attendance upon Chingis, the emperor's son, who (he should say) had unexpectedly arrived that night. Achmac was much astonished at the intelligence, but, being greatly in awe of the prince, instantly obeyed. Upon passing the gate of the (new) city, he met a Tartar officer named Kogatai, the commandant of the guard of twelve thousand men, who asked him whither he was going at that late hour. He replied that he was proceeding to wait upon Chingis, of whose arrival he had just heard. 'How is it possible,' said the officer, 'that he can have arrived in so secret a manner, that I should not have been aware of his approach in time to order a party of his guards to attend him?' In the meanwhile the two Cathaians felt assured that if they could but succeed in despatching Achmac they had nothing further to apprehend. Upon his entering the palace and seeing so many lights burning, he made his prostrations before Van-ku, supposing him to be the prince, when Chen-ku, who stood there provided with a sword, severed his head from his body. Kogatai had stopped at the door, but upon observing what had taken place, exclaimed that there was treason going forward, and instantly let fly an arrow at Van-ku as he sat upon the throne, which slew him. He then called to his men, who seized Chen-ku, and despatched an order into the city, that every person found out of doors should be put to death. The Cathaians perceiving, however, that the Tartars had discovered the conspiracy, and being deprived of their leaders, one of whom was killed and the other a prisoner, kept within their houses, and were unable to make the signals to the other towns, as had been concerted. Kogatai immediately sent messengers to the Grand Khan, with a circumstantial relation of all that had passed, who, in return, directed him to make a diligent investigation of the treason, and to punish, according to the degree of their guilt, those whom he should find to have been concerned. On the following day, Kogatai examined all the Cathaians, and upon such as were principals in the conspiracy he inflicted capital punishment. The same was done with respect to the other cities that were known to have participated in the guilt.

When the Grand Khan returned to Kanbalu, he was desirous of knowing the causes of what had happened, and then learned that the infamous Achmac and seven of his sons (for all were not equally culpable) had committed those enormities which have been described. He gave orders for removing the treasure which had been accumulated by the deceased to an incredible amount, from the place of his residence in the old city to the new, where it was deposited in his own treasury. He likewise directed that his body should be taken from the tomb, and thrown into the street to be torn in pieces by the dogs. The sons who had followed the steps of their father in his iniquities he caused to be flayed alive. Reflecting also upon the principles of the accursed sect of the Saracens, which indulge them in the commission of every crime, and allow them to murder those who differ from them on points of faith, so that even the nefarious Achmac and his sons might have supposed themselves guiltless, he held them in contempt and abomination. Summoning, therefore, these people to his presence, he forbade them to continue many practices enjoined to them by their law, commanding that in future their marriages should be regulated by the custom of the Tartars, and that instead of the mode of killing animals for food, by cutting their throats, they should be obliged to open the belly. At the time that these events took place Marco Polo was on the spot. We shall now proceed to what relates to the establishment of the court kept by the Grand Khan.

CHAPTER IX

Of the Personal Guard of the Grand Khan

The bodyguard of the Grand Khan consists, as is well known to everyone, of twelve thousand horsemen, who are termed *kasitan*, which signifies 'soldiers devoted to their master.' It is not, however, from any apprehensions entertained by him that he is surrounded by this guard, but as matter of state. These twelve thousand men are commanded by four superior officers, each of whom is at the head of three thousand; and each three thousand does constant duty in the palace during three successive days and nights, at the expiration of which they are relieved by another division. When all the four have completed their period of duty, it comes again to the turn of the first. During the daytime, the nine thousand who are off guard do not, however, quit the palace, unless when employed upon the service of his majesty, or when the individuals are called away for their domestic concerns, in which case they must obtain leave of absence through their commanding officer; and if, in consequence of any serious occurrence, such as that of a father, a brother, or any near relation being at the point of death, their immediate return should be prevented, they must apply to his majesty for an extension of their leave. But in the night-time these nine thousand retire to their quarters.

CHAPTER X

Of the Style in which the Grand Khan holds his Public Courts, and sits at Table with all his Nobles — Of the Manner in which the Drinking Vessels of Gold and Silver, filled with the Milk of Mares and Camels, are disposed in the Hall — And of the Ceremony that takes place when he Drinks

When his majesty holds a grand and public court, those who attend it are seated in the following order. The table of the sovereign is placed before his elevated throne, and he takes his seat on the northern side, with his face turned towards the south; and next to him, on his left hand, sits the empress. On his right hand, upon seats somewhat lower, are placed his sons, grandsons, and other persons connected with him by blood, that is to say, who are descended from the imperial stock. The seat, however, of Chingis, his eldest son, is raised a little above those of his other sons, whose heads are nearly on a level with the feet of the Grand Khan. The other princes and the nobility have their places at still lower tables; and the same rules are observed with respect to the females, the wives of the sons, grandsons, and other relatives of the Grand Khan being seated on the left hand, at tables in like manner gradually lower; then follow the wives of the nobility and military officers: so that all are seated according to their respective ranks and dignities, in the places assigned to them, and to which they are entitled. The tables are arranged in such a manner that the Grand Khan, sitting on his elevated throne, can overlook the whole. It is not, however, to be understood that all who assemble on such occasions can be accommodated at tables. The greater part of the officers, and even of the nobles, on the contrary, eat, sitting upon carpets, in the hall; and on the outside stand a great multitude of persons who come from different countries, and bring with them many rare and curious articles. Some of these are feudatories, who desire to be reinstated in possessions that have been taken from them, and who always make their appearance upon the appointed days of public festivity, or occasions of royal marriages.

In the middle of the hall, where the Grand Khan sits at table, there is a magnificent piece of furniture, made in the form of a square coffer, each side of which is three paces in length, exquisitely carved in figures of animals, and gilt. It is hollow within, for the purpose of receiving a capacious vase, shaped like a jar, and of precious materials, calculated to hold about a tun, and filled with wine. On each of its four sides stands a smaller vessel, containing about a hogshead, one of which is filled with mare's milk, another with that of the camel, and so of the others, according to the kinds of beverage in use. Within this buffet are also the cups or flagons belonging to his majesty, for serving the liquors. Some of them are of beautiful gilt plate. Their size is such that, when filled with wine or other liquor, the quantity would be sufficient for eight or ten men. Before every two persons who have seats at the tables, one of these flagons is placed, together with a kind of ladle, in the form of a cup with a handle, also of plate; to be used not only for taking the wine out of the flagon, but for lifting it to the head. This is observed as well with respect to the women as the men. The quantity and richness of the plate belonging to his majesty is quite incredible. Officers of rank are likewise appointed, whose duty it is to see that all strangers who happen to arrive at the time of the festival, and are unacquainted with the etiquette of the court, are suitably accommodated with places; and these stewards are continually visiting every part of the hall, enquiring of the guests if there is anything with which they are unprovided, or whether any of them wish for wine, milk, meat, or other articles, in which case it is immediately brought to them by the attendants.

At each door of the grand hall, or of whatever part the Grand Khan happens to be in, stand two officers, of a gigantic figure, one on each side, with staves in their hands, for the purpose of preventing persons from touching the threshold with their feet, and obliging them to step beyond it. If by chance anyone is guilty of this offence, these janitors take from him his garment, which he must redeem for money; or, when they do not take the garment, they inflict on him such number of blows as they have authority for doing. But, as strangers may be unacquainted with the prohibition, officers are appointed to introduce them, by whom they are warned of it; and this precaution is used because touching the threshold is there regarded as a bad omen. In departing from the hall, as some of the company may be affected by the liquor, it is impossible to guard against the accident, and the order is not then strictly enforced. The numerous persons who attend at the sideboard of his majesty, and who serve him with victuals and drink, are all obliged to cover their noses and mouths with handsome veils or cloths of worked silk, in order that his victuals or his wine may not be affected by their breath. When drink is called for by him, and the page in waiting has presented it, he retires three paces and kneels down, upon which the courtiers, and all who are present, in like manner make their prostration. At the same moment all the musical instruments, of which there is a numerous band, begin to play, and continue to do so until he has ceased drinking, when all the company recover their posture; and this reverential salutation is made so often as his majesty drinks. It is unnecessary to say anything of the victuals, because it may well be imagined that their abundance is excessive. When the repast is finished, and the tables have been removed, persons of various descriptions enter the hall, and amongst these a troop of comedians and performers on different instruments, as also tumblers and jugglers, who exhibit their skill in the presence of the Grand Khan, to the high amusement and gratification of all the spectators. When these sports are concluded, the people separate, and each returns to his own house.

CHAPTER XI

Of the Festival that is kept throughout the Dominions of the Grand Khan on the Twenty-eighth of September, being the Anniversary of his Nativity

All the Tartar and other subjects of the Grand Khan celebrate as a festival the day of his majesty's birth, which took place on the twenty-eighth day of the month of September; and this is their greatest festival, excepting only that kept on the first day of the year, which shall be hereafter described. Upon this anniversary the Grand Khan appears in a superb dress of cloth of gold, and on the same occasion full twenty thousand nobles and military officers are clad by him in dresses similar to his own in point of colour and form; but the materials are not equally rich. They are, however, of silk, and of the colour of gold; and along with the vest they likewise receive a girdle of chamois leather, curiously worked with gold and silver thread, and also a pair of boots. Some of the dresses are ornamented with precious stones and pearls to the value of a thousand bezants of gold, and are given to those nobles who, from their confidential employments, are nearest to his majesty's person, and are termed *quiécitari*. These dresses are appointed to be worn on the thirteen solemn festivals celebrated in the thirteen (lunar) months of the year, when those who are clad in them make an appearance that is truly royal. When his majesty assumes any particular dress, the nobles of his court wear corresponding, but less costly, dresses, which are always in readiness. They are not annually renewed, but on the contrary are made to last about ten years. From this parade an idea may be formed of the magnificence of the Grand Khan, which is unequalled by that of any monarch in the world.

On the occasion of this festival of the Grand Khan's nativity, all his Tartar subjects, and likewise the people of every kingdom and province throughout his dominions, send him valuable presents, according to established usage. Many persons who repair to court in order to solicit principalities to which they have pretensions, also bring presents, and his majesty accordingly gives direction to the tribunal of twelve, who have cognisance of such matters, to assign to them such territories and governments as may be proper. Upon this day likewise all the Christians, idolaters, and Saracens, together with every other description of people, offer up devout prayers to their respective gods and idols, that they may bless and preserve the sovereign, and bestow upon him long life, health, and prosperity. Such, and so extensive, are the rejoicings on the return of his majesty's birthday. We shall now speak of another festival, termed the White Feast, celebrated at the commencement of the year.

CHAPTER XII

Of the White Feast, held on the First Day of the Month of February, being the Commencement of their Year — Of the Number of Presents then brought — And of the Ceremonies that take Place at a Table whereon is inscribed the Name of the Grand Khan

It is well ascertained that the Tartars date the commencement of their year from the month of February, and on that occasion it is customary for the Grand Khan, as well as all who are subject to him, in their several countries, to clothe themselves in white garments, which, according to their ideas, are the emblem of good fortune; and they assume this dress at the beginning of the year, in the hope that, during the whole course of it, nothing but what is fortunate may happen to them, and that they may enjoy pleasure and comfort. Upon this day the inhabitants of all the provinces and kingdoms who hold lands or rights of jurisdiction under the Grand Khan, send him valuable presents of gold, silver, and precious stones, together with many pieces of white cloth, which they add, with the intent that his majesty may experience throughout the year uninterrupted felicity, and possess treasures adequate to all his expenses. With the same view the nobles, princes, and all ranks of the community, make reciprocal presents, at their respective houses, of white articles; embracing each other with demonstrations of joy and festivity, and saying (as we ourselves are accustomed to do), 'May good fortune attend you through the coming year, and may everything you undertake succeed to your wish.' On this occasion great numbers of beautiful white horses are presented to the Grand Khan; or if not perfectly white, it is at least the prevailing colour. In this country white horses are not uncommon.

It is moreover the custom in making presents to the Grand Khan, for those who have it in their power to furnish nine times nine of the article of which the present consists. Thus, for instance, if a province sends a present of horses, there are nine times nine, or eighty-one head in the drove; so also of gold, or of cloth, nine times nine pieces. By such means his majesty receives at this festival no fewer than a hundred thousand horses. On this day it is that all his elephants, amounting to five thousand, are exhibited in procession, covered with housings of cloth, fancifully and richly worked with gold and silk, in figures of birds and beasts. Each of these supports upon its shoulders two coffers filled with vessels of plate and other apparatus for the use of the court. Then follows a train of camels, in like manner laden with various necessary articles of furniture. When the whole are properly arranged, they pass in review before his majesty, and form a pleasing spectacle.

On the morning of the festival, before the tables are spread, all the princes, the nobility of various ranks, the cavaliers, astrologers, physicians, and falconers, with many others holding public offices, the prefects of the people and of the lands, together with the officers of the army, make their entry into the grand hall, in front of the emperor. Those who cannot find room within, stand on the outside of the building, in such a situation as to be within sight of their sovereign. The assemblage is marshalled in the following order. The first places are assigned to the sons and grandsons of his majesty and all the imperial family. Next to these are the provincial kings and the nobility of the empire, according to their several degrees, in regular succession. When all have been disposed in the places appointed for them, a person of high dignity, or as we should express it, a great prelate, rises and says with a loud voice: 'Bow down and do reverence'; when instantly all bend their bodies until their foreheads touch the floor. Again the prelate cries: 'God bless our lord, and long preserve him in the enjoyment of felicity.' To which the people answer: 'God grant it.' Once more the prelate says: 'May God increase the grandeur and prosperity of his empire; may he preserve all those who are his subjects in the blessings of peace and contentment; and in all their lands may abundance prevail.' The people again reply: 'God grant it.' They then make their prostrations four times. This being done, the prelate advances to an altar, richly adorned, upon which is placed a red tablet inscribed with the name of the Grand Khan. Near to this stands a censer of burning incense, with which the prelate, on the behalf of all who are assembled, perfumes the tablet and the altar, in a reverential manner; when everyone present humbly prostrates himself before the tablet. This ceremony being concluded, they return to their places, and then make the presentation of their respective gifts; such as have been mentioned. When a display has been made of these, and the Grand Khan has cast his eyes upon them, the tables are prepared for the feast, and the company, as well women as men, arrange themselves there in the manner and order described in a former chapter. Upon the removal of the victuals, the musicians and theatrical performers exhibit for the amusement of the court, as has been already related. But on this occasion a lion is conducted into the presence of his majesty, so tame, that it is taught to lay itself down at his feet. The sports being finished, everyone returns to his own home.

CHAPTER XIII

Of the Quantity of Game taken and sent to the Court, during the Winter Months

At the season when the Grand Khan resides in the capital of Cathay, or during the months of December, January, and February, at which time the cold is excessive, he gives orders for general hunting parties to take place in all the countries within forty stages of the court; and the governors of districts are required to send thither all sorts of game of the larger kind, such as wild boars, stags, fallow deer, roebucks, and bears, which are taken in the following manner: All persons possessed of land in the province repair to the places where these animals are to be found, and proceed to enclose them within a circle, when they are killed, partly with dogs, but chiefly by shooting them with arrows. Such of them as are intended for his majesty's use are first paunched for that purpose, and then forwarded on carriages, in large quantities, by those who reside within thirty stages of the capital. Those, in fact, who are at the distance of forty stages, do not, on account of the length of the journey, send the carcasses, but only the skins, some dressed and others raw, to be made use of for the service of the army as his majesty may judge proper.

CHAPTER XIV

Of Leopards and Lynxes used for Hunting Deer — Of Lions habituated to the Chase of various Animals — And of Eagles taught to seize Wolves

The Grand Khan has many leopards and lynxes kept for the purpose of chasing deer, and also many lions, which are larger than the Babylonian lions, have good skins and of a handsome colour — being streaked lengthways with white, black, and red stripes. They are active in seizing boars, wild oxen and asses, bears, stags, roebucks, and other beasts that are the objects of sport. It is an admirable sight, when the lion is let loose in pursuit of the animal, to observe the savage eagerness and speed with which he overtakes it. His majesty has them conveyed for this purpose, in cages placed upon cars, and along with them is confined a little dog, with which they become familiarised. The reason for thus shutting them up is, that they would otherwise be so keen and furious at the sight of the game that it would be impossible to keep them under the necessary constraint. It is proper that they should be led in a direction opposite to the wind, in order that they may not be scented by the game, which would immediately run off, and afford no chance of sport. His majesty has eagles also, which are trained to stoop at wolves, and such is their size and strength that none, however large, can escape from their talons.

CHAPTER XV

Of two Brothers who are principal Officers of the Chase to the Grand Khan

His majesty has in his service two persons, brothers both by the father and mother, one of them named Bayan and the other Mingan, who are, what in the language of the Tartars are called, *chivichi*, that is to say, 'masters of the chase', having charge of the hounds fleet and slow, and of the mastiffs. Each of these has under his orders a body of ten thousand chasseurs; those under the one brother wearing a red uniform, and those under the other, a sky-blue, whenever they are upon duty. The dogs of different descriptions which accompany them to the field are not fewer than five thousand. The one brother, with his division, takes the ground to the right hand of the emperor, and the other to the left, with his division, and each advances in regular order, until they have enclosed a tract of country to the extent of a day's march. By this means no beast can escape them. It is a beautiful and an exhilarating sight to watch the exertions of the huntsmen and the sagacity of the dogs, when the emperor is within the circle, engaged in the sport, and they are seen pursuing the stags, bears, and other animals, in every direction. The two brothers are under an engagement to furnish the court daily, from the commencement of October to the end of March, with a thousand pieces of game, quails being excepted; and also with fish, of which as large a quantity as possible is to be supplied, estimating the fish that three men can eat at a meal as equivalent to one piece of game.

CHAPTER XVI

Of the Grand Khan's proceeding to the Chase, with his Gerfalcons and Hawks — Of his Falconers — And of his Tents

When his majesty has resided the usual time in the metropolis, and leaves it in the month of March, he proceeds in a north-easterly direction, to within two days' journey of the ocean, attended by full ten thousand falconers, who carry with them a vast number of gerfalcons, peregrine falcons, and sakers, as well as many vultures, in order to pursue the game along the banks of the river. It must be understood that he does not keep all this body of men together in one place, but divides them into several parties of one or two hundred or more, who follow the sport in various directions, and the greater part of what they take is brought to his majesty. He has likewise with him ten thousand men of those who are termed *taskaol*, implying that their business is to be upon the watch, and, who, for this purpose, are detached in small parties of two or three to stations not far distant from each other, in such a manner as to encompass a considerable tract of country. Each of them is provided with a call and a hood, by which they are enabled, when necessary, to call in and to secure the birds. Upon the command being given for flying the hawks, those who let them loose are not under the necessity of following them, because the others, whose duty it is, look out so attentively that the birds cannot direct their flight to any quarter where they are not secured, or promptly assisted if there should be occasion. Every bird belonging to his majesty, or to any of his nobles, has a small silver label fastened to its leg, on which is engraved the name of the owner and also the name of the keeper. In consequence of this precaution, as soon as the hawk is secured, it is immediately known to whom it belongs, and restored accordingly. If it happens that, although the name appears, the owner, not being personally known to the finder, cannot be ascertained in the first instance, the bird is, in that case, carried to an officer termed *bulangazi*, whose title imports that he is the 'guardian of unclaimed property'. If a horse, therefore, a sword, a bird, or any other article is found, and it does not appear to whom it belongs, the finder carries it directly to this officer, by whom it is received in charge and carefully preserved. If, on the other hand, a person finds any article that has been lost, and fails to carry it to the proper depositary, he is accounted a thief. Those by whom any property has been lost make their application to this officer, by whom it is restored to them. His situation is always in the most elevated part of the camp, and distinguished by a particular flag, in order that he may be the more readily found by such as have occasion to apply to him. The effect of this regulation is, that no articles are ultimately lost.

When his majesty makes his progress in this manner, towards the shores of the ocean, many interesting occurrences attend the sport, and it may truly be said that it is unrivalled by any other amusement in the world. On account of the narrowness of the passes in some parts of the country where the Grand Khan follows the chase, he is borne upon two elephants only, or sometimes a single one, being more convenient than a greater number; but under other circumstances he makes use of four, upon the backs of which is placed a pavilion of wood, handsomely carved, the inside being lined with cloth of gold, and the outside covered with the skins of lions, a mode of conveyance which is rendered necessary to him during his hunting excursions, in consequence of the gout, with which he is troubled. In the pavilion he always carries with him twelve of his best gerfalcons, with twelve officers, from amongst his favourites, to bear him company and amuse him. Those who are on horseback by his side give him notice of the approach of cranes or other birds, upon which he raises the curtain of the pavilion, and when he espies the game, gives direction for letting fly the gerfalcons, which seize the cranes and overpower them after a long struggle. The view of this sport, as he lies upon his couch, affords extreme satisfaction to his majesty, as well as to the officers who attend him, and to the horsemen by whom he is surrounded. After having thus enjoyed the amusement for some hours, he repairs to a place named Kakzarmodin, where are pitched the pavilions and tents of his sons, and also of the nobles, the lifeguards, and the falconers; exceeding ten thousand in number, and making a handsome appearance. The tent of his majesty, in which he gives his audiences, is so long and wide that under it ten thousand soldiers might be drawn up, leaving room for the superior officers and other persons of rank. Its entrance fronts the south, and on the eastern side it has another tent connected with it, forming a capacious saloon, which the emperor usually occupies, with a few of his nobility, and when he thinks proper to speak to any other persons, they are introduced to him in that apartment. In the rear of this there is a large and handsome chamber, where he sleeps; and there are many other tents and apartments (for the different branches of the household), but which are not immediately connected with the great tent. These halls and chambers are all constructed and fitted up in the following manner. Each of them is supported by three pillars of wood, richly carved and gilt. The tents are covered on the outside with the skins of lions, streaked white, black, and red, and so well joined together that neither wind nor rain can penetrate. Withinside they are lined with the skins of ermines and sables, which are the most costly of all furs; for the latter, if of a size to trim a dress, is valued at two thousand besants of gold, provided it be perfect; but if otherwise, only one thousand. It is esteemed by Tartars the queen of furs. The animal, which in their language is named *rondes*, is about the size of a polecat. With these two kinds of skin, the halls as well as the sleeping-rooms are handsomely fitted up in compartments, arranged with much taste and skill. The tent-ropes, or cords by which they stretch the tents, are all of silk. Near to the grand tent of his majesty are situated those of his ladies, also very handsome and splendid. They have in like manner their gerfalcons, their hawks, and other birds and beasts, with which they partake in the amusement. The number of persons collected in these encampments is quite incredible, and a spectator might conceive himself to be in the midst of a populous city, so great is the assemblage from every part of the empire. The Grand Khan is attended on the occasion by the whole of his family and household; that is to say, his physicians, astronomers, falconers, and every other description of officer.

In these parts of the country he remains until the first vigil of our Easter, during which period he never ceases to frequent the lakes and rivers, where he takes storks, swans, herons, and a variety of other birds. His people also being detached to several different places, procure for him a large quantity of game. In this manner, during the season of his diversion, he enjoys himself to a degree that no person who is not an eyewitness can conceive; the excellence and the extent of the sport being greater than it is possible to express. It is strictly forbidden to every tradesman, mechanic, or husbandman throughout his majesty's dominions, to keep a vulture, hawk, or any other bird used for the pursuit of game, or any sporting dog; nor is a nobleman or cavalier to presume to chase beast or bird in the neighbourhood of the place where his majesty takes up his residence (the distance being limited to five miles, for example, on one side, ten on another, and perhaps fifteen in a third direction), unless his name be inscribed in a list kept by the grand falconer, or he has a special privilege to that effect. Beyond those limits it is permitted. There is an order, however, which prohibits every person throughout all the countries subject to the Grand Khan, whether prince, nobleman, or peasant, from daring to kill hares, roebucks, fallow deer, stags, or other animals of that kind, or any large birds, between the months of March and October; to the intent that they may increase and multiply; and as the breach of this order is attended with punishment, game of every description increases prodigiously. When the usual time is elapsed, his majesty returns to the capital by the road he went; continuing his sport during the whole of the journey.

CHAPTER XVII

Of the Multitude of Persons who continually resort to and depart from the City of Kanbalu – And of the Commerce of the Place

Upon the return of the Grand Khan to his capital, he holds a great and splendid court, which lasts three days, in the course of which he gives feasts and otherwise entertains those by whom he is surrounded. The amusements of these three days are indeed admirable. The multitude of inhabitants, and the number of houses in the city, as also in the suburbs without the city (of which there are twelve, corresponding to the twelve gates), is greater than the mind can comprehend. The suburbs are even more populous than the city, and it is there that the merchants and others whose business leads them to the capital, and who, on account of its being the residence of the court, resort thither in great numbers, take up their abode. Wherever, indeed, his majesty holds his court, thither these people flock from all quarters, in pursuit of their several objects. In the suburbs there are also as handsome houses and stately buildings as in the city, with the exception only of the palace of the Grand Khan. No corpse is suffered to be interred within the precincts of the city; and those of the idolaters, with whom it is customary to burn their dead, are carried to the usual spot beyond the suburbs. There likewise all public executions take place. Women who live by prostituting themselves for money dare not, unless it be secretly, to exercise their profession in the city, but must confine themselves to the suburbs, where, as has already been stated, there reside above five-and-twenty thousand; nor is this number greater than is necessary for the vast concourse of merchants and other strangers, who, drawn thither by the court, are continually arriving and departing. To this city everything that is most rare and valuable in all parts of the world finds its way; and more especially does this apply to India, which furnishes precious stones, pearls, and various drugs and spices. From the provinces of Cathay itself, as well as from the other provinces of the empire, whatever there is of value is carried thither, to supply the demands of those multitudes who are induced to establish their residence in the vicinity of the court. The quantity of merchandise sold there exceeds also the traffic of any other place; for no fewer than a thousand carriages and pack-horses, loaded with raw silk, make their daily entry; and gold tissues and silks of various kinds are manufactured to an immense extent. In the vicinity of the capital are many walled and other towns, whose inhabitants live chiefly by the court, selling the articles which they produce in the markets of the former, and procuring from thence in return such as their own occasions require.

CHAPTER XVIII

*Of the kind of Paper Money issued by the Grand Khan, and
made to pass current throughout his Dominions*

In this city of Kanbalu is the mint of the Grand Khan, who may truly
be said to possess the secret of the alchemists, as he has the art of
producing money by the following process. He causes the bark to be
stripped from those mulberry trees the leaves of which are used for
feeding silk-worms, and takes from it that thin inner rind which lies
between the coarser bark and the wood of the tree. This being
steeped, and afterwards pounded in a mortar, until reduced to a pulp,
is made into paper, resembling (in substance) that which is manufactured from cotton, but quite black. When ready for use, he has it cut
into pieces of money of different sizes, nearly square, but somewhat
longer than they are wide. Of these, the smallest pass for a denier
tournois; the next size for a Venetian silver groat; others for two,
five, and ten groats; others for one, two, three, and as far as ten
besants of gold. The coinage of this paper money is authenticated
with as much form and ceremony as if it were actually of pure gold
or silver; for to each note a number of officers, specially appointed,
not only subscribe their names, but affix their signets also; and when
this has been regularly done by the whole of them, the principal
officer, deputed by his majesty, having dipped into vermilion the
royal seal committed to his custody, stamps with it the piece of
paper, so that the form of the seal tinged with the vermilion remains
impressed upon it, by which it receives full authenticity as current
money, and the act of counterfeiting it is punished as a capital
offence. When thus coined in large quantities, this paper currency is
circulated in every part of the Grand Khan's dominions; nor dares
any person, at the peril of his life, refuse to accept it in payment. All
his subjects receive it without hesitation, because, wherever their
business may call them, they can dispose of it again in the purchase of
merchandise they may have occasion for; such as pearls, jewels, gold,

or silver. With it, in short, every article may be procured.

Several times in the course of the year, large caravans of merchants arrive with such articles as have just been mentioned, together with gold tissues, which they lay before the Grand Khan. He thereupon calls together twelve experienced and skilful persons, selected for this purpose, whom he commands to examine the articles with great care, and to fix the value at which they should be purchased. Upon the sum at which they have been thus conscientiously appraised he allows a reasonable profit, and immediately pays for them with this paper; to which the owners can have no objection, because, as has been observed, it answers the purpose of their own disbursements; and even though they should be inhabitants of a country where this kind of money is not current, they invest the amount in other articles of merchandise suited to their own markets. When any persons happen to be possessed of paper money which from long use has become damaged, they carry it to the mint, where, upon the payment of only three per cent, they may receive fresh notes in exchange. Should any be desirous of procuring gold or silver for the purposes of manufacture, such as of drinking-cups, girdles, or other articles wrought of these metals, they in like manner apply at the mint, and for their paper obtain the bullion they require. All his majesty's armies are paid with this currency, which is to them of the same value as if it were gold or silver. Upon these grounds, it may certainly be affirmed that the Grand Khan has a more extensive command of treasure than any other sovereign in the universe.

CHAPTER XIX

Of the Council of Twelve great Officers appointed for the Affairs of the Army, and of Twelve others, for the general Concerns of the Empire

The Grand Khan selects twelve noblemen of high rank and consequence (as has been mentioned), whose duty it is to decide upon every point respecting the army; such as the removal of troops from one station to another; the change of officers commanding them; the employment of a force where it may be judged necessary; and the numbers which it may be proper to detach upon any particular service, according to the degree of its importance. Besides these objects, it is their business to distinguish between officers who have given proofs of valour in combat, and those who have shown themselves base and cowardly, in order to advance the former and to degrade the latter. Thus, if the commander of a thousand has been found to conduct himself in an unbecoming manner, this tribunal, considering him to be unworthy of the rank he held, reduce him to the command of an hundred men; or, on the contrary, if he has displayed such qualities as give claim to promotion, they appoint him commander of ten thousand. All this, however, is done with the knowledge and subject to the approval of his majesty, to whom they report their opinion of the officer's merit or demerit, and who, upon confirming their decision, grants to him who is promoted to the command of ten thousand men (for example) the tablet or warrant belonging to his rank, as before described; and also confers on him large presents, in order to excite others to merit the same rewards.

The tribunal composed of these twelve nobles is named Thai, denoting a supreme court, as being responsible to no other than the sovereign. Besides this, there is another tribunal, likewise of twelve nobles, appointed for the superintendence of everything that respects the government of the thirty-four provinces of the empire. These have in Kanbalu a large and handsome palace or court, containing many chambers and halls. For the business of each province there is a presiding law-officer, together with several clerks, who have their respective apartments in the court, and there transact whatever business is necessary to be done for the province to which they belong, according to the directions they receive from the tribunal of twelve. These have authority to make choice of persons for the governments of the several provinces, whose names are presented to the Grand Khan for confirmation of their appointments and delivery of the tablets of gold or of silver appropriated to their ranks. They have also the superintendence of every matter that regards the collection of the revenue, both from land and customs, together with its disposal, and have the control of every other department of the state; with the exception only of what relates to the army. This tribunal is named Sing, implying that it is a second high court, and, like the other, responsible only to the Grand Khan. But the former tribunal, named Thai, which has the administration of military affairs, is regarded as superior in rank and dignity to the latter.

CHAPTER XX

Of the Places established on all the great Roads for supplying Post-Horses — Of the Couriers on Foot — And of the Mode in which the Expense is defrayed

From the city of Kanbalu there are many roads leading to the different provinces, and upon each of these, that is to say, upon every great high road, at the distance of twenty-five or thirty miles, accordingly as the towns happen to be situated, there are stations, with houses of accommodation for travellers, called *yamb* or post-houses. These are large and handsome buildings, having several well-furnished apartments, hung with silk, and provided with everything suitable to persons of rank. Even kings may be lodged at these stations in a becoming manner, as every article required may be obtained from the towns and strong places in the vicinity; and for some of them the court makes regular provision. At each station four hundred good horses are kept in constant readiness, in order that all messengers going and coming upon the business of the Grand Khan, and all ambassadors, may have relays, and, leaving their jaded horses, be supplied with fresh ones. Even in mountainous districts, remote from the great roads, where there were no villages, and the towns are far distant from each other, his majesty has equally caused buildings of the same kind to be erected, furnished with everything necessary, and provided with the usual establishment of horses. He sends people to dwell upon the spot, in order to cultivate the land, and attend to the service of the post; by which means large villages are formed. In consequence of these regulations, ambassadors to the court, and the royal messengers, go and return through every province and kingdom of the empire with the greatest convenience and facility; in all which the Grand Khan exhibits a superiority over every other emperor, king, or human being. In his dominions no fewer than two hundred thousand horses are thus employed in the department of the post, and ten thousand buildings, with suitable furniture, are kept up. It is indeed so wonderful a system, and so effective in its operation, as it is scarcely possible to describe. If it be questioned how the population of the country can supply sufficient numbers for these duties, and by what means they can be victualled, we may answer, that all the idolaters, and likewise the Saracens, keep six, eight, or ten women, according to their circumstances, by whom they have a prodigious number of children; some of them as many as thirty sons capable of following their fathers in arms; whereas with us a man has only one wife, and even although she should prove barren, he is obliged to pass his life with her, and is by that means deprived of the chance of raising a family. Hence it is that our population is so much inferior to theirs. With regard to food, there is no deficiency of it, for these people, especially the Tartars, Cathaians, and inhabitants of the province of Manji (or Southern China), subsist, for the most part, upon rice, panicum, and millet; which three grains yield, in their soil, an hundred measures for one. Wheat, indeed, does not yield a similar increase, and bread not being in use with them, it is eaten only in the form of vermicelli or of pastry. The former grains they boil in milk or stew with their meat. With them no spot of earth is suffered to lie idle, that can possibly be cultivated; and their cattle of different kinds multiply exceedingly, insomuch that when they take the field, there is scarcely an individual that does not carry with him six, eight, or more horses, for his own personal use. From all this may be seen the causes of so large a population, and the circumstances that enable them to provide so abundantly for their subsistence.

In the intermediate space between the post-houses, there are small villages settled at the distance of every three miles, which may contain, one with another, about forty cottages. In these are stationed the foot messengers, likewise employed in the service of his majesty. They wear girdles round their waists, to which several small bells are attached, in order that their coming may be perceived at a distance; and as they run only three miles, that is, from one of these foot-stations to another next adjoining, the noise serves to give notice of their approach, and preparation is accordingly made by a fresh courier to proceed with the packet instantly upon the arrival of the former. Thus it is so expeditiously conveyed from station to station, that in the course of two days and two nights his majesty receives distant intelligence that in the ordinary mode could not be obtained in less than ten days; and it often happens that in the fruit season, what is gathered in the morning at Kanbalu is conveyed to the Grand Khan, at Shan-du, by the evening of the following day; although the distance is generally considered as ten days' journey. At each of these three-mile stations there is a clerk, whose business it is to note the day and hour at which the one courier arrives and the other departs; which is likewise done at all the post-houses. Besides this, officers are directed to pay monthly visits to every station, in order to examine into the management of them, and to punish those couriers who have neglected to use proper diligence. All these couriers are not only exempt from the (capitation) tax, but also receive from his majesty good allowances. The horses employed in this service are not attended with any (direct) expense; the cities, towns, and villages in the neighbourhood being obliged to furnish, and also to maintain them. By his majesty's command the governors of the cities cause examination to be made by well-informed persons, as to the number of horses the inhabitants, individually, are capable of supplying. The same is done with respect to the towns and villages; and according to their means the requisition is enforced; those on each side of the station contributing their due proportion. The charge of the maintenance of the horses is afterwards deducted by the cities out of the revenue payable to the Grand Khan; inasmuch as the sum for which each inhabitant would be liable is commuted for an equivalent of horses or share of horses, which he maintains at the nearest adjoining station.

It must be understood, however, that of the four hundred horses the whole are not constantly on service at the station, but only two hundred, which are kept there for the space of a month, during which period the other half are at pasture; and at the beginning of the month, these in their turn take the duty, whilst the former have time to recover their flesh; each alternately relieving the other. Where it happens that there is a river or a lake which the couriers on foot, or the horsemen, are under the necessity of passing, the neighbouring cities are obliged to keep three or four boats in continual readiness for that purpose; and where there is a desert of several days' journey, that does not admit of any habitation, the city on its borders is obliged to furnish horses to such persons as ambassadors to and from the court, that they may be enabled to pass the desert, and also to supply provisions to them and their suite; but cities so circumstanced have a remuneration from his majesty. Where the post stations lie at a distance from the great road, the horses are partly those of his majesty, and are only in part furnished by the cities and towns of the district.

When it is necessary that the messengers should proceed with extraordinary despatch, as in the cases of giving information of disturbance in any part of the country, the rebellion of a chief, or other important matter, they ride two hundred, or sometimes two hundred and fifty miles in the course of a day. On such occasions they carry with them the tablet of the gerfalcon as a signal of the urgency of their business and the necessity for despatch. And when there are two messengers, they take their departure together from the same place, mounted upon good fleet horses; and they gird their bodies tight, bind a cloth round their heads, and push their horses to the greatest speed. They continue thus till they come to the next post-house, at twenty-five miles distant, where they find two other horses, fresh and in a state for work; they spring upon them without taking any repose, and changing in the same manner at every stage, until the day closes, they perform a journey of two hundred and fifty miles. In cases of great emergency they continue their course during the night, and if there should be no moon, they are accompanied to the next station by persons on foot, who run before them with lights; when of course they do not make the same expedition as in the daytime, the light-bearers not being able to exceed a certain pace. Messengers qualified to undergo this extraordinary degree of fatigue are held in high estimation. Now we will leave this subject, and I will tell you of a great act of benevolence which the Grand Khan performs twice a year.

CHAPTER XXI

*Of the Relief afforded by the Grand Khan to all the
Provinces of his Empire, in Times of Dearth or Mortality of
Cattle*

The Grand Khan sends every year his commissioners to ascertain
whether any of his subjects have suffered in their crops of corn from
unfavourable weather, from storms of wind or violent rains, or by
locusts, worms, or any other plague; and in such cases he not only
refrains from exacting the usual tribute of that year, but furnishes
them from his granaries with so much corn as is necessary for their
subsistence, as well as for sowing their land. With this view, in times
of great plenty, he causes large purchases to be made of such kinds of
grain as are most serviceable to them, which is stored in granaries
provided for the purpose in the several provinces, and managed with
such care as to ensure its keeping for three or four years without
damage. It is his command, that these granaries be always kept full,
in order to provide against times of scarcity; and when, in such
seasons, he disposes of the grain for money, he requires for four
measures no more than the purchaser would pay for one measure in
the market. In like manner where there has been a mortality of cattle
in any district, he makes good the loss to the sufferers from those
belonging to himself, which he has received as his tenth of produce
in other provinces. All his thoughts, indeed, are directed to the
important object of assisting the people whom he governs, that they
may be enabled to live by their labour and improve their substance.
We must not omit to notice a peculiarity of the Grand Khan, that
where an accident has happened by lightning to any herd of cattle,
flock of sheep, or other domestic animals, whether the property of
one or more persons, and however large the herd may be, he does
not demand the tenth of the increase of such cattle during three
years; and so also if a ship laden with merchandise has been struck by
lightning, he does not collect from her any custom or share of her

cargo, considering the accident as an ill omen. God, he says, has shown himself to be displeased with the owner of the goods, and he is unwilling that property bearing the mark of divine wrath should enter his treasury.

CHAPTER XXII

Of the Trees which he causes to be planted at the Sides of the Roads, and of the Order in which they are kept

There is another regulation adopted by the Grand Khan, equally ornamental and useful. At both sides of the public roads he causes trees to be planted, of a kind that become large and tall, and being only two paces asunder, they serve (besides the advantage of their shade in summer) to point out the road (when the ground is covered with snow); which is of great assistance and affords much comfort to travellers. This is done along all the high roads, where the nature of the soil admits of plantation; but when the way lies through sandy deserts or over rocky mountains, where it is impossible to have trees, he orders stones to be placed and columns to be erected, as marks for guidance. He also appoints officers of rank, whose duty it is to see that all these are properly arranged and the roads constantly kept in good order. Besides the motives that have been assigned for these plantations, it may be added that the Grand Khan is the more disposed to make them, from the circumstance of his diviners and astrologers having declared that those who plant trees are rewarded with long life.

CHAPTER XXIII

Of the kind of Wine made in the Province of Cathay – And of the Stones used there for burning in the manner of Charcoal

The greater part of the inhabitants of the province of Cathay drink a sort of wine made from rice mixed with a variety of spices and drugs. This beverage, or wine as it may be termed, is so good and well flavoured that they do not wish for better. It is clear, bright, and pleasant to the taste, and being (made) very hot, has the quality of inebriating sooner than any other.

Throughout this province there is found a sort of black stone, which they dig out of the mountains, where it runs in veins. When lighted, it burns like charcoal, and retains the fire much better than wood; insomuch that it may be preserved during the night, and in the morning be found still burning. These stones do not flame, excepting a little when first lighted, but during their ignition give out a considerable heat. It is true there is no scarcity of wood in the country, but the multitude of inhabitants is so immense, and their stoves and baths, which they are continually heating, so numerous, that the quantity could not supply the demand; for there is no person who does not frequent the warm bath at least three times in the week, and during the winter daily, if it is in their power. Every man of rank or wealth has one in his house for his own use; and the stock of wood must soon prove inadequate to such consumption; whereas these stones may be had in the greatest abundance, and at a cheap rate.

CHAPTER XXIV

*Of the great and admirable Liberality exercised by the Grand
Khan towards the Poor of Kanbalu, and other Persons who
apply for Relief at his Court*

It has been already stated that the Grand Khan distributes large
quantities of grain to his subjects (in the provinces). We shall now
speak of his great charity to and provident care of the poor in the city
of Kanbalu. Upon his being apprised of any respectable family, that
had lived in easy circumstances, being by misfortunes reduced to
poverty, or who, in consequence of infirmities, are unable to work
for their living or to raise a supply of any kind of grain: to a family in
that situation he gives what is necessary for their year's consumption,
and at the customary period they present themselves before the
officers who manage the department of his majesty's expenses and
who reside in a palace where that business is transacted, to whom
they deliver a statement in writing of the quantity furnished to them
in the preceding year, according to which they receive also for the
present. He provides in like manner for their clothing, which he has
the means of doing from his tenths of wool, silk, and hemp. These
materials he has woven into the different sorts of cloth, in a house
erected for that purpose, where every artisan is obliged to work one
day in the week for his majesty's service. Garments made of stuffs thus
manufactured he orders to be given to the poor families above
described, as they are wanted for their winter and their summer
dresses. He also has clothing prepared for his armies, and in every city
has a quantity of woollen cloth woven, which is paid for from the
amount of the tenths levied at the place.

It should be known that the Tartars, when they followed their
original customs, and had not yet adopted the religion of the
idolaters, were not in the practice of bestowing alms, and when a
necessitous man applied to them, they drove him away with injurious
expressions, saying, 'Begone with your complaint of a bad season
which God has sent you; had he loved you, as it appears he loves me,

you would have prospered as I do.' But since the wise men of the idolaters, and especially the baksis, already mentioned, have represented to his majesty that providing for the poor is a good work and highly acceptable to their deities, he has relieved their wants in the manner stated, and at his court none are denied food who come to ask it. Not a day passes in which there are not distributed, by the regular officers, twenty thousand vessels of rice, millet, and panicum. By reason of this admirable and astonishing liberality which the Grand Khan exercises towards the poor, the people all adore him as a divinity.

CHAPTER XXV

Of the Astrologers of the City of Kanbalu

There are in the city of Kanbalu, amongst Christians, Saracens, and Cathaians, about five thousand astrologers and prognosticators, for whose food and clothing the Grand Khan provides in the same manner as he does for the poor families above mentioned, and who are in the constant exercise of their art. They have their astrolabes, upon which are described the planetary signs, the hours (at which they pass the meridian), and their several aspects for the whole year. The astrologers (or almanac-makers) of each distinct sect annually proceed to the examination of their respective tables, in order to ascertain from thence the course of the heavenly bodies, and their relative positions for every lunation. They discover therein what the state of the weather shall be, from the paths and configurations of the planets in the different signs, and thence foretell the peculiar phenomena of each month: that in such a month, for instance, there shall be thunder and storms; in such another, earthquakes; in another, strokes of lightning and violent rains; in another, diseases, mortality, wars, discords, conspiracies. As they find the matter in their astrolabes, so they declare it will come to pass; adding, however, that God, according to his good pleasure, may do more or less than they have set down. They write their predictions for the year upon certain small squares, which are called *takuini*, and these they sell, for a groat apiece, to all persons who are desirous of peeping into futurity. Those whose predictions are found to be the more generally correct are esteemed the most perfect masters of their art, and are consequently the most honoured. When any person forms the design of executing some great work, of performing a distant journey in the way of commerce, or of commencing any other undertaking, and is desirous of knowing what success may be likely to attend it, he has recourse to one of these astrologers, and, informing him that he is about to proceed on such an expedition, enquires in what disposition the heavens appear to be at the time. The latter thereupon tells him, that before he can answer it is necessary he should be informed of the year, the month, and the hour in which he was born; and that, having learned these particulars, he will then proceed to ascertain in what respects the constellation that was in the ascendant at his nativity corresponds with the aspect of the celestial bodies at the time of making the enquiry. Upon this comparison he grounds his prediction of the favourable or unfavourable termination of the adventure.

It should be observed that the Tartars compute their time by a cycle of twelve years; to the first of which they give the name of the lion; to the second year, that of the ox; to the third, the dragon; to the fourth, the dog; and so of the rest, until the whole of the twelve have elapsed. When a person, therefore, is asked in what year he was born, he replies, In the course of the year of the lion, upon such a day, at such an hour and minute; all of which has been carefully noted by his parents in a book. Upon the completion of the twelve years of the cycle, they return to the first, and continually repeat the same series.

CHAPTER XXVI

Of the Religion of the Tartars — Of the Opinions they hold respecting the Soul — And of some of their Customs

As has already been observed, these people are idolaters, and for deities, each person has a tablet fixed up against a high part of the wall of his chamber, upon which is written a name, that serves to denote the high, celestial, and sublime God; and to this they pay daily adoration, with incense burning. Lifting up their hands and then striking their faces against the floor three times, they implore from him the blessings of sound intellect and health of body; without any further petition. Below this, on the floor, they have a statue which they name *Natigai*, which they consider as the God of all terrestrial things or whatever is produced from the earth. They give him a wife and children, and worship him in a similar manner, burning incense, raising their hands, and bending to the floor. To him they pray for seasonable weather, abundant crops, increase of family, and the like. They believe the soul to be immortal, in this sense, that immediately upon the death of a man, it enters into another body, and that accordingly as he has acted virtuously or wickedly during his life, his future state will become, progressively, better or worse. If he be a poor man, and has conducted himself worthily and decently, he will be re-born, in the first instance, from the womb of a gentlewoman, and become, himself, a gentleman; next, from the womb of a lady of rank, and become a nobleman; thus continually ascending in the scale of existence, until he be united to the divinity. But if, on the contrary, being the son of a gentleman, he has behaved unworthily, he will, in his next state, be a clown, and at length a dog, continually descending to a condition more vile than the preceding.

Their style of conversation is courteous; they salute each other politely, with countenances expressive of satisfaction, have an air of good breeding, and eat their victuals with particular cleanliness. To their parents they show the utmost reverence; but should it happen that a child acts disrespectfully to or neglects to assist his parents in their necessity, there is a public tribunal, whose especial duty it is to punish with severity the crime of filial ingratitude, when the circumstance is known. Malefactors guilty of various crimes, who are apprehended and thrown into prison, are executed by strangling; but such as remain till the expiration of three years, being the time appointed by his majesty for a general gaol delivery, and are then liberated, have a mark imprinted upon one of their cheeks, that they may be recognised.

The present Grand Khan has prohibited all species of gambling and other modes of cheating, to which the people of this country are addicted more than any others upon earth; and as an argument for deterring them from the practice, he says to them (in his edict), 'I subdued you by the power of my sword, and consequently whatever you possess belongs of right to me: if you gamble, therefore, you are sporting with my property.' He does not, however, take anything arbitrarily in virtue of this right. The order and regularity observed by all ranks of people, when they present themselves before his majesty, ought not to pass unnoticed. When they approach within half a mile of the place where he happens to be, they show their respect for his exalted character by assuming a humble, placid, and quiet demeanour, insomuch that not the least noise, nor the voice of any person calling out, or even speaking aloud, is heard. Every man of rank carries with him a small vessel, into which he spits, so long as he continues in the hall of audience, no one daring to spit on the floor; and this being done, he replaces the cover, and makes a salutation. They are accustomed likewise to take with them handsome buskins made of white leather, and when they reach the court, but before they enter the hall (for which they wait a summons from the Grand Khan), they put on these white buskins, and give those in which they had walked to the care of the servants. This practice is observed that they may not soil the beautiful carpets, which are curiously wrought with silk and gold, and exhibit a variety of colours.

CHAPTER XXVII

Of the River named Pulisangan, and of the Bridge over it

Having thus completed the account of the government and police of the province of Cathay and city of Kanbalu, as well as of the magnificence of the Grand Khan, we shall now proceed to speak of other parts of the empire. You must know then that the Grand Khan sent Marco as his ambassador to the west; and leaving Kanbalu, he travelled westward during full four months; we shall now tell you all he saw going and coming.

Upon leaving the capital and travelling ten miles, you come to a river named Pulisangan, which discharges itself into the ocean, and is navigated by many vessels entering from thence, with considerable quantities of merchandise. Over this river there is a very handsome bridge of stone, perhaps unequalled by another in the world. Its length is three hundred paces, and its width eight paces; so that ten men can, without inconvenience, ride abreast. It has twenty-four arches, supported by twenty-five piers erected in the water, all of serpentine stone, and built with great skill. On each side, and from one extremity to the other, there is a handsome parapet, formed of marble slabs and pillars arranged in a masterly style. At the commencement of the ascent the bridge is something wider than at the summit, but from the part where the ascent terminates, the sides run in straight lines and parallel to each other. Upon the upper level there is a massive and lofty column, resting upon a tortoise of marble, and having near its base a large figure of a lion, with a lion also on the top. Towards the slope of the bridge there is another handsome column or pillar, with its lion, at the distance of a pace and a half from the former; and all the spaces between one pillar and another, throughout the whole length of the bridge, are filled up with slabs of marble, curiously sculptured, and mortised into the next adjoining pillars, which are, in like manner, a pace and a half asunder, and equally surmounted with lions, forming altogether a beautiful spectacle. These parapets serve to prevent accidents that might otherwise happen to passengers. What has been said applies to the descent as well as to the ascent of the bridge.

CHAPTER XXVIII

Of the City of Gouza

After having passed this bridge, proceeding thirty miles in a westerly direction, through a country abounding with fine buildings, amongst vineyards and much cultivated and fertile grounds, you arrive at a handsome and considerable city, named Gouza, where there are many convents of the idolaters. The inhabitants in general live by commerce and manual arts. They have manufactures of gold tissues and the finest kind of gauze. The inns for accommodating travellers are there numerous. At the distance of a mile beyond this place, the roads divide; the one going in a westerly, and the other in a south-easterly direction, the former through the provinces of Cathay, and the latter towards the province of Manji. From the city of Gouza it is a journey of ten days through Cathay to the kingdom of Ta-in-fu; in the course of which you pass many fine cities and strong places, in which manufactures and commerce flourish, and where you see many vineyards and much cultivated land. From hence grapes are carried into the interior of Cathay, where the vine does not grow. Mulberry trees also abound, the leaves of which enable the inhabitants to produce large quantities of silk. A degree of civilisation prevails amongst all the people of this country, in consequence of their frequent intercourse with the towns, which are numerous and but little distant from each other. To these the merchants continually resort, carrying their goods from one city to another, as the fairs are successively held at each. At the end of five days' journey beyond the ten that have been mentioned, it is said there is another city still larger and more handsome (than Ta-in-fu), named Achbaluch, to which the limits of his majesty's hunting grounds extend, and within which no persons dare to sport, excepting the princes of his own family, and those whose names are inscribed on the grand falconer's list; but beyond these limits, all persons qualified by their rank are at liberty to pursue game. It happens, however, that the Grand Khan scarcely ever takes the amusement of the chase on this side of the country; and the consequence is, that the wild animals, especially hares, multiply to such a degree as to occasion the destruction of all the growing corn of the province. When this came to the knowledge of the Grand Khan, he repaired thither, with the whole of his court, and innumerable multitudes of these animals were taken.

CHAPTER XXIX

Of the Kingdom of Ta-in-fu

At the end of ten days' journey from the city of Gouza, you arrive (as has been said) at the kingdom of Ta-in-fu, whose chief city, the capital of the province, bears the same name. It is of the largest size, and very beautiful. A considerable trade is carried on here, and a variety of articles are manufactured, particularly arms and other military stores, which are at this place conveniently situated for the use of the Grand Khan's armies. Vineyards are numerous, from which grapes in vast abundance are gathered; and although within all the jurisdiction of Ta-in-fu no other vines are found than those produced in the district immediately surrounding the capital, there is yet a sufficient supply for the whole of the province. Other fruits also grow here in plenty, as does the mulberry tree, together with the worms that yield the silk.

CHAPTER XXX

Of the City of Pi-an-fu

Leaving Ta-in-fu, and travelling westward, seven days' journey, through a fine country in which there are many cities and strong places, where commerce and manufactures prevail, and whose merchants, travelling over various parts of the country, obtain considerable profits, you reach a city named Pi-an-fu, which is of a large size and much celebrated. It likewise contains numerous merchants and artisans. Silk is produced here also in great quantity. We shall not say anything further of these places, but proceed to speak of the distinguished city of Ka-chan-fu; first noticing, however, a noble fortress named Thai-gin.

CHAPTER XXXI

Of the Fortress of Thai-gin or Tai-gin

In a western direction from Pi-an-fu there is a large and handsome fortress named Thai-gin, which is said to have been built, at a remote period, by a king who was called Dor. Within the walls of the fort stands a spacious and highly-ornamented palace, the hall of which contains paintings of all the renowned princes who, from ancient times, have reigned at this place, forming together a superb exhibition. A remarkable circumstance in the history of this King Dor shall now be related. He was a powerful prince, assumed much state, and was always waited upon by young women of extraordinary beauty, a vast number of whom he entertained at his court. When, for recreation, he went about the fortress, he was drawn in his carriage by these damsels, which they could do with facility, as it was of a small size. They were devoted to his service, and performed every office that administered to his convenience or amusement. In his government he was not wanting in vigour, and he ruled with dignity and justice. The works of his castle, according to the report of the people of the country, were beyond example strong. He was, however, a vassal of Un-khan, who, as we have already stated, was known by the appellation of Prester John; but, influenced by pride, he rebelled against him. When this came to the knowledge of Prester John, he was exceedingly grieved, being sensible that, from the strong situation of the castle, it would be in vain to march against it, or even to proceed to any act of hostility. Matters had remained some time in this state, when seven cavaliers belonging to his retinue presented themselves before him, and declared their resolution to attempt the seizure of King Dor's person, and to bring him alive to his majesty. To this they were encouraged by the promise of a large reward. They accordingly took their departure for the place of his residence, and feigning to have arrived from a distant country, made him an offer of their services. In his employment they so ably and diligently performed their duties that they gained the esteem of their new master, who showed them distinguished favour, insomuch that when he took the diversion of hunting, he always had them near his person. One day when the king was engaged in the chase, and had crossed a river which separated him from the rest of his party, who remained on the opposite side, these cavaliers perceived that the opportunity now presented itself of executing their design. They drew their swords, surrounded the king, and led him away by force towards the territory of Prester John, without its being possible for him to receive assistance from his own people. When they reached the court of that monarch, he gave orders for clothing his prisoner in the meanest apparel, and, with the view of humiliating him by the indignity, committed to him the charge of his herds. In this wretched condition he remained for two years, strict care being taken that he should not effect his escape. At the expiration of that period, Prester John caused him to be again brought before him, trembling from apprehension that they were going to put him to death. But on the contrary, Prester John, after a sharp and severe admonition, in which he warned him against suffering pride and arrogance to make him swerve from his allegiance in future, granted him a pardon, directed that he should be dressed in royal apparel, and sent him back to his principality with an honourable escort. From that time forward he always preserved his loyalty, and lived on amicable terms with Prester John. The foregoing is what was related to me on the subject of King Dor.

CHAPTER XXXII

Of the very large and noble River called the Kara-moran

Upon leaving the fortress of Thai-gin, and travelling about twenty miles, you come to a river called the Kara-moran, which is of such magnitude, both in respect to width and depth, that no solid bridge can be erected upon it. Its waters are discharged into the ocean, as shall hereafter be more particularly mentioned. On its banks are many cities and castles, in which a number of trading people reside, who carry on an extensive commerce. The country bordering upon it produces ginger, and silk also in large quantities. Of birds the multitude is incredible, especially of pheasants, which are sold at the rate of three for the value of a Venetian groat. Here likewise grows a species of large cane, in infinite abundance, some of a foot, and others a foot and a half (in circumference), which are employed by the inhabitants for a variety of useful purposes.

CHAPTER XXXIII

Of the City of Ka-chan-fu

Having crossed this river and travelled three days' journey, you arrive at a city named Ka-chan-fu, whose inhabitants are idolaters. They carry on a considerable traffic, and work at a variety of manufactures. The country produces in great abundance, silk, ginger, galangal, spikenard, and many drugs that are nearly unknown in our part of the world. Here they weave gold tissues, as well as every other kind of silken cloth. We shall speak in the next place of the noble and celebrated city of Ken-zan-fu, in the kingdom of the same name.

CHAPTER XXXIV

Of the City of Ken-zan-fu

Departing from Ka-chan-fu, and proceeding eight days journey in a westerly direction, you continually meet with cities and commercial towns, and pass many gardens and cultivated grounds, with abundance of the mulberry or tree that contributes to the production of silk. The inhabitants in general worship idols, but there are also found here Nestorian Christians, Turkomans, and Saracens. The wild beasts of the country afford excellent sport, and a variety of birds also are taken. At the end of those eight stages you arrive at the city of Ken-zan-fu, which was anciently the capital of an extensive, noble, and powerful kingdom, the seat of many kings, highly descended and distinguished in arms. At the present day it is governed by a son of the Grand Khan, named Mangalu, upon whom his father has conferred the sovereignty. It is a country of great commerce, and eminent for its manufactures. Raw silk is produced in large quantities, and tissues of gold and every other kind of silk are woven there. At this place likewise they prepare every article necessary for the equipment of an army. All species of provisions are in abundance, and to be procured at a moderate price. The inhabitants in general worship idols, but there are some Christians, Turkomans, and Saracens. In a plain, about five miles from the city, stands a beautiful palace belonging to king Mangalu, embellished with many fountains and rivulets, both within and on the outside of the buildings. There is also a fine park, surrounded by a high wall, with battlements, enclosing an extent of five miles, where all kinds of wild animals, both beasts and birds, are kept for sport. In its centre is this spacious palace, which, for symmetry and beauty, cannot be surpassed. It contains many halls and chambers, ornamented with paintings in gold and the finest azure, as well as with great profusion of marble. Mangalu, pursuing the footsteps of his father, governs his principality with strict equity, and is beloved by his people. He also takes much delight in hunting and hawking.

CHAPTER XXXV

Of the Boundaries of Cathay and Manji

Travelling westward three days from the residence of Mangalu, you still find towns and castles, whose inhabitants subsist by commerce and manufactures, and where there is an abundance of silk; but at the end of these three stages you enter upon a region of mountains and valleys, which lie within the province of Kun-kin. This tract, however, has no want of inhabitants, who are worshippers of idols, and cultivate the earth. They live also by the chase, the land being much covered with woods. In these are found many wild beasts, such as lions (tigers), bears, lynxes, fallow deer, antelopes, stags, and many other animals, which are made to turn to good account. This region extends to the distance of twenty days' journey, during which the way lies entirely over mountains and through valleys and woods, but still interspersed with towns where travellers may find convenient accommodation. This journey of twenty days towards the west being performed, you arrive at a place called Ach-baluch Manji, which

signifies, the white city on the confines of Manji, where the country
becomes level, and is very populous. The inhabitants live by trade
and manual arts. Large quantities of ginger are produced here, which
is conveyed through all the province of Cathay, with great advantage
to the merchants. The country yields wheat, rice, and other grain
plentifully, and at a reasonable rate. This plain, thickly covered with
habitations, continues for two stages, after which you again come to
high mountains, valleys, and forests. Travelling twenty days still
further to the west, you continue to find the country inhabited, by
people who worship idols, and subsist upon the produce of their soil,
as well as that of the chase. Here also, besides the wild animals above
enumerated, there are great numbers of that species which produces
the musk.

CHAPTER XXXVI

Of the Province of Sin-din-fu, and of the great River Kian

Having travelled those twenty stages through a mountainous country,
you reach a plain on the confines of Manji, where there is a district
named Sin-din-fu, by which name also the large and noble city, its
capital, formerly the seat of many rich and powerful kings, is called.
The circumference of the city is twenty miles; but at the present day
it is divided in consequence of the following circumstances. The late
old king had three sons; and it being his wish that each of them
should reign after his death, he made a partition of the city amongst
them, separating one part from the other by walls, although the
whole continued to be surrounded by one general enclosure. These
three brothers accordingly became kings, and each had for his portion
a considerable tract of country, the territory of their father having
been extensive and rich. But, upon its conquest by the Grand Khan,
he destroyed these three princes, and possessed himself of their
inheritance.

The city is watered by many considerable streams, which, descending from the distant mountains, surround and pass through it in a
variety of directions. Some of these rivers are half a mile in width,

others are two hundred paces, and very deep, over which are built several large and handsome stone bridges, eight paces in breadth, their length being greater or less according to the size of the stream. From one extremity to the other there is a row of marble pillars on each side, which support the roof; for here the bridges have very handsome roofs, constructed of wood, ornamented with paintings of a red colour, and covered with tiles. Throughout the whole length also there are neat apartments and shops, where all sorts of trades are carried on. One of the buildings, larger than the rest, is occupied by the officers who collect the duties upon provisions and merchandise, and a toll from persons who pass the bridge. In this way, it is said, his majesty receives daily the sum of a hundred besants of gold. These rivers, uniting their streams below the city, contribute to form the mighty river called the Kian, whose course, before it discharges itself into the ocean, is equal to a hundred days' journey; but of its properties occasion will be taken to speak in a subsequent part of this book.

On these rivers and in the parts adjacent are many towns and fortified places, and the vessels are numerous, in which large quantities of merchandise are transported to and from the city. The people of the province are idolaters. Departing from thence you travel five stages, partly along a plain, and partly through valleys, where you see many respectable mansions, castles, and small towns. The inhabitants subsist by agriculture. In the city there are manufactures, particularly of very fine cloths and of crapes or gauzes. This country, like the districts already mentioned, is infested with lions (tigers), bears, and other wild animals. At the end of these five days' journey you reach the desolated country of Thebeth.

CHAPTER XXXVII

Of the Province of Thebeth

The province named Thebeth was laid entirely waste at the time that Mangu-khan carried his arms into that country. To the distance of twenty days' journey you see numberless towns and castles in a state of ruin; and in consequence of the want of inhabitants, wild beasts, and especially tigers, have multiplied to such a degree that merchants and other travellers are exposed there to great danger during the night. They are not only under the necessity of carrying their provisions along with them, but are obliged, upon arriving at their halting places, to employ the utmost circumspection, and to take the following precautions, that their horses may not be devoured. In this region, and particularly in the neighbourhood of rivers, are found canes (bamboos) of the length of ten paces, three palms in circumference, and three palms also in the space between each knot or joint. Several of these, in their green state, the travellers tie together, and place them, when evening approaches, at a certain distance from their quarters, with a fire lighted around them, when, by the action of the heat, they burst with a tremendous explosion. The noise is so loud as to be heard at the distance of two miles, which has the effect of terrifying the wild beasts and making them fly from the neighbourhood. The merchants also provide themselves with iron shackles, in order to fasten the legs of their horses, which would otherwise, when alarmed by the noise, break their halters and run away; and, from the neglect of this precaution, it has happened that many owners have lost their cattle. Thus you travel for twenty days through a desolated country, finding neither inns nor provisions, unless perhaps once in three or four days, when you take the opportunity of replenishing your stock of necessaries. At the end of that period you begin to discover a few castles and strong towns, built upon rocky heights, or upon the summits of mountains, and gradually enter an inhabited and cultivated district, where there is no longer any danger from beasts of prey.

A scandalous custom, which could only proceed from the blindness of idolatry, prevails amongst the people of these parts, who are disinclined to marry young women so long as they are in their virgin state, but require, on the contrary, that they should have had previous commerce with many of the other sex; and this, they assert, is pleasing to their deities, and that a woman who has not had the company of men is worthless. Accordingly, upon the arrival of a caravan of merchants, and as soon as they have set up their tents for the night, those mothers who have marriageable daughters conduct them to the place, and each, contending for a preference, entreats the strangers to accept of her daughter and enjoy her society so long as they remain in the neighbourhood. Such as have most beauty to recommend them are of course chosen, and the others return home disappointed and chagrined, whilst the former continue with the travellers until the period of their departure. They then restore them to their mothers, and never attempt to carry them away. It is expected, however, that the merchants should make them presents of trinkets, rings, or other complimentary tokens of regard, which the young women take home with them. When, afterwards, they are designed for marriage, they wear all these ornaments about the neck or other part of the body, and she who exhibits the greatest number of them is considered to have attracted the attention of the greatest number of men, and is on that account in the higher estimation with the young men who are looking out for wives; nor can she bring to her husband a more acceptable portion than a quantity of such gifts. At the solemnisation of her nuptials, she accordingly makes a display of them to the assembly, and he regards them as a proof that their idols have rendered her lovely in the eyes of men. From thenceforward no person can dare to meddle with her who has become the wife of another, and this rule is never infringed. These idolatrous people are treacherous and cruel, and holding it no crime or turpitude to rob, are the greatest thieves in the world. They subsist by the chase and by fowling, as well as upon the fruits of the earth.

Here are found the animals that produce the musk, and such is the quantity, that the scent of it is diffused over the whole country. Once in every month the secretion takes place, and it forms itself, as has already been said, into a sort of imposthume, or boil full of blood, near the navel; and the blood thus issuing, in consequence of excessive repletion, becomes the musk. Throughout every part of this region the animal abounds, and the odour generally prevails. They are called *gudderi* in the language of the natives, and are taken with dogs. These people use no coined money, nor even the paper money of the Grand Khan, but for their currency employ coral. Their dress is homely, being of leather, undressed skins, or of canvas. They have a language peculiar to the province of Thebeth, which borders on Manji. This was formerly a country of so much importance as to be divided into eight kingdoms, containing many cities and castles. Its rivers, lakes, and mountains are numerous. In the rivers gold-dust is found in very large quantities. Not only is the coral, before mentioned, used for money, but the women also wear it about their necks, and with it ornament their idols. There are manufactures of camlet and of gold cloth, and many drugs are produced in the country that have not been brought to ours. These people are necromancers, and by their infernal art perform the most extraordinary and delusive enchantments that were ever seen or heard of. They cause tempests to arise, accompanied with flashes of lightning and thunderbolts, and produce many other miraculous effects. They are altogether an ill-conditioned race. They have dogs of the size of asses, strong enough to hunt all sorts of wild beasts, particularly the wild oxen, which are called *beyamini*, and are extremely large and fierce. Some of the best laner falcons are bred here, and also sakers, very swift of flight, and the natives have good sport with them. This province of Thebeth is subject to the Grand Khan, as well as all the other kingdoms and provinces that have been mentioned. Next to this is the province of Kain-du.

CHAPTER XXXVIII

Of the Province of Kain-du

Kain-du a western province, which was formerly subject to its own princes; but, since it has been brought under the dominion of the Grand Khan, it is ruled by the governors whom he appoints. We are not to understand, however, that it is situated in the western part (of Asia), but only that it lies westward with respect to our course from the northeastern quarter. Its inhabitants are idolaters. It contains many cities and castles, and the capital city, standing at the commencement of the province, is likewise named Kain-du. Near to it there is a large lake of salt water, in which are found abundance of pearls, of a white colour, but not round. So great indeed is the quantity, that, if his majesty permitted every individual to search for them, their value would become trifling; but the fishery is prohibited to all who do not obtain his licence. A mountain in the neighbourhood yields the turquoise stone, the mines of which cannot be worked without the same permission.

The inhabitants of this district are in the shameful and odious habit of considering it no mark of disgrace that those who travel through the country should have connection with their wives, daughters, or sisters; but, on the contrary, when strangers arrive, each householder endeavours to conduct one of them home with him, and, giving up all the females of the family to him, leaves him in the situation of master of the house, and takes his departure. And while the stranger is in the house, he places a signal at the window, as his hat or some other thing; and as long as this signal is seen in the house, the husband remains absent. And this custom prevails throughout that province. This they do in honour of their idols, believing that by such acts of kindness and hospitality to travellers a blessing is obtained, and that they shall be rewarded with a plentiful supply of the fruits of the earth.

The money or currency they make use of is thus prepared. Their gold is formed into small rods, and (being cut into certain lengths) passes according to its weight, without any stamp. This is their greater money: the smaller is of the following description. In this country there are salt-springs, from which they manufacture salt by boiling it in small pans. When the water has boiled for an hour, it becomes a kind of paste, which is formed into cakes of the value of twopence each. These, which are flat on the lower, and convex on the upper side, are placed upon hot tiles, near a fire, in order to dry and harden. On this latter species of money the stamp of the Grand Khan is impressed, and it cannot be prepared by any other than his own officers. Eighty of the cakes are made to pass for a saggio of gold. But when these are carried by the traders amongst the inhabitants of the mountains and other parts little frequented, they obtain a saggio of gold for sixty, fifty, or even forty of the salt cakes, in proportion as they find the natives less civilised, further removed from the towns, and more accustomed to remain on the same spot; inasmuch as people so circumstanced cannot always have a market for their gold, musk, and other commodities. And yet even at this rate it answers well to them who collect the gold-dust from the beds of the rivers, as has been mentioned. The same merchants travel in like manner through the mountainous and other parts of the province of Thebeth, last spoken of, where the money of salt has equal currency. Their profits are considerable, because these country people consume the salt with their food, and regard it as an indispensable necessary; whereas the inhabitants of the cities use for the same purpose only the broken fragments of the cakes, putting the whole cakes into circulation as money. Here also the animals called *gudderi*, which yield the musk, are taken in great numbers, and the article is proportionably abundant. Many fish, of good kinds, are caught in the lake. In the country are found tigers, bears, deer, stags, and antelopes. There are numerous birds also, of various sorts. The wine is not made from grapes, but from wheat and rice, with a mixture of spices, which is an excellent beverage.

This province likewise produces cloves. The tree is small; the branches and leaves resemble those of the laurel, but are somewhat longer and narrower. Its flowers are white and small, as are the cloves themselves, but as they ripen they become dark-coloured. Ginger grows there and also cassia in abundance, besides many other drugs, of which no quantity is ever brought to Europe. Upon leaving the city of Kain-du, the journey is fifteen days to the opposite boundary of the province; in the course of which you meet with respectable habitations, many fortified posts, and also places adapted to hunting and fowling. The inhabitants follow the customs and manners that have already been described. At the end of these fifteen days, you come to the great river Brius, which bounds the province, and in which are found large quantities of gold-dust. It discharges itself into the ocean. We shall now leave this river, as nothing further that is worthy of observation presents itself, and shall proceed to speak of the province of Karaian.

CHAPTER XXXIX

Of the great Province of Karaian, and of Yachi its principal City

Having passed the river above mentioned, you enter the province of Karaian, which is of such extent as to be divided into seven governments. It is situated towards the west; the inhabitants are idolaters; and it is subject to the dominion of the Grand Khan, who has constituted as its king his son named Cen-Temur, a rich, magnificent, and powerful prince, endowed with consummate wisdom and virtue, and by whom the kingdom is ruled with great justice. In travelling from this river five days' journey, in a westerly direction, you pass through a country fully inhabited, and see many castles. The inhabitants live upon flesh meat and upon the fruits of the earth. Their language is peculiar to themselves, and is difficult to be acquired. The best horses are bred in this province. At the end of these five days you arrive at its capital city, which is named Yachi, and is large and noble. In it are found merchants and artisans, with a mixed population, consisting of (the native) idolaters, Nestorian Christians, and Saracens or Mahometans; but the first is the most numerous class. The land is fertile in rice and wheat. The people, however, do not use wheaten bread, which they esteem unwholesome, but eat rice; and of the other grain, with the addition of spices, they make wine, which is clear, light-coloured, and most pleasant to the taste. For money they employ the white porcelain shell, found in the sea, and these they also wear as ornaments about their necks. Eighty of the shells are equal in value to a saggio of silver or two Venetian groats, and eight saggi of good silver to one of pure gold. In this country also there are salt-springs, from which all the salt used by the inhabitants is procured. The duty levied on this salt produces a large revenue to the king.

The natives do not consider it as an injury done to them, when others have connection with their wives, provided the act be voluntary on the woman's part. Here there is a lake nearly a hundred miles in circuit, in which great quantities of various kinds of fish are caught; some of them being of a large size. The people are accustomed to eat the undressed flesh of fowls, sheep, oxen, and buffaloes, but cured in the following manner. They cut the meat into very small particles, and then put it into a pickle of salt, with the addition of several of their spices. It is thus prepared for persons of the higher class, but the poorer sort only steep it, after mincing, in a sauce of garlic, and then eat it as if it were dressed.

CHAPTER XL

Of the Province named Karazan

Leaving the city of Yachi, and travelling ten days in a westerly direction, you reach the province of Karazan, which is also the name of its chief city. The inhabitants are idolaters. The country belongs to the dominion of the Grand Khan, and the royal functions are exercised by his son, named Kogatin. Gold is found in the rivers, both in small particles and in lumps; and there are also veins of it in the mountains. In consequence of the large quantity obtained, they give a saggio of gold for six saggi of silver. They likewise use the before-mentioned porcelain shells in currency; which, however, are not found in this part of the world, but are brought from India. As I have said before, these people never take virgins for their wives.

Here are seen huge serpents, ten paces in length, and ten spans in the girt of the body. At the fore part, near the head, they have two short legs, having three claws like those of a tiger, with eyes larger than a fourpenny loaf (*pane da quattro denari*) and very glaring. The jaws are wide enough to swallow a man, the teeth are large and sharp, and their whole appearance is so formidable, that neither man, nor any kind of animal, can approach them without terror. Others are met with of a smaller size, being eight, six, or five paces long; and the following method is used for taking them. In the daytime, by reason of the great heat, they lurk in caverns, from whence, at night, they issue to seek their food, and whatever beast they meet with and can lay hold of, whether tiger, wolf, or any other, they devour; after which they drag themselves towards some lake, spring of water, or river, in order to drink. By their motion in this way along the shore, and their vast weight, they make a deep impression, as if a heavy beam had been drawn along the sands. Those whose employment it is to hunt them observe the track by which they are most frequently accustomed to go, and fix into the ground several pieces of wood, armed with sharp iron spikes, which they cover with the sand in such a manner as not to be perceptible. When therefore the animals make their way towards the places they usually haunt, they are wounded by these instruments, and speedily killed. The crows, as soon as they perceive them to be dead, set up their scream; and this serves as a signal to the hunters, who advance to the spot, and proceed to separate the skin from the flesh, taking care immediately to secure the gall, which is most highly esteemed in medicine. In cases of the bite of a mad dog, a pennyweight of it, dissolved in wine, is administered. It is also useful in accelerating parturition, when the labour pains of women have come on. A small quantity of it being applied to carbuncles, pustules, or other eruptions on the body, they are presently dispersed; and it is efficacious in many other complaints. The flesh also of the animal is sold at a dear rate, being thought to

have a higher flavour than other kinds of meat, and by all persons it is
esteemed a delicacy. In this province the horses are of a large size, and
whilst young, are carried for sale to India. It is the practice to deprive
them of one joint of the tail, in order to prevent them from lashing it
from side to side, and to occasion its remaining pendent; as the
whisking it about, in riding, appears to them a vile habit. These
people ride with long stirrups, as the French do in our part of the
world; whereas the Tartars, and almost all other people, wear them
short, for the more conveniently using the bow; as they rise in their
stirrups above the horse, when they shoot their arrows. They have
complete armour of buffalo-leather, and carry lances, shields, and
cross-bows. All their arrows are poisoned. I was assured, as a certain
fact, that many persons, and especially those who harbour bad
designs, always carry poison about them, with the intention of
swallowing it, in the event of their being apprehended for any
delinquency, and exposed to the torture, that, rather than suffer it,
they may effect their own destruction. But their rulers, who are
aware of this practice, are always provided with the dung of dogs,
which they oblige the accused to swallow immediately after, as it
occasions their vomiting up the poison, and thus an antidote is ready
against the arts of these wretches. Before the time of their becoming
subject to the dominion of the Grand Khan, these people were
addicted to the following brutal custom. When any stranger of
superior quality, who united personal beauty with distinguished
valour, happened to take up his abode at the house of one of them,
he was murdered during the night; not for the sake of his money, but
in order that the spirit of the deceased, endowed with his accomplish-
ments and intelligence, might remain with the family, and that
through the efficacy of such an acquisition, all their concerns might
prosper. Accordingly the individual was accounted fortunate who
possessed in this manner the soul of any noble personage; and many
lost their lives in consequence. But from the time of his majesty's
beginning to rule the country, he has taken measures for suppressing
the horrid practice, and from the effect of severe punishments that
have been inflicted, it has ceased to exist.

CHAPTER XLI

Of the Province of Kardandan and the City of Vochang

Proceeding five days' journey in a westerly direction from Karazan, you enter the province of Kardandan, belonging to the dominion of the Grand Khan, and of which the principal city is named Vochang. The currency of this country is gold by weight, and also the porcelain shells. An ounce of gold is exchanged for five ounces of silver, and a saggio of gold for five saggi of silver; there being no silver mines in this country, but much gold; and consequently the merchants who import silver obtain a large profit. Both the men and the women of this province have the custom of covering their teeth with thin plates of gold, which are fitted with great nicety to the shape of the teeth, and remain on them continually. The men also form dark stripes or bands round their arms and legs, by puncturing them in the following manner. They have five needles joined together, which they press into the flesh until blood is drawn; and they then rub the punctures with a black colouring matter, which leaves an indelible mark. To bear these dark stripes is considered as an ornamental and honourable distinction. They pay little attention to anything but horsemanship, the sports of the chase, and whatever belongs to the use of arms and a military life; leaving the entire management of their domestic concerns to their wives, who are assisted in their duties by slaves, either purchased or made prisoners in war.

These people have the following singular usage. As soon as a woman has been delivered of a child, and, rising from her bed, has washed and swathed the infant, her husband immediately takes the place she has left, has the child laid beside him, and nurses it for forty days. In the meantime, the friends and relations of the family pay to him their visits of congratulation; whilst the woman attends to the business of the house, carries victuals and drink to the husband in his bed, and suckles the infant at his side. These people eat their meat raw, or prepared in the manner that has been described, and along with it eat rice. Their wine is manufactured from rice, with a mixture of spices, and is a good beverage.

In this district they have neither temples nor idols, but pay their worship to the elder or ancestor of the family, from whom, they say, as they derive their existence, so to him they are indebted for all that they possess. They have no knowledge of any kind of writing, nor is this to be wondered at, considering the rude nature of the country, which is a mountainous tract covered with the thickest forests. During the summer season, the atmosphere is so gloomy and unwholesome, that merchants and other strangers are obliged to leave the district, in order to escape from death. When the natives have transactions of business with each other, which require them to execute any obligation for the amount of a debt or credit, their chief takes a square piece of wood, and divides it in two. Notches are then cut on it, denoting the sum in question, and each party receives one of the corresponding pieces, as is practised in respect to our tallies. Upon the expiration of the term, and payment made by the debtor, the creditor delivers up his counterpart, and both remain satisfied.

Neither in this province, nor in the cities of Kain-du, Vochang, or Yachi, are to be found persons professing the art of physic. When a person of consequence is attacked with a disorder, his family send for those sorcerers who offer sacrifices to the idols, to whom the sick person gives an account of the nature of his complaint. The sorcerers thereupon give directions for the attendance of persons who perform on a variety of loud instruments, in order that they may dance and sing hymns in honour and praise of their idols; and which they continue to do, until the evil spirit has taken possession of one of them, when their musical exertions cease. They then enquire of the person so possessed the cause of the man's indisposition, and the means that should be used for effecting his cure. The evil spirit answers by the mouth of him into whose body he has entered, that the sickness has been occasioned by an offence given to a certain deity. Upon which the sorcerers address their prayers to that deity, beseeching him to pardon the sinner, on the condition that when cured he shall offer a sacrifice of his own blood. But if the demon perceives that there is no prospect of a recovery, he pronounces the deity to be so grievously offended that no sacrifice can appease him. If, on the contrary, he judges that a cure is likely to take place, he requires that an offering be made of so many sheep with black heads;

that so many sorcerers, with their wives, be assembled, and that the sacrifice be performed by their hands; by which means, he says, the favour of the deity may be conciliated. The relations comply immediately with all that has been demanded, the sheep are slain, their blood is sprinkled towards the heavens, the sorcerers (male and female) light up and perfume with incense the whole house of the sick person, making a smoke with wood of aloes. They cast into the air the water in which the flesh has been seethed, together with some of the liquor brewed with spices; and then laugh, sing, and dance about, with the idea of doing honour to their idol or divinity. They next enquire of the demoniac whether, by the sacrifice that has been made, the idol is satisfied, or if it is his command that another be yet performed. When the answer is, that the propitiation has been satisfactory, the sorcerers of both sexes, who had not ceased their songs, thereupon seat themselves at the tables and proceed to feast on the meat that had been offered in sacrifice, and to drink the spiced liquor, of which a libation had been made, with signs of great hilarity. Having finished their meal, and received their fees, they return to their homes; and if, through God's providence, the patient recovers, they attribute his cure to the idol for whom the sacrifice was performed; but if he happens to die, they then declare that the rites had been rendered ineffective by those who dressed the victuals having presumed to taste them before the deity's portion had been presented to him. It must be understood that ceremonies of this kind are not practised upon the illness of every individual, but only perhaps once or twice in the course of a month, for noble or wealthy personages. They are common, however, to all the idolatrous inhabitants of the whole provinces of Cathay and Manji, amongst whom a physician is a rare character. And thus do the demons sport with the blindness of these deluded and wretched people.

CHAPTER XLII

Of the Manner in which the Grand Khan effected the
Conquest of the Kingdom of Mien and Bangala

Before we proceed further (in describing the country), we shall speak
of a memorable battle that was fought in this kingdom of Vochang
(Unchang, or Yun-chang). It happened that in the year 1272 the
Grand Khan sent an army into the countries of Vochang and
Karazan, for their protection and defence against any attack that
foreigners might attempt to make; for at this period he had not as yet
appointed his own sons to the governments, which it was afterwards
his policy to do; as in the instance of Cen-temur, for whom those
places were erected into a principality. When the king of Mien and
Bangala, in India, who was powerful in the number of his subjects, in
extent of territory, and in wealth, heard that an army of Tartars had
arrived at Vochang, he took the resolution of advancing immediately
to attack it, in order that by its destruction the Grand Khan should be
deterred from again attempting to station a force upon the borders of
his dominions. For this purpose he assembled a very large army,
including a multitude of elephants (an animal with which his country
abounds), upon whose backs were placed battlements or castles, of
wood, capable of containing to the number of twelve or sixteen in
each. With these, and a numerous army of horse and foot, he took
the road to Vochang, where the Grand Khan's army lay, and
encamping at no great distance from it, intended to give his troops a
few days of rest. As soon as the approach of the king of Mien, with so
great a force, was known to Nestardin, who commanded the troops
of the Grand Khan, although a brave and able officer, he felt much
alarmed, not having under his orders more than twelve thousand
men (veterans, indeed, and valiant soldiers); whereas the enemy had
sixty thousand, besides the elephants armed as has been described. He
did not, however, betray any sign of apprehension, but descending
into the plain of Vochang, took a position in which his flank was
covered by a thick wood of large trees, whither, in case of a furious

charge by the elephants, which his troops might not be able to sustain, they could retire, and from thence, in security, annoy them with their arrows. Calling together the principal officers of his army, he exhorted them not to display less valour on the present occasion than they had done in all their preceding engagements, reminding them that victory did not depend upon the number of men, but upon courage and discipline. He represented to them that the troops of the king of Mien and Bangala were raw and unpractised in the art of war, not having had the opportunities of acquiring experience that had fallen to their lot; that instead of being discouraged by the superior number of their foes, they ought to feel confidence in their own valour so often put to the test; that their very name was a subject of terror, not merely to the enemy before them, but to the whole world; and he concluded by promising to lead them to certain victory. Upon the king of Mien's learning that the Tartars had descended into the plain, he immediately put his army in motion, took up his ground at the distance of about a mile from the enemy, and made a disposition of his force, placing the elephants in the front, and the cavalry and infantry, in two extended wings, in their rear, but leaving between them a considerable interval. Here he took his own station, and proceeded to animate his men and encourage them to fight valiantly, assuring them of victory, as well from the superiority of their numbers, being four to one, as from their formidable body of armed elephants, whose shock the enemy, who had never before been engaged with such combatants, could by no means resist. Then giving orders for sounding a prodigious number of warlike instruments, he advanced boldly with his whole army towards that of the Tartars, which remained firm, making no movement, but suffering them to approach their entrenchments. They then rushed out with great spirit and the utmost eagerness to engage; but it was soon found that the Tartar horses, unused to the sight of such huge animals, with their castles, were terrified, and wheeling about endeavoured to fly; nor could their riders by any exertions restrain them, whilst the king, with the whole of his forces, was every moment gaining ground. As soon as the prudent commander perceived this unexpected disorder, without losing his presence of mind, he instantly adopted the measure of ordering his men to dismount and their horses to be taken into the wood, where they were fastened to the trees. When dismounted, the men, without loss of time, advanced on foot towards the line of elephants, and commenced a brisk discharge of arrows; whilst, on the other side, those who were stationed in the castles, and the rest of the king's army, shot volleys in return with great activity; but their arrows did not make the same impression as those of the Tartars, whose bows were drawn with a stronger arm. So incessant were the discharges of the latter, and all their weapons (according to the instructions of their commander) being directed against the elephants, these were soon covered with arrows, and, suddenly giving way, fell back upon their own people in the rear, who were thereby thrown into confusion. It soon became impossible for their drivers to manage them, either by force or address. Smarting under the pain of their wounds, and terrified by the shouting of the assailants, they were no longer governable, but without guidance or control ran about in all directions, until at length, impelled by rage and fear, they rushed into a part of the wood not occupied by the Tartars. The consequence of this was, that from the closeness of the branches of large trees, they broke, with loud crashes, the battlements or castles that were upon their backs, and involved in the destruction those who sat upon them. Upon seeing the rout of the elephants the Tartars acquired fresh courage, and filing off by detachments, with perfect order and regularity, they remounted their horses, and joined their several divisions, when a sanguinary and dreadful combat was renewed. On the part of the king's troops there was no want of valour, and he himself went amongst the ranks entreating them to stand firm, and not to be alarmed by the accident that had befallen the elephants. But the Tartars, by their consummate skill in archery, were too powerful for them, and galled them the more exceedingly, from their not being provided with such armour as was worn by the former. The arrows having been expended on both sides, the men grasped their swords and iron maces, and violently encountered each other. Then in an instant were to be seen many horrible wounds, limbs dismembered, and multitudes falling to the ground, maimed and dying; with such effusion of blood as was dreadful to behold. So great also was the clangour of arms, and such the shoutings and the shrieks, that the noise seemed to ascend to the skies. The king of Mien, acting as became a valiant chief, was present wherever the greatest danger appeared, animating his soldiers, and beseeching them to maintain their ground with resolution. He ordered fresh squadrons from the reserve to advance to the support of those that were exhausted; but perceiving at length that it was impossible any longer to sustain the conflict or to withstand the impetuosity of the Tartars, the greater part of his troops being either killed or wounded, and all the field covered with the carcasses of men and horses, whilst those who survived were beginning to give way, he also found himself compelled to take to flight with the wreck of his army, numbers of whom were afterwards slain in the pursuit.

The losses in this battle, which lasted from the morning till noon, were severely felt on both sides; but the Tartars were finally victorious; a result that was materially to be attributed to the troops of the king of Mien and Bangala not wearing armour as the Tartars did, and to their elephants, especially those of the foremost line, being equally without that kind of defence, which, by enabling them to sustain the first discharges of the enemy's arrows, would have allowed them to break his ranks and throw him into disorder. A point perhaps of still greater importance is, that the king ought not to have made his attack on the Tartars in a position where their flank was supported by a wood, but should have endeavoured to draw them into the open country, where they could not have resisted the first impetuous onset of the armed elephants, and where, by extending the cavalry of his two wings, he might have surrounded them. The Tartars having collected their force after the slaughter of the enemy, returned towards the wood into which the elephants had fled for shelter, in order to take possession of them, where they found that the men who had escaped from the overthrow were employed in cutting down trees and barricading the passages, with the intent of defending themselves. But their ramparts were soon demolished by the Tartars, who slew many of them, and with the assistance of the persons accustomed to the management of the elephants, they possessed themselves of these to the number of two hundred or more. From the period of this battle the Grand Khan has always chosen to employ elephants in his armies, which before that time he had not done. The consequences of the victory were, that he acquired possession of the whole of the territories of the king of Bangala and Mien, and annexed them to his dominions.

CHAPTER XLIII

Of an Uninhabited Region, and of the Kingdom of Mien

Leaving the province of Kardandan, you enter upon a vast descent, which you travel without variation for two days and a half, in the course of which no habitations are to be found. You then reach a spacious plain, whereon, three days in every week, a number of trading people assemble, many of whom come down from the neighbouring mountains, bringing their gold to be exchanged for silver, which the merchants who repair thither from distant countries carry with them for this purpose; and one saggio of gold is given for five of silver. The inhabitants are not allowed to be the exporters of their own gold, but must dispose of it to the merchants, who furnish them with such articles as they require; and as none but the natives themselves can gain access to the places of their residence, so high and strong are the situations, and so difficult of approach, it is on this account that the transactions of business are conducted in the plain. Beyond this, in a southerly direction, towards the confines of India, lies the city of Mien. The journey occupies fifteen days, through a country much depopulated, and forests abounding with elephants, rhinoceroses, and other wild beasts, where there is not the appearance of any habitation.

CHAPTER XLIV

Of the City of Mien, and of a grand Sepulchre of its King

After the journey of fifteen days that has been mentioned, you reach the city of Mien, which is large, magnificent, and the capital of the kingdom. The inhabitants are idolaters, and have a language peculiar to themselves. It is related that there formerly reigned in this country a rich and powerful monarch, who, when his death was drawing near, gave orders for erecting on the place of his interment, at the head and foot of the sepulchre, two pyramidal towers, entirely of marble, ten paces in height, of a proportionate bulk, and each terminating with a ball. One of these pyramids was covered with a plate of gold an inch in thickness, so that nothing besides the gold was visible; and the other with a plate of silver, of the same thickness. Around the balls were suspended small bells of gold and of silver, which sounded when put in motion by the wind. The whole formed a splendid object. The tomb was in like manner covered with a plate, partly of gold and partly of silver. This the king commanded to be prepared for the honour of his soul, and in order that his memory might not perish. The Grand Khan, having resolved upon taking possession of this city, sent thither a valiant officer to effect it, and the army, at its own desire, was accompanied by some of the jugglers or sorcerers, of whom there were always a great number about the court. When these entered the city, they observed the two pyramids so richly ornamented, but would not meddle with them until his majesty's pleasure respecting them should be known. The Grand Khan, upon being informed that they had been erected in pious memory of a former king, would not suffer them to be violated nor injured in the smallest degree; the Tartars being accustomed to consider as a heinous sin the removal of any article appertaining to the dead. In this country were found many elephants, large and handsome wild oxen, with stags, fallow deer, and other animals in great abundance.

CHAPTER XLV

Of the Province of Bangala

The province of Bangala is situated on the southern confines of India, and was (not yet) brought under the dominion of the Grand Khan at the time of Marco Polo's residence at his court; (although) the operations against it occupied his army for a considerable period, the country being strong and its king powerful, as has been related. It has its peculiar language. The people are worshippers of idols, and amongst them there are teachers, at the head of schools for instruction in the principles of their idolatrous religion and of necromancy, whose doctrine prevails amongst all ranks, including the nobles and chiefs of the country. Oxen are found here almost as tall as elephants, but not equal to them in bulk. The inhabitants live upon flesh, milk, and rice, of which they have abundance. Much cotton is grown in the country, and trade flourishes. Spikenard, galangal, ginger, sugar, and many sorts of drugs are amongst the productions of the soil; to purchase which the merchants from various parts of India resort thither. They likewise make purchases of eunuchs, of whom there are numbers in the country, as slaves; for all the prisoners taken in war are presently emasculated; and as every prince and person of rank is desirous of having them for the custody of their women, the merchants obtain a large profit by carrying them to other kingdoms, and there disposing of them. This province is thirty days' journey in extent, and at the eastern extremity of it lies a country named Kangigu.

CHAPTER XLVI

Of the Province of Kangigu

Kangigu is a province situated towards the east, and is governed by a king. The people are idolaters, have a peculiar language, and make a voluntary submission to the Grand Khan, to whom they pay an annual tribute. The king is so devoted to sensual pleasures, that he has about four hundred wives; and when he hears of any handsome woman, he sends for her, and adds her to the number. Gold is found here in large quantities, and also many kinds of drugs; but, being an inland country, distant from the sea, there is little opportunity of vending them. There are elephants in abundance, and other beasts. The inhabitants live upon flesh, rice, and milk. They have no wine made from grapes, but prepare it from rice and a mixture of drugs. Both men and women have their bodies punctured all over, in figures of beasts and birds; and there are among them practitioners whose sole employment it is to trace out these ornaments with the point of a needle, upon the hands, the legs, and the breast. When a black colouring stuff has been rubbed over these punctures, it is impossible, either by water or otherwise, to efface the marks. The man or woman who exhibits the greatest profusion of these figures, is esteemed the most handsome.

CHAPTER XLVII

Of the Province of Amu

Amu, also, is situated towards the east, and its inhabitants are subjects of the Grand Khan. They are idolaters, and live upon the flesh of their cattle and the fruits of the earth. They have a peculiar language. The country produces many horses and oxen, which are sold to the itinerant merchants, and conveyed to India. Buffaloes also, as well as oxen, are numerous, in consequence of the extent and excellence of the pastures. Both men and women wear rings, of gold and silver, upon their wrists, arms, and legs; but those of the females are the more costly. The distance between this province and that of Kangigu is twenty-five days' journey, and thence to Bangala is twenty days' journey. We shall now speak of a province named Tholoman, situated eight days' journey from the former.

CHAPTER XLVIII

Of Tholoman

The province of Tholoman lies towards the east, and its inhabitants are idolaters. They have a peculiar language, and are subjects of the Grand Khan. The people are tall and good-looking; their complexions inclining rather to brown than fair. They are just in their dealings, and brave in war. Many of their towns and castles are situated upon lofty mountains. They burn the bodies of their dead;

and the bones that are not reduced to ashes, they put into wooden
boxes, and carry them to the mountains, where they conceal them in
caverns of the rocks, in order that no wild animal may disturb them.
Abundance of gold is found here. For the ordinary small currency
they use the porcelain shells that come from India; and this sort of
money prevails also in the two before-mentioned provinces of
Kangigu and Amu. Their food and drink are the same that has been
already mentioned.

CHAPTER XLIX

Of the Cities of Chintigui, Sidin-fu, Gin-gui, and Pazan-fu

Leaving the province of Tholoman, and pursuing a course towards
the east, you travel for twelve days by a river, on each side of which
lie many towns and castles; when at length you reach the large and
handsome city of Chintigui, the inhabitants of which are idolaters,
and are the subjects of the Grand Khan. They are traders and artisans.
They make cloth of the bark of certain trees, which looks well, and is
the ordinary summer clothing of both sexes. The men are brave
warriors. They have no other kind of money than the stamped paper
of the Grand Khan.

In this province the tigers are so numerous, that the inhabitants,
from apprehension of their ravages, cannot venture to sleep at night
out of their towns; and those who navigate the river dare not go to
rest with their boats moored near the banks; for these animals have
been known to plunge into the water, swim to the vessel, and drag
the men from thence; but find it necessary to anchor in the middle of
the stream, where, in consequence of its great width, they are in
safety. In this country are likewise found the largest and fiercest dogs
that can be met with: so courageous and powerful are they, that a
man, with a couple of them, may be an over-match for a tiger.
Armed with a bow and arrows, and thus attended, should he meet a
tiger, he sets on his intrepid dogs, who instantly advance to the attack.
The animal instinctively seeks a tree, against which to place himself,
in order that the dogs may not be able to get behind him, and that he

may have his enemies in front. With this intent, as soon as he perceives the dogs, he makes towards the tree, but with a slow pace, and by no means running, that he may not show any signs of fear, which his pride would not allow. During this deliberate movement, the dogs fasten upon him, and the man plies him with his arrows. He, in his turn, endeavours to seize the dogs, but they are too nimble for him, and draw back, when he resumes his slow march; but before he can gain his position, he has been wounded by so many arrows, and so often bitten by the dogs, that he falls through weakness and from loss of blood. By these means it is that he is at length taken.

There is here an extensive manufacture of silks, which are exported in large quantities to other parts by the navigation of the river, which continues to pass amongst towns and castles; and the people subsist entirely by trade. At the end of twelve days, you arrive at the city of Sidin-fu, of which an account has been already given. From thence, in twenty days, you reach Gin-gui, in which we were, and in four days more the city of Pazan-fu, which belongs to Cathay, and lies towards the south, in returning by the other side of the province. The inhabitants worship idols, and burn the bodies of their dead. There are here also certain Christians, who have a church. They are subjects of the Grand Khan, and his paper money is current among them. They gain their living by trade and manufacture, having silk in abundance, of which they weave tissues mixed with gold, and also very fine scarfs. This city has many towns and castles under its jurisdiction: a great river flows beside it, by means of which large quantities of merchandise are conveyed to the city of Kanbalu; for by the digging of many canals it is made to communicate with the capital. But we shall take our leave of this, and, proceeding three days' journey, speak of another city named Chan-glu.

CHAPTER L

Of the City of Chan-glu

Chan-glu is a large city situated towards the south, and is in the province of Cathay. It is under the dominion of the Grand Khan. The inhabitants worship idols, and burn the bodies of their dead. The stamped paper of the emperor is current amongst them. In this city and the district surrounding it they make great quantities of salt, by the following process: in the country is found a salsuginous earth; upon this, when laid in large heaps, they pour water, which in its passage through the mass imbibes the particles of salt, and is then collected in channels, from whence it is conveyed to very wide pans, not more than four inches in depth. In these it is well boiled, and then left to crystallise. The salt thus made is white and good, and is exported to various parts. Great profits are made by those who manufacture it, and the Grand Khan derives from it a considerable revenue. This district produces abundance of well-flavoured peaches, of such a size that one of them will weigh two pounds troy-weight. We shall now speak of another city, named Chan-gli.

CHAPTER LI

Of the City of Chan-gli

Chan-gli also is a city of Cathay, situated towards the south, and belonging to the Grand Khan, the inhabitants of which are idolaters, and in like manner make use of the khan's paper currency. Its distance from Chan-glu is five days' journey, in the course of which you pass many cities and castles likewise in the dominions of the Grand Khan. They are places of great commerce, and the customs levied at them amount to a large sum. Through this city passes a wide and deep river, which affords conveyance to vast quantities of merchandise, consisting of silk, drugs, and other valuable articles. We shall now take leave of this place, and give an account of another city named Tudin-fu.

CHAPTER LII

Of the City of Tudin-fu

When you depart from Chan-gli, and travel southwards six days' journey, you pass many towns and castles of great importance and grandeur, whose inhabitants worship idols, and burn the bodies of their dead. They are the subjects of the Grand Khan, and receive his paper money as currency. They subsist by trade and manufactures, and have provisions in abundance. At the end of these six days you arrive at a city named Tudin-fu, which was formerly a magnificent capital, but the Grand Khan reduced it to his subjection by force of arms. It is rendered a delightful residence by the gardens which surround it, stored as they are with handsome shrubs and excellent fruits. Silk is produced here in wonderfully large quantities. It has under its jurisdiction eleven cities and considerable towns of the empire, all places of great trade, and having abundance of silk. It was the seat of government of its own king, before the period of its reduction by the Grand Khan. In 1272 the latter appointed one of his officers of the highest rank, named Lucansor, to the government of this city, with a command of seventy thousand horse, for the protection of that part of the country. This man upon finding himself master of a rich and highly productive district, and at the head of so powerful a force, became intoxicated with pride, and formed schemes of rebellion against his sovereign. With this view he tampered with the principal persons of the city, persuaded them to become partakers in his evil designs, and by their means succeeded in producing a revolt throughout all the towns and fortified places of the province. As soon as the Grand Khan became acquainted with these traitorous proceedings, he despatched to that quarter an army of a hundred thousand men, under the orders of two others of his nobles, one of whom was named Angul and the other Mongatai. When the approach of this force was known to Lucansor, he lost no time in assembling an army no less numerous than that of his opponents, and brought them as speedily as possible to action. There was much slaughter on both sides, when at length, Lucansor being killed, his troops betook themselves to flight. Many were slain in the pursuit, and many were made prisoners. These were conducted to the presence of the Grand Khan, who caused the principals to be put to death, and pardoning the others took them into his own service, to which they ever afterwards continued faithful.

CHAPTER LIII

Of the City of Singui-matu

Travelling from Tudin-fu three days, in a southerly direction, you pass many considerable towns and strong places, where commerce and manufactures flourish. The inhabitants are idolaters, and are subjects of the Grand Khan. The country abounds with game, both beasts and birds, and produces an ample supply of the necessaries of life. At the end of three days you arrive at the city of Singui-matu, which is noble, large, and handsome, and rich in merchandise and manufactures; all the inhabitants of this city are idolaters, and are subjects of the Grand Khan and use paper money; within it, but on the southern side, passes a large and deep river, which the inhabitants divided into two branches, one of which, taking its course to the east, runs through Cathay, whilst the other, taking a westerly course, passes towards the province of Manji. This river is navigated by so many vessels that the number might seem incredible, and serves to convey from both provinces, that is, from the one province to the other, every requisite article of consumption. It is indeed surprising to observe the multitude and the size of the vessels that are continually passing and repassing, laden with merchandise of the greatest value. On leaving Singui-matu and travelling towards the south for sixteen days, you unceasingly meet with commercial towns and with castles. The people throughout the country are idolaters, and subjects of the

Grand Khan. They burn the bodies of their dead and use paper money. At the end of eight days' journey you find a city named Lingui. It is a very noble and great city; the men are warlike; and it has manufactures and commerce. There are plenty of animals, and abundance of everything for eating and drinking. After leaving Lingui you proceed three days' journey to the south, passing plenty of cities and castles, all under the Grand Khan. All the inhabitants are idolaters, and burn their dead. At the end of these three days you find a good city called Pingui, where there are all the necessaries of life, and this city furnishes a great revenue to the Grand Khan. You go thence two days' journey to the south, through fair and rich countries, to a city called Cingui, which is very large, and abounding in commerce and manufactures. All its inhabitants are idolaters and burn their dead; they use paper money, and are subjects of the Grand Khan. They have much grain and wheat. In the country through which you pass subsequently, you find cities, towns, and castles, and very handsome and useful dogs, and abundance of wheat. The people resemble those just described.

CHAPTER LIV

*Of the great River called the Kara-moran, and of the Cities
of Koi-gan-zu and Kuan-zu*

At the end of two days' journey you reach, once more, the great river Kara-moran, which has its source in the territories that belonged to Prester John. It is a mile wide and of vast depth, and upon its waters great ships freely sail with their full loading. Large fish in considerable quantities are caught there. At a place in this river, about a mile distant from the sea, there is a station for fifteen thousand vessels, each of them capable of carrying fifteen horses and twenty men, besides the crews to navigate them, and the necessary stores and provisions. These the Grand Khan causes to be kept in a constant state of readiness for the conveyance of an army to any of the islands in the (neighbouring) ocean that may happen to be in rebellion, or for expeditions to any more distant region. These vessels are moored close to the bank of the river, not far from a city named Koi-gan-zu, on the opposite side to which is another named Kuan-zu, but the former is a large place, and the latter a small one. Upon crossing this river you enter the noble province of Manji; but it must not be understood that a complete account has been given of the province of Cathay. Not the twentieth part have I described. Marco Polo, in travelling through the province, has only noted such cities as lay in his route, omitting those situated on the one side and the other, as well as many intermediate places, because a relation of them all would be a work of too great length, and prove fatiguing to the reader. Leaving these parts we shall therefore proceed to speak, in the first instance, of the manner in which the province of Manji was acquired, and then of its cities, the magnificence and riches of which shall be set forth in the subsequent part of our discourse.

CHAPTER LV

Of the most noble Province of Manji, and of the Manner in which it was Subdued by the Grand Khan

The province of Manji is the most magnificent and the richest that is known in the eastern world. About the year 1269 it was subject to a prince who was styled Facfur, and who surpassed in power and wealth any other that for a century had reigned in that country. His disposition was pacific, and his actions benevolent. So much was he beloved by his people, and such the strength of his kingdom, enclosed by rivers of the largest size, that his being molested by any power upon earth was regarded as an impossible event. The effect of this opinion was, that he neither paid any attention himself to military affairs, nor encouraged his people to become acquainted with military exercises. The cities of his dominions were remarkably well fortified, being surrounded by deep ditches, a bow-shot in width and full of water. He did not keep up any force in cavalry, because he was not apprehensive of attack. The means of increasing his enjoyments and multiplying his pleasures were the chief employment of his thoughts. He maintained at his court, and kept near his person, about a thousand beautiful women, in whose society he took delight. He was a friend to peace and to justice, which he administered strictly. The smallest act of oppression, or injury of any kind, committed by one man against another, was punished in an exemplary manner, without respect of persons. Such indeed was the impression of his justice, that when shops, filled with goods, happened, through the negligence of the owners, to be left open, no person dared to enter them, or to rob them of the smallest article. Travellers of all descriptions might pass through every part of the kingdom, by night as well as by day, freely and without apprehension of danger. He was religious, and charitable to the poor and needy. Children whom their wretched mothers exposed in consequence of their inability to rear them, he caused to be saved and taken care of, to the number of twenty thousand annually. When the boys attained a sufficient age, he had them instructed in some handicraft, and afterwards married them to young women who were brought up in the same manner.

Very different from the temper and habits of Facfur were those of Kublai-khan, emperor of the Tartars, whose whole delight consisted in thoughts of a warlike nature, of the conquest of countries, and of extending his renown. After having annexed to his dominions a number of provinces and kingdoms, he now directed his views to the subduing that of Manji, and for this purpose assembled a numerous army of horse and foot, the command of which he gave to a general named Chin-san Bay-an, which signifies in our language, the 'Hundred-eyed'. This occurred in the year 1273. A number of vessels were put under his orders, with which he proceeded to the invasion of Manji. Upon landing there, he immediately summoned the inhabitants of the city of Koi-gan-zu to surrender to the authority of his sovereign. Upon their refusal to comply, instead of giving orders for an assault, he advanced to the next city, and when he there received a similar answer, proceeded to a third and a fourth, with the same result. Deeming it no longer prudent to leave so many cities in his rear, whilst not only his army was strong, but he expected to be soon joined by another of equal force, which the Grand Khan was to send to him from the interior, he resolved upon the attack of one of these cities; and having, by great exertions and consummate skill, succeeded in carrying the place, he put every individual found in it to the sword. As soon as the intelligence of this event reached the other cities, it struck their inhabitants with such consternation and terror, that of their own accord they hastened to declare their submission. This being effected, he advanced, with the united force of his two armies, against the royal city of Kinsai, the residence of king Facfur, who felt all the agitation and dread of a person who had never seen a battle, nor been engaged in any sort of warfare. Alarmed for the safety of his person, he made his escape to a fleet of vessels that lay in readiness for the purpose, and embarking all his treasure and valuable effects, left the charge of the city to his queen, with directions for its being defended to the utmost; feeling assured that her sex would be a protection to her, in the event of her falling into the hands of the enemy. He from thence proceeded to sea, and reaching certain islands, where were some strongly fortified posts, he continued there till his death. After the queen had been left in the manner related, it is said to have come to her knowledge that the king had been told by his astrologers that he could never be deprived of his sovereignty by any other than a chief who should have a hundred eyes. On the strength of this declaration she felt confident, notwithstanding that the city became daily more and more straitened, that it could not be lost, because it seemed a thing impossible that any mortal could have that number of eyes. Enquiring, however, the name of the general who commanded the enemy's troops, and being told it was Chin-san Bay-an, which means a hundred eyes, she was seized with horror at hearing it pronounced, as she felt a conviction that this must be the person who, according to the saying of the astrologers, might drive her husband from his throne. Overcome by womanish fear, she no longer attempted to make resistance, but immediately surrendered. Being thus in possession of the capital, the Tartars soon brought the remainder of the province under their subjection. The queen was sent to the presence of Kublai-khan, where she was honourably received by him, and an allowance was by his orders assigned, that enabled her to support the dignity of her rank. Having stated the manner in which the conquest of Manji was effected, we shall now speak of the different cities of that province, and first of Koi-gan-zu.

CHAPTER LVI

Of the City of Koi-gan-zu

Koi-gan-zu is a very handsome and wealthy city, lying in a direction between south-east and east, at the entrance of the province of Manji, where a prodigious number of vessels are continually passing, its situation (as we have already observed) being near the bank of the river Kara-moran. Large consignments of merchandise are forwarded to this city, in order that the goods may be transported, by means of this river, to various other places. Salt is manufactured here in great quantities, not only for the consumption of the city itself, but for exportation to other parts; and from this salt the Grand Khan derives an ample revenue.

CHAPTER LVII

Of the Town of Pau-ghin

Upon leaving Koi-gan-zu, you travel one day's journey towards the south-east, by a handsome stone causeway, leading into the province of Manji. On both sides of the causeway there are very extensive marshy lakes, the waters of which are deep, and may be navigated; nor is there besides this any other road by which the province can be entered. It is, however, accessible by means of shipping; and in this manner it was that the officer who commanded the Grand Khan's armies invaded it, by effecting a landing with his whole force. At the end of the day's journey, you reach a considerable town named Pau-ghin. The inhabitants worship idols, burn their dead, use paper money, and are the subjects of the Grand Khan. They gain their living by trade and manufacture: they have much silk, and weave gold tissues. The necessaries of life are there in abundance.

CHAPTER LVIII

Of the City of Kain

At the distance of a day's journey from Pau-ghin, towards the south-east, stands the large and well-built city of Kain. Its inhabitants are idolaters, use the paper money as their currency, and are the subjects of the Grand Khan. Trade and manufactures flourish amongst them. They have fish in abundance, and game also, both beasts and birds. Pheasants, in particular, are in such plenty, that for a bit of silver equal in value to a Venetian groat you may purchase three of these birds, of the size of pea-fowls.

CHAPTER LIX

Of the Cities of Tin-gui and Chin-gui

At the end of a day's journey from the last-mentioned place, in the course of which many villages and much tilled land are met with, you reach a city named Tin-gui, not of any great size, but plentifully furnished with all the necessaries of life. The people are idolaters, the subjects of the Grand Khan, and use his paper money. They are merchants, and have many trading vessels. Both beasts and birds are here found in plenty. The situation of this city is towards the south-east, and on the left-hand – that is, on the eastern side of it, at the distance of three days' journey – you find the sea. In the intermediate space there are many salt-works, where large quantities of salt are manufactured. You next come to the large and well-built town of Chin-gui, from whence salt is exported sufficient for the supply of all the neighbouring provinces. On this article the Grand Khan raises a revenue, the amount of which would scarcely be credited. Here also the inhabitants worship idols, use paper money, and are the subjects of his majesty.

CHAPTER LX

Of the City of Yan-gui, of which Marco Polo held the Government

Proceeding in a south-easterly direction from Chin-gui, you come to the important city of Yan-gui, which, having twenty-four towns under its jurisdiction, must be considered as a place of great consequence. It belongs to the dominion of the Grand Khan. The people are idolaters, and subsist by trade and manual arts. They manufacture arms and all sorts of warlike accoutrements; in consequence of which many troops are stationed in this part of the country. The city is the place of residence of one of the twelve nobles before spoken of, who are appointed by his majesty to the government of the provinces; and in the room of one of these, Marco Polo, by special order of the Grand Khan, acted as governor of this city during the space of three years.

CHAPTER LXI

Of the Province of Nan-ghin

Nan-ghin is the name of a large and distinguished province of Manji, situated towards the west. The people are idolaters, use paper money in currency, are subjects of the Grand Khan, and are largely engaged in commerce. They have raw silk, and weave tissues of silver and gold in great quantities, and of various patterns. The country produces abundance of corn, and is stored as well with domestic cattle as with beasts and birds that are the objects of the chase, and plenty of tigers. It supplies the sovereign with an ample revenue, and chiefly from the imposts levied upon the rich articles in which the merchants trade. We shall now speak of the noble city of Sa-yan-fu.

CHAPTER LXII

Of the City of Sa-yan-fu, that was taken by the means of
Nicolo and Maffeo Polo

Sa-yan-fu is a considerable city of the province of Manji, having
under its jurisdiction twelve wealthy and large towns. It is a place of
great commerce and extensive manufactures. The inhabitants burn
the bodies of their dead, and are idolaters. They are the subjects of the
Grand Khan, and use his paper currency. Raw silk is there produced
in great quantity, and the finest silks, intermixed with gold, are
woven. Game of all kinds abounds. The place is amply furnished with
everything that belongs to a great city, and by its uncommon strength
it was enabled to stand a siege of three years; refusing to surrender to
the Grand Khan, even after he had obtained possession of the
province of Manji. The difficulties experienced in the reduction of it
were chiefly occasioned by the army's not being able to approach it,
excepting on the northern side; the others being surrounded with
water, by means of which the place continually received supplies,
which it was not in the power of the besiegers to prevent. When the
operations were reported to his majesty, he felt extremely hurt that
this place alone should obstinately hold out, after all the rest of the
country had been reduced to obedience. The circumstance having
come to the knowledge of the brothers Nicolo and Maffeo, who
were then resident at the imperial court, they immediately presented
themselves to the Grand Khan, and proposed to him that they should
be allowed to construct machines, such as were made use of in the
West, capable of throwing stones of three hundred pounds weight,
by which the buildings of the city might be destroyed and the
inhabitants killed. Their memorial was attended to by the Grand
Khan, who, warmly approving of the scheme, gave orders that the
ablest smiths and carpenters should be placed under their direction;
amongst whom were some Nestorian Christians, who proved to be
most able mechanics. In a few days they completed their mangonels,
according to the instructions furnished by the two brothers; and a trial

being made of them in the presence of the Grand Khan, and of his whole court, an opportunity was afforded of seeing them cast stones, each of which weighed three hundred pounds. They were then put on board of vessels, and conveyed to the army. When set up in front of the city of Sa-yan-fu, the first stone projected by one of them fell with such weight and violence upon a building, that a great part of it was crushed, and fell to the ground. So terrified were the inhabitants by this mischief, which to them seemed to be the effect of a thunderbolt from heaven, that they immediately deliberated upon the expediency of surrendering. Persons authorised to treat were accordingly sent from the place, and their submission was accepted on the same terms and conditions as had been granted to the rest of the province. This prompt result of their ingenuity increased the reputation and credit of these two Venetian brothers in the opinion of the Grand Khan and of all his courtiers.

CHAPTER LXIII

Of the City of Sin-gui and of the very great River Kiang

Leaving the city of Sa-yan-fu, and proceeding fifteen days' journey towards the south-east, you reach the city of Sin-gui, which, although not large, is a place of great commerce. The number of vessels that belong to it is prodigious, in consequence of its being situated near the Kiang, which is the largest river in the world, its width being in some places ten, in others eight, and in others six miles. Its length, to the place where it discharges itself into the sea, is upwards of one hundred days' journey. It is indebted for its great size to the vast number of other navigable rivers that empty their waters into it, which have their sources in distant countries. A great number of cities and large towns are situated upon its banks, and more than two hundred, with sixteen provinces, partake of the advantages of its navigation, by which the transport of merchandise is to an extent that might appear incredible to those who have not had an opportunity of witnessing it. When we consider, indeed, the length of its course, and the multitude of rivers that communicate with it (as has been observed), it is not surprising that the quantity and value of articles for the supply of so many places, lying in all directions, should be incalculable. The principal commodity, however, is salt, which is not only conveyed by means of the Kiang, and the rivers connected with it, to the towns upon their banks, but afterwards from thence to all places in the interior of the country. On one occasion, when Marco Polo was at the city of Sin-gui, he saw there not fewer than fifteen thousand vessels; and yet there are other towns along the river where the number is still more considerable. All these vessels are covered with a kind of deck, and have a mast with one sail. Their burthen is in general about four thousand *cantari*, or quintals, of Venice, and from that upwards to twelve thousand cantari, which some of them are capable of loading. They do not employ hempen cordage, excepting for the masts and sails (standing and running rigging). They have canes of the length of fifteen paces, such as have been already described, which they split, in their whole length, into very thin pieces, and these, by twisting them together, they form into ropes three hundred paces long. So skilfully are they manufactured, that they are equal in strength to cordage made of hemp. With these ropes the vessels are tracked along the rivers, by means of ten or twelve horses to each, as well upwards, against the current, as in the opposite direction. At many places near the banks of this river there are hills and small rocky eminences, upon which are erected idol temples and other edifices, and you find a continual succession of villages and inhabited places.

CHAPTER LXIV

Of the City of Kayn-gui

Kayn-gui is a small town on the southern bank of the before-mentioned river, where annually is collected a very large quantity of corn and rice, the greatest part of which is conveyed from thence to the city of Kanbalu, for the supply of the establishment of the Grand Khan; for through this place is the line of communication with the province of Cathay, by means of rivers, lakes, and a wide and deep

canal which the Grand Khan has caused to be dug, in order that
vessels may pass from one great river to the other, and from the
province of Manji, by water, as far as Kanbalu, without making any
part of the voyage by sea. This magnificent work is deserving of
admiration; and not so much from the manner in which it is
conducted through the country, or its vast extent, as from its utility
and the benefit it produces to those cities which lie in its course. On
its banks, likewise, are constructed strong and wide terraces, or
chaussées, upon which the travelling by land also is rendered perfectly
convenient. In the midst of the river, opposite to the city of Kayn-
gui, there is an island entirely of rock, upon which are built a grand
temple and monastery, where two hundred monks, as they may be
termed, reside, and perform service to the idols; and this is the
supreme head of many other temples and monasteries. We shall now
speak of the city of Chan-ghian-fu.

CHAPTER LXV

Of the City of Chan-ghian-fu

Chan-ghian-fu is a city of the province of Manji, the inhabitants of
which are idolaters, subjects of the Grand Khan, and use his paper
money. They gain their living by trade and manufacture, and are
wealthy. They weave tissues of silk and gold. The field sports are
there most excellent in every species of game, and provisions are
abundant. There are in this city three churches of Nestorian
Christians, which were built in the year 1278, when his majesty
appointed a Nestorian, named Mar-Sachis, to the government of it
for three years. By him these churches were established, where there
had not been any before; and they still subsist. Leaving this place, we
shall now speak of Tin-gui-gui.

CHAPTER LXVI

Of the City of Tin-gui-gui

Departing from Chan-ghian-fu, and travelling four days towards the south-east, you pass many towns and fortified places, the inhabitants of which are idolaters, live by arts and commerce, are the subjects of the Grand Khan, and use his paper money. At the end of these four days, you reach the city of Tin-gui-gui, which is large and handsome, and produces much raw silk, of which tissues of various qualities and patterns are woven. The necessaries of life are here in plenty, and the variety of game affords excellent sport. The inhabitants were a vile, inhuman race. At the time that Chinsan Ba-yan, or the hundred-eyed, subdued the country of Manji, he despatched certain Alanian Christians, along with a party of his own people, to possess themselves of this city; who, as soon as they appeared before it, were suffered to enter without resistance. The place being surrounded by a double wall, one of them within the other, the Alanians occupied the first enclosure, where they found a large quantity of wine, and having previously suffered much from fatigue and privation, they were eager to quench their thirst, and, without any consideration, proceeded to drink to such excess, that, becoming intoxicated, they fell asleep. The people of the city, who were within the second enclosure, as soon as they perceived that their enemies lay slumbering on the ground, took the opportunity of murdering them, not suffering one to escape. When Chinsan Ba-yan learned the fate of his detachment, his indignation and anger were raised to the highest pitch, and he sent another army to attack the place. When it was carried, he gave orders for putting to the sword all the inhabitants, great and small, without distinction of sex, as an act of retaliation.

CHAPTER LXVII

Of the Cities of Sin-gui and Va-giu

Sin-gui is a large and magnificent city, the circumference of which is twenty miles. The inhabitants are idolaters, subjects of the Grand Khan, and use his paper money. They have vast quantities of raw silk, and manufacture it, not only for their own consumption, all of them being clothed in dresses of silk, but also for other markets. There are amongst them some very rich merchants, and the number of inhabitants is so great as to be a subject of astonishment. They are, however, a pusillanimous race, and solely occupied with their trade and manufacture. In these indeed they display considerable ability, and if they were as enterprising, manly, and warlike, as they are ingenious, so prodigious is their number, that they might not only subdue the whole of the province (Manji), but might carry their views still further. They have amongst them many physicians of eminent skill, who can ascertain the nature of the disorder, and know how to apply the proper remedies. There are also persons distinguished as professors of learning, or, as we should term them, philosophers, and others who may be called magicians or enchanters. On the mountains near the city, rhubarb grows in the highest perfection, and is from thence distributed throughout the province. Ginger is likewise produced in large quantities, and is sold at so cheap a rate, that forty pounds weight of the fresh root may be had for the value, in their money, of a Venetian silver groat. Under the jurisdiction of Sin-gui there are sixteen respectable and wealthy cities and towns, where trade and arts flourish. By the name of Sin-gui is to be understood 'the city of the earth', as by that of Kin-sai, 'the city of heaven'. Leaving Sin-gui, we shall now speak of another city, distant from it only a day's journey, named Va-giu, where, likewise, there is a vast abundance of raw silk, and where there are many merchants as well as artificers. Silks of the finest quality are woven here, and are afterwards carried to every part of the province. No other circumstances presenting themselves as worthy of remark, we shall now proceed to the description of the principal city and metropolis of the province of Manji, named Kin-sai.

CHAPTER LXVIII

Of the noble and magnificent City of Kin-sai

§1. Upon leaving Va-giu you pass, in the course of three days' journey, many towns, castles, and villages, all of them well inhabited and opulent. The people are idolaters, and the subjects of the Grand Khan, and they use paper money and have abundance of provisions. At the end of three days you reach the noble and magnificent city of Kin-sai, a name that signifies 'the celestial city', and which it merits from its pre-eminence to all others in the world, in point of grandeur and beauty, as well as from its abundant delights, which might lead an inhabitant to imagine himself in paradise. This city was frequently visited by Marco Polo, who carefully and diligently observed and enquired into every circumstance respecting it, all of which he entered in his notes, from whence the following particulars are briefly stated. According to common estimation, this city is an hundred miles in circuit. Its streets and canals are extensive, and there are squares, or market-places, which, being necessarily proportioned in size to the prodigious concourse of people by whom they are frequented, are exceedingly spacious. It is situated between a lake of fresh and very clear water on the one side, and a river of great magnitude on the other, the waters of which, by a number of canals, large and small, are made to run through every quarter of the city, carrying with them all the filth into the lake, and ultimately to the sea. This, whilst it contributes much to the purity of the air, furnishes a communication by water, in addition to that by land, to all parts of the town; the canals and the streets being of sufficient width to allow of boats on the one, and carriages in the other, conveniently passing, with articles necessary for the consumption of the inhabitants. It is commonly said that the number of bridges, of all sizes, amounts to twelve thousand. Those which are thrown over the principal canals and are connected with the main streets, have arches so high, and built with so much skill, that vessels with their masts can pass under them, whilst, at the same time, carts and horses are passing over their heads – so well is the slope from the street adapted to the height of the arch. If they were not in fact so numerous, there would be no convenience of crossing from one place to another.

§2. Beyond the city, and enclosing it on that side, there is a fosse about forty miles in length, very wide, and full of water that comes from the river before mentioned. This was excavated by the ancient kings of the province, in order that when the river should overflow its banks, the superfluous water might be diverted into this channel; and to serve at the same time as a measure of defence. The earth dug out from thence was thrown to the inner side, and has the appearance of many hillocks surrounding the place. There are within the city ten principal squares or market-places, besides innumerable shops along the streets. Each side of these squares is half a mile in length, and in front of them is the main street, forty paces in width, and running in a direct line from one extremity of the city to the other. It is crossed by many low and convenient bridges. These market-squares (two miles their whole dimension) are at the distance of four miles from each other. In a direction parallel to that of the main street, but on the opposite side of the squares, runs a very large canal, on the nearer bank of which capacious warehouses are built of stone, for the accommodation of the merchants who arrive from India and other parts, together with their goods and effects, in order that they may be conveniently situated with respect to the market-places. In each of these, upon three days in every week, there is an assemblage of from forty to fifty thousand persons, who attend the markets and supply them with every article of provision that can be desired. There is an abundant quantity of game of all kinds, such as roebucks, stags, fallow deer, hares, and rabbits, together with partridges, pheasants, francolins, quails, common fowls, capons, and such numbers of ducks and geese as can scarcely be expressed; for so easily are they bred and reared on the lake, that, for the value of a Venetian silver groat, you may purchase a couple of geese and two couple of ducks. There, also, are the shambles, where they slaughter cattle for food, such as oxen, calves, kids, and lambs, to furnish the tables of rich persons and of the great magistrates. As to people of the lower classes, they do not scruple to eat every other kind of flesh, however unclean, without any discrimination. At all seasons there is in the markets a great variety of herbs and fruits, and especially pears of an extraordinary size, weighing ten pounds each, that are white in the inside, like paste, and have a very fragrant smell. There are peaches also, in their season, both of the yellow and the white kind, and of a delicious flavour. Grapes are not produced there, but are brought in a dried state, and very good, from other parts. This applies also to wine, which the natives do not hold in estimation, being accustomed to their own liquor prepared from rice and spices. From the sea, which is fifteen miles distant, there is daily brought up the river, to the city, a vast quantity of fish; and in the lake also there is abundance, which gives employment at all times to persons whose sole occupation it is to catch them. The sorts are various according to the season of the year, and, in consequence of the offal carried thither from the town, they become large and rich. At the sight of such an importation of fish, you would think it impossible that it could be sold; and yet, in the course of a few hours, it is all taken off, so great is the number of inhabitants, even of those classes which can afford to indulge in such luxuries, for fish and flesh are eaten at the same meal. Each of the ten market-squares is surrounded with high dwelling-houses, in the lower part of which are shops, where every kind of manufacture is carried on, and every article of trade is sold; such, amongst others, as spices, drugs, trinkets, and pearls. In certain shops nothing is vended but the wine of the country, which they are continually brewing, and serve out fresh to their customers at a moderate price. The streets connected with the market-squares are numerous, and in some of them are many cold baths, attended by servants of both sexes, to perform the offices of ablution for the men and women who frequent them, and who from their childhood have been accustomed at all times to wash in cold water, which they reckon highly conducive to health. At these bathing places, however, they have apartments provided with warm water, for the use of strangers, who, from not being habituated to it, cannot bear the shock of the cold. All are in the daily practice of washing their persons, and especially before their meals.

§3. In other streets are the habitations of the courtesans, who are here in such numbers as I dare not venture to report; and not only near the squares, which is the situation usually appropriated for their residence, but in every part of the city they are to be found, adorned with much finery, highly perfumed, occupying well-furnished houses, and attended by many female domestics. These women are accomplished, and are perfect in the arts of blandishment and dalliance, which they accompany with expressions adapted to every description of person, insomuch that strangers who have once tasted of their charms, remain in a state of fascination, and become so enchanted by their meretricious arts, that they can never divest themselves of the impression. Thus intoxicated with sensual pleasures, when they return to their homes they report that they have been in Kin-sai, or the celestial city, and pant for the time when they may be enabled to revisit paradise. In other streets are the dwellings of the physicians and the astrologers, who also give instructions in reading and writing, as well as in many other arts. They have apartments also amongst those which surround the market-squares. On opposite sides of each of these squares there are two large edifices, where officers appointed by the Grand Khan are stationed, to take immediate cognisance of any differences that may happen to arise between the foreign merchants, or amongst the inhabitants of the place. It is their duty likewise to see that the guards upon the several bridges in their respective vicinities (of whom mention shall be made hereafter) are duly placed, and in cases of neglect, to punish the delinquents at their discretion.

On each side of the principal street, already mentioned as extending from one end of the city to the other, there are houses and mansions of great size, with their gardens, and near to these, the dwellings of the artisans, who work in shops, at their several trades; and at all hours you see such multitudes of people passing and repassing, on their various avocations, that the providing food in sufficiency for their maintenance might be deemed an impossibility; but other ideas will be formed when it is observed that, on every market-day, the squares are crowded with tradespeople, who cover the whole space with the articles brought by carts and boats, for all of which they find a sale. By instancing the single article of pepper, some notion may be formed of the whole quantity of provisions, meat, wine, groceries, and the like, required for the consumption of the inhabitants of Kin-sai; and of this, Marco Polo learned from an officer employed in the Grand Khan's customs, the daily amount was forty-three loads, each load being two hundred and forty-three pounds.

§4. The inhabitants of the city are idolaters, and they use paper money as currency. The men as well as the women have fair complexions, and are handsome. The greater part of them are always clothed in silk, in consequence of the vast quantity of that material produced in the territory of Kin-sai, exclusively of what the merchants import from other provinces. Amongst the handicraft trades exercised in the place, there are twelve considered to be superior to the rest, as being more generally useful; for each of which there are a thousand workshops, and each shop furnishes employment for ten, fifteen, or twenty workmen, and in a few instances as many as forty, under their respective masters. The opulent principals in these manufactories do not labour with their own hands, but, on the contrary, assume airs of gentility and affect parade. Their wives equally abstain from work. They have much beauty as has been remarked, and are brought up with delicate and languid habits. The costliness of their dresses, in silks and jewellery, can scarcely be imagined. Although the laws of their ancient kings ordained that each citizen should exercise the profession of his father, yet they were allowed, when they acquired wealth, to discontinue the manual labour, provided they kept up the establishment, and employed persons to work at their paternal trades. Their houses are well built and richly adorned with carved work. So much do they delight in ornaments of this kind, in paintings, and fancy buildings, that the sums they lavish on such objects are enormous. The natural disposition of the native inhabitants of Kin-sai is pacific, and by the example of their former kings, who were themselves unwarlike, they have been accustomed to habits of tranquillity. The management of arms is unknown to them, nor do they keep any in their houses. Contentious broils are never heard among them. They conduct their mercantile and manufacturing concerns with perfect candour and probity. They are friendly towards each other, and persons who inhabit the same street, both men and women, from the mere circumstance of neighbourhood, appear like one family. In their domestic manners they are free from jealousy or suspicion of their wives, to whom great respect is shown, and any man would be accounted infamous who should presume to use indecent expressions to a married woman. To strangers also, who visit their city in the way of commerce, they give proofs of cordiality, inviting them freely to their houses, showing them hospitable attention, and furnishing them with the best advice and assistance in their mercantile transactions. On the other hand, they dislike the sight of soldiery, not excepting the guards of the Grand Khan, as they preserve the recollection that by them they were deprived of the government of their native kings and rulers.

§5. On the borders of the lake are many handsome and spacious edifices belonging to men of rank and great magistrates. There are likewise many idol temples, with their monasteries, occupied by a number of monks, who perform the service of the idols. Near the central part are two islands, upon each of which stands a superb building, with an incredible number of apartments and separate pavilions. When the inhabitants of the city have occasion to celebrate a wedding, or to give a sumptuous entertainment, they resort to one of these islands, where they find ready for their purpose every article that can be required, such as vessels, napkins, table-linen, and the like, which are provided and kept there at the common expense of the citizens, by whom also the buildings were erected. It may happen that at one time there are a hundred parties assembled there, at wedding or other feasts, all of whom, notwithstanding, are accommodated with separate rooms or pavilions, so judiciously arranged that they do not interfere with or incommode each other. In addition to this, there are upon the lake a great number of pleasure vessels or barges, calculated for holding ten, fifteen, to twenty persons, being from fifteen to twenty paces in length, with a wide and flat flooring, and not liable to heel to either side in passing through the water. Such persons as take delight in the amusement, and mean to enjoy it, either in the company of their women or that of their male companions, engage one of these barges, which are always kept in the nicest order, with proper seats and tables, together with every other kind of furniture necessary for giving an entertainment. The cabins have a flat roof or upper deck, where the boatmen take their place, and by means of long poles, which they thrust to the bottom of the lake (not more than one or two fathoms in depth), they shove the barges along, until they reach the intended spot. These cabins are painted within-side of various colours and with a variety of figures; all parts of the vessel are likewise adorned with painting. There are windows on each side, which may either be kept shut, or opened, to give an opportunity to the company, as they sit at table, of looking out in every direction and feasting their eyes on the variety and beauty of the scenes as they pass them. And truly the gratification afforded in this manner, upon the water, exceeds any that can be derived from the amusements on the land; for as the lake extends the whole length of the city, on one side, you have a view, as you stand in the boat, at a certain distance from the shore, of all its grandeur and beauty, its palaces, temples, convents, and gardens, with trees of the largest size growing down to the water's edge, whilst at the same time you enjoy the sight of other boats of the same description, continually passing you, filled in like manner with parties in pursuit of amusement. In fact, the inhabitants of this place, as soon as the labours of the day have ceased, or their mercantile transactions are closed, think of nothing else than of passing the remaining hours in parties of pleasure, with their wives or their mistresses, either in these barges, or about the city in carriages, of which it will here be proper to give some account, as constituting one of the amusements of these people.

It must be observed, in the first place, that the streets of Kin-sai are all paved with stones and bricks, and so likewise are all the principal roads extending from thence through the province of Manji, by means of which passengers can travel to every part without soiling their feet; but as the couriers of his majesty, who go on horseback with great speed, cannot make use of the pavement, a part of the road, on one side, is on their account left unpaved. The main street of the city, of which we have before spoken, as leading from one extremity to the other, is paved with stone and brick to the width of ten paces on each side, the intermediate part being filled up with small gravel, and provided with arched drains for carrying off the rain-water that falls, into the neighbouring canals, so that it remains always dry. On this gravel it is that the carriages are continually passing and repassing. They are of a long shape, covered at top, have curtains and cushions of silk, and are capable of holding six persons. Both men and women who feel disposed to take their pleasure, are in the daily practice of hiring them for that purpose, and accordingly at every hour you may see vast numbers of them driven along the middle part of the street. Some of them proceed to visit certain gardens, where the company are introduced, by those who have the management of the place, to shady recesses contrived by the gardeners for that purpose; and here the men indulge themselves all day in the society of their women, returning home, when it becomes late, in the manner they came.

§6. It is the custom of the people of Kin-sai, upon the birth of a child, for the parents to make a note, immediately, of the day, hour, and minute at which the delivery took place. They then enquire of an astrologer under what sign or aspect of the heavens the child was born; and his answer is likewise committed carefully to writing. When therefore he is grown up, and is about to engage in any mercantile adventure, voyage, or treaty of marriage, this document is carried to the astrologer, who, having examined it, and weighed all the circumstances, pronounces certain oracular words, in which these people, who sometimes find them justified by the event, place great confidence. Of these astrologers, or rather magicians, great numbers are to be met with in every market-place, and no marriage is ever celebrated until an opinion has been pronounced upon it by one of that profession.

It is also their custom, upon the death of any great and rich personage, to observe the following ceremonies. The relations, male and female, clothe themselves in coarse dresses, and accompany the body to the place appointed for burning it. The procession is likewise attended by performers on various musical instruments, which are sounded as it moves along, and prayers to their idols are chanted in a loud voice. When arrived at the spot, they throw into the flame many pieces of cotton-paper, upon which are painted representations of male and female servants, horses, camels, silk wrought with gold, as well as of gold and silver money. This is done, in consequence of their belief that the deceased will possess in the other world all these conveniences, the former in their natural state of flesh and bones, together with the money and the silks. As soon as the pile has been consumed, they sound all the instruments of music at the same time, producing a loud and long-continued noise; and they imagine that by these ceremonies their idols are induced to receive the soul of the man whose corpse has been reduced to ashes, in order to its being regenerated in the other world, and entering again into life.

§7. In every street of this city there are stone buildings or towers, to which, in case of a fire breaking out in any quarter (an accident by no means unusual, as the houses are mostly constructed of wood), the inhabitants may remove their effects for security. By a regulation which his majesty has established, there is a guard of ten watchmen stationed, under cover, upon all the principal bridges, of whom five do duty by day and five by night. Each of these guard-rooms is provided with a sonorous wooden instrument as well as one of metal, together with a *clepsydra* (*horiuolo*), by means of which latter the hours of the day and night are ascertained. As soon as the first hour of the night is expired, one of the watchmen gives a single stroke upon the wooden instrument, and also upon the metal *gong* (*bacino*), which announces to the people of the neighbouring streets that it is the first hour. At the expiration of the second, two strokes are given; and so on progressively, increasing the number of strokes as the hours advance. The guard is not allowed to sleep, and must be always on the alert. In the morning, as soon as the sun begins to appear, a single stroke is again struck, as in the evening, and so onwards from hour to hour. Some of these watchmen patrol the streets, to observe whether any person has a light or fire burning after the hour appointed for extinguishing them. Upon making the discovery, they affix a mark to the door, and in the morning the owner of the house is taken before the magistrates, by whom, if he cannot assign a legitimate excuse for his offence, he is condemned to punishment. Should they find any person abroad at an unseasonable hour, they arrest and confine him, and in the morning he is carried before the same tribunal. If, in the course of the day, they notice any person who from lameness or other infirmity is unable to work, they place him in one of the hospitals, of which there are several in every part of the city, founded by the ancient kings, and liberally endowed. When cured, he is obliged to work at some trade. Immediately upon the appearance of fire breaking out in a house, they give the alarm by beating on the wooden machine, when the watchmen from all the bridges within a certain distance assemble to extinguish it, as well as to save the effects of the merchants and others, by removing them to the stone towers that have been mentioned. The goods are also sometimes put into boats, and conveyed to the islands in the lake. Even on such occasions the inhabitants dare not stir out of their houses, when the fire happens in the night-time, and only those can be present whose goods are actually removing, together with the guard collected to assist, which seldom amounts to a smaller number than from one to two thousand men. In cases also of tumult or insurrection amongst the citizens, the services of this police guard are necessary; but independently of them, his majesty always keeps on foot a large body of troops, both infantry and cavalry, in the city and its vicinity, the command of which he gives to his ablest officers, and those in whom he can place the greatest confidence, on account of the extreme importance of this province, and especially its noble capital, which surpasses in grandeur and wealth every other city in the world. For the purposes of nightly watch, there are mounds of earth thrown up, at the distance of above a mile from each other, on the top of which a wooden frame is constructed, with a sounding board, which being struck with a mallet by the guard stationed there, the noise is heard to a great distance. If precautions of this nature were not taken upon occasions of fire, there would be danger of half the city being consumed; and their use is obvious also in the event of popular commotion, as, upon the signal being given, the guards at the several bridges arm themselves, and repair to the spot where their presence is required.

§8. When the Grand Khan reduced to his obedience the province of Manji, which until that time had been one kingdom, he thought proper to divide it into nine parts, over each of which he appointed a king or viceroy, who should act as supreme governor of that division, and administer justice to the people. These make a yearly report to commissioners acting for his majesty, of the amount of the revenue, as well as of every other matter pertaining to their jurisdiction. Upon the third year they are changed, as are all other public officers. One of these nine viceroys resides and holds his court in the city of Kin-sai, and has authority over more than a hundred and forty cities and towns, all large and rich. Nor is this number to be wondered at, considering that in the whole of the province of Manji there are no fewer than twelve hundred, containing a large population of industrious and wealthy inhabitants. In each of these, according to its size and other circumstances, his majesty keeps a garrison, consisting, in some places, of a thousand, in others of ten or twenty thousand men, accordingly as he judges the city to be, in its own population, more or less powerful. It is not to be understood that all these troops are Tartars. On the contrary, they are chiefly natives of the province of Cathay. The Tartars are universally horsemen, and cavalry cannot be quartered about those cities which stand in the low, marshy parts of the province, but only in firm, dry situations, where such troops can be properly exercised. To the former, he sends Cathaians, and such men of the province of Manji as appear to have a military turn; for it is his practice to make an annual selection amongst all his subjects of such as are best qualified to bear arms; and these he enrols to serve in his numerous garrisons, that may be considered as so many armies.

But the soldiers drawn from the province of Manji he does not employ in the duty of their native cities; on the contrary, he marches them to others at the distance of perhaps twenty days' journey, where they are continued for four or five years, at the expiration of which they are allowed to return to their homes, and others are sent to replace them. This regulation applies equally to the Cathaians. The greater part of the revenues of the cities, paid into the treasury of the Grand Khan, is appropriated to the maintenance of these garrisons. When it happens that a city is in a state of rebellion (and it is not an uncommon occurrence for these people, actuated by some sudden exasperation, or when intoxicated, to murder their governors), a part of the garrison of a neighbouring city is immediately despatched with orders to destroy the place where such guilty excesses have been committed; whereas it would be a tedious operation to send an army from another province, that might be two months on its march. For such purposes, the city of Kin-sai constantly supports a garrison of thirty thousand soldiers; and the smallest number stationed at any place is one thousand.

§9. It now remains to speak of a very fine palace that was formerly the residence of king Facfur, whose ancestors enclosed with high walls an extent of ground ten miles in compass, and divided it into three parts. That in the centre was entered by a lofty portal, on each side of which was a magnificent colonnade, on a flat terrace, the roofs of which were supported by rows of pillars, highly ornamented with the most beautiful azure and gold. The colonnade opposite to the entrance, at the further side of the court, was still grander than the others, its roof being richly adorned, the pillars gilt, and the walls on the inner side ornamented with exquisite paintings, representing the histories of former kings. Here, annually, upon certain days consecrated to the service of their idols, king Facfur was accustomed to hold his court, and to entertain at a feast his principal nobles, the chief magistrates, and the opulent citizens of Kin-sai. Under these colonnades might be seen, at one time, ten thousand persons suitably accommodated at table. This festival lasted ten or twelve days, and the magnificence displayed on the occasion, in silks, gold, and precious stones, exceeded all imagination; for every guest, with a spirit of emulation, endeavoured to exhibit as much finery as his circumstances would possibly allow. Behind the colonnade last mentioned, or that which fronted the grand portal, there was a wall, with a passage, that divided this exterior court of the palace from an interior court, which formed a kind of large cloister, with its rows of pillars sustaining a portico that surrounded it, and led to various apartments for the use of the king and queen. These pillars were ornamented in a similar manner, as were also the walls. From this cloister you entered a covered passage or corridor, six paces in width, and of such a length as to reach to the margin of the lake. On each side of this there were corresponding entrances to ten courts, in the form of long cloisters, surrounded by their porticoes, and each cloister or court had fifty apartments, with their respective gardens, the residence of a thousand young women, whom the king retained in his service. Accompanied sometimes by his queen, and on other occasions by a party of these females, it was his custom to take amusement on the lake, in barges covered with silk, and to visit the idol temples on its borders. The other two divisions of this seraglio were laid out in groves, pieces of water, beautiful gardens stored with fruit trees, and also enclosures for all sorts of animals that are the objects of sport, such as antelopes, deer, stags, hares, and rabbits. Here likewise the king amused himself, in company with his damsels, some in carriages and some on horseback. No male person was allowed to be of these parties, but on the other hand, the females were practised in the art of coursing with dogs, and pursuing the animals that have been mentioned. When fatigued with these exercises, they retired into the groves on the banks of the lake, and there quitting their dresses, rushed into the water in a state of nudity, sportively swimming about, some in one direction and some in another, whilst the king remained a spectator of the exhibition. After this they returned to the palace. Sometimes he ordered his repast to be provided in one of these groves, where the foliage of lofty trees afforded a thick shade, and was there waited upon by the same damsels. Thus was his time consumed amidst the enervating charms of his women, and in profound ignorance of whatever related to martial concerns, the consequence of which was, that his depraved habits and his pusillanimity enabled the Grand Khan to deprive him of his splendid possessions, and to expel him with ignominy from his throne as has been already stated. All these particulars were communicated to me, when I was in that city, by a rich merchant of Kin-sai, then very old, who had been a confidential servant of king Facfur, and was acquainted with every circumstance

of his life. Having known the palace in its original state, he was
desirous of conducting me to view it. Being at present the residence
of the Grand Khan's viceroy, the colonnades are preserved in the
style in which they had formerly subsisted, but the chambers of the
females had been suffered to go to ruin, and the foundations only
were visible. The wall likewise that enclosed the park and gardens
was fallen to decay, and neither animals nor trees were any longer to
be found there.

§10. At the distance of twenty-five miles from this city, in a
direction to the northward of east, lies the sea, near to which is a
town named Gan-pu, where there is an extremely fine port,
frequented by all the ships that bring merchandise from India. The
river that flows past the city of Kin-sai forms this port, at the place
where it falls into the sea. Boats are continually employed in the
conveyance of goods up and down the river, and those intended for
exportation are there put on board of ships bound to various parts of
India and of Cathay.

Marco Polo, happening to be in the city of Kin-sai at the time of
making the annual report to his majesty's commissioners of the
amount of revenue and the number of inhabitants, had an opportunity of observing that the latter were registered at one hundred and
sixty *tomans* of fireplaces, that is to say, of families dwelling under the
same roof; and as a *toman* is ten thousand, it follows that the whole
city must have contained one million six hundred thousand families,
amongst which multitude of people there was only one church of
Nestorian Christians. Every father of a family, or housekeeper, is
required to affix a writing to the door of his house, specifying the
name of each individual of his family, whether male or female, as well
as the number of his horses. When any person dies, or leaves the
dwelling, the name is struck out, and upon the occasion of a birth, it
is added to the list. By these means the great officers of the province
and governors of the cities are at all times acquainted with the exact
number of the inhabitants. The same regulation is observed throughout the province of Cathay as well as of Manji. In like manner, all the
keepers of inns and public hotels inscribe in a book the names of
those who take up their occasional abode with them, particularising
the day and the hour of their arrival and departure; a copy of which is
transmitted daily to those magistrates who have been spoken of as
stationed in the market-squares. It is a custom in the province of

Manji, with the indigent class of the people, who are unable to support their families, to sell their children to the rich, in order that they may be fed and brought up in a better manner than their own poverty would admit.

CHAPTER LXIX

Of the Revenues of the Grand Khan

We shall now speak of the revenue which the Grand Khan draws from the city of Kin-sai and the places within its jurisdiction, constituting the ninth division or kingdom of Manji. In the first place, upon salt, the most productive article, he levies a yearly duty of eighty tomans of gold, each toman being eighty thousand saggi, and each saggio fully equal to a gold florin and consequently amounting to six million four hundred thousand ducats. This vast produce is occasioned by the vicinity of the province to the sea, and the number of salt lakes or marshes, in which, during the heat of summer the water becomes crystallised, and from whence a quantity of salt is taken, sufficient for the supply of five of the other divisions of the province. There is here cultivated and manufactured a large quantity of sugar, which pays, as do all other groceries, three and one-third per cent. The same is also levied upon the wine, or fermented liquor, made of rice. The twelve classes of artisans, of whom we have already spoken, as having each a thousand shops, and also the merchants, as well those who import the goods into the city, in the first instance, as those who carry them from thence to the interior, or who export them by sea, pay, in like manner, a duty of three and one-third per cent; but goods coming by sea from distant countries and regions, such as from India, pay ten per cent. So likewise all native articles of the country, as cattle, the vegetable produce of the soil, and silk, pay a tithe to the king. The account being made up in the presence of Marco Polo, he had an opportunity of seeing that the revenue of his majesty, exclusively of that arising from salt, already stated, amounted in the year to the sum of two hundred and ten tomans (each toman being eighty thousand saggi of gold), or sixteen million eight hundred thousand ducats.

CHAPTER LXX

Of the City of Ta-pin-zu

Leaving the city of Kin-sai, and travelling one day's journey towards the south-east, continually passing houses, villas, and delightful gardens, where every kind of vegetable is produced in abundance, you arrive at the city of Ta-pin-zu, which is very handsome and large, and belongs to the jurisdiction of Kin-sai. The inhabitants worship idols, use paper money, burn the bodies of their dead, are subjects of the Grand Khan, and gain their subsistence by trade and manual arts. This place not demanding any more particular notice, we shall proceed to speak of the city of Uguiu.

CHAPTER LXXI

Of the City of Uguiu

From Ta-pin-zu, travelling three days towards the south-east, you come to the city of Uguiu, and still further, in the same direction, two days' journey, you pass in continual succession so many towns, castles, and other inhabited places, and such is their vicinity to each other, that to a stranger they have the appearance of one extended city. All of them are dependent upon Kin-sai. The people are idolaters, and the country supplies the necessaries of life in great abundance. Here are found canes of greater bulk and length than those already noticed, being four spans in girth and fifteen paces long.

CHAPTER LXXII

Of the Cities of Gen-gui, Zen-gian, and Gie-za

Proceeding further, three days' journey in the same direction, you reach the town of Gen-gui, and still advancing to the south-east, you never cease to meet with towns full of inhabitants, who are employed at their trades, and cultivate the soil. In this part of the province of Manji there are not any sheep to be seen, but many oxen, cows, buffaloes, and goats, and of swine a vast number. At the end of the fourth day you arrive at the city of Zen-gian, built upon a hill that stands insulated in the river, which, by dividing itself into two branches, appears to embrace it. These streams take opposite directions, one of them pursuing its course to the south-east, and the other to the north-west. The cities last mentioned are likewise under the dominion of the Grand Khan, and dependent upon Kin-sai. The people worship idols, and subsist by trade. There is in the country abundance of game, both beasts and birds. Proceeding further, three days' journey, you reach the large and noble city of Gie-za, which is the last within the jurisdiction of Kin-sai. Having passed this city, you enter upon another kingdom or viceroyalty of Manji, named Kon-cha.

CHAPTER LXXIII

Of the Kingdom or Viceroyalty of Kon-cha, and its Capital City named Fu-giu

Upon leaving the last city of the kingdom or viceroyalty of Kin-sai, named Gie-za, you enter that of Kon-cha, the principal city of which is named Fu-giu. In the course of six days' journey through this country, in a south-east direction, over hills and along valleys, you continually pass towns and villages, where the necessaries of life are in abundance, and there is much field sport, particularly of birds. The people are idolaters, the subjects of the Grand Khan, and are engaged in commerce and manufactures. In these parts there are tigers of great size and strength. Ginger and also galangal are produced in large quantities, as well as other drugs. For money equal in value to a Venetian silver groat you may have eighty pounds weight of fresh ginger, so common is its growth. There is also a vegetable which has all the properties of the true saffron, as well the smell as the colour, and yet it is not really saffron. It is held in great estimation, and being an ingredient in all their dishes, it bears, on that account, a high price.

The people in this part of the country are addicted to eating human flesh, esteeming it more delicate than any other, provided the death of the person has not been occasioned by disease. When they advance to combat they throw loose their hair about their ears, and they paint their faces of a bright blue colour. They arm themselves with lances and swords, and all march on foot excepting their chief, who rides on horseback. They are a most savage race of men, insomuch that when they slay their enemies in battle, they are anxious to drink their blood, and afterwards they devour their flesh. Leaving this subject, we shall now speak of the city of Kue-lin-fu.

CHAPTER LXXIV

Of the City of Kue-lin-fu

The journey of six days (mentioned in the preceding chapter) being accomplished, you arrive at the city of Kue-lin-fu, which is of considerable size, and contains three very handsome bridges, upwards of a hundred paces in length, and eight paces in width. The women of the place are very handsome, and live in a state of luxurious ease. There is much raw silk produced here, and it is manufactured into silk pieces of various sorts. Cottons are also woven, of coloured threads, which are carried for sale to every part of the province of Manji. The people employ themselves extensively in commerce, and export quantities of ginger and galangal. I have been told, but did not myself see the animal, that there are found at this place a species of domestic fowls which have no feathers, their skins being clothed with black hair, resembling the fur of cats. Such a sight must be extraordinary. They lay eggs like other fowls, and they are good to eat. The multitude of tigers renders travelling through the country dangerous, unless a number of persons go in company.

CHAPTER LXXV

Of the City of Un-guen

Upon leaving the city of Kue-lin-fu, and travelling three days, during which you are continually passing towns and castles, of which the inhabitants are idolaters, have silk in abundance, and export it in considerable quantities, you reach the city of Un-guen. This place is remarkable for a great manufacture of sugar, which is sent from thence to the city of Kanbalu for the supply of the court. Previously to its being brought under the dominion of the Grand Khan, the natives were unacquainted with the art of manufacturing sugar of a fine quality, and boiled it in such an imperfect manner, that when left to cool it remained in the state of a dark-brown paste. But at the time this city became subject to his majesty's government, there happened to be at the court some persons from Babylon who were skilled in the process, and who, being sent thither, instructed the inhabitants in the mode of refining the sugar by means of the ashes of certain woods.

CHAPTER LXXVI

Of the City of Kan-giu

Travelling fifteen miles further in the same direction, you come to the city of Kan-giu, which belongs to the kingdom or viceroyalty of Kon-cha, one of the nine divisions of Manji. In this place is stationed a large army for the protection of the country, and to be always in readiness to act, in the event of any city manifesting a disposition to rebel. Through the midst of it passes a river, a mile in breadth, upon the banks of which, on either side, are extensive and handsome buildings. In front of these, great numbers of ships are seen lying, having merchandise on board, and especially sugar, of which large quantities are manufactured here also. Many vessels arrive at this port from India, freighted by merchants who bring with them rich assortments of jewels and pearls, upon the sale of which they obtain a considerable profit. This river discharges itself into the sea, at no great distance from the port named Zai-tun. The ships coming from India ascend the river as high up as the city, which abounds with every sort of provision, and has delightful gardens, producing exquisite fruits.

CHAPTER LXXVII

Of the City and Port of Zai-tun, and the City of Tin-gui

Upon leaving the city of Kan-giu and crossing the river to proceed in a south-easterly direction, you travel during five days through a well-inhabited country, passing towns, castles, and substantial dwellings, plentifully supplied with all kinds of provisions. The road lies over hills, across plains, and through woods, in which are found many of those shrubs from whence the camphor is procured. The country abounds also with game. The inhabitants are idolaters. They are the subjects of the Grand Khan, and within the jurisdiction of Kan-giu. At the end of five days' journey, you arrive at the noble and handsome city of Zai-tun, which has a port on the sea-coast celebrated for the resort of shipping, loaded with merchandise, that is afterwards distributed through every part of the province of Manji. The quantity of pepper imported there is so considerable, that what is carried to Alexandria, to supply the demand of the western parts of the world, is trifling in comparison, perhaps not more than the hundredth part. It is indeed impossible to convey an idea of the concourse of merchants and the accumulation of goods, in this which is held to be one of the largest and most commodious ports in the world. The Grand Khan derives a vast revenue from this place, as every merchant is obliged to pay ten per cent upon the amount of his investment. The ships are freighted by them at the rate of thirty per cent for fine goods, forty-four for pepper, and for lignum-aloes, sandalwood, and other drugs, as well as articles of trade in general, forty per cent; so that it is computed by the merchants, that their charges, including customs and freight, amount to half the value of the cargo; and yet upon the half that remains to them their profit is so considerable, that they are always disposed to return to the same market with a further stock of merchandise. The country is delightful. The people are idolaters, and have all the necessaries of life in plenty: their disposition is peaceable, and they are fond of ease and indulgence. Many persons arrive in this city from the interior parts of India for the purpose of having their persons ornamented by puncturing with needles (in the manner before described), as it is celebrated for the number of its artists skilled in that practice.

The river that flows by the port of Zai-tun is large and rapid, and is a branch of that which passes the city of Kin-sai. At the place where it separates from the principal channel stands the city of Tin-gui. Of this place there is nothing further to be observed, than that cups or bowls and dishes of porcelain-ware are there manufactured. The process was explained to be as follows. They collect a certain kind of earth, as it were, from a mine, and laying it in a great heap, suffer it to be exposed to the wind, the rain, and the sun, for thirty or forty years, during which time it is never disturbed. By this it becomes refined and fit for being wrought into the vessels above mentioned. Such colours as may be thought proper are then laid on, and the ware is afterwards baked in ovens or furnaces. Those persons, therefore, who cause the earth to be dug, collect it for their children and grand-children. Great quantities of the manufacture are sold in the city, and for a Venetian groat you may purchase eight porcelain cups.

We have now described the viceroyalty of Kon-cha, one of the nine divisions of Manji, from whence the Grand Khan draws as ample a revenue as even from that of Kin-sai. Of the others we shall not attempt to speak, because Marco Polo did not himself visit any of their cities, as he has done those of Kinsai and Kon-cha. It should be observed that throughout the province of Manji one general language prevails, and one uniform manner of writing, yet in the different parts of the country there is a diversity of dialect, similar to what is found between the Genoese, the Milanese, the Florentine, and the dialects of other Italian states, whose inhabitants, although they have each their peculiar speech, can make themselves reciprocally understood.

Not having yet completed the subjects upon which Marco Polo purposed to write, he will now bring this Second Book to a close, and will commence another with a description of the countries and provinces of India, distinguishing it into the Greater, the Lesser, and the Middle India, parts of which he visited whilst employed in the service of the Grand Khan, who ordered him thither upon different occasions of business, and afterwards when, accompanied by his father and uncle, in their returning journey they escorted the queen destined for king Argon. He will have the opportunity of relating many extraordinary circumstances observed by himself personally in those countries, but at the same time will not omit to notice others of which he was informed by persons worthy of credit, or which were pointed out to him in the sea-chart of the coasts of India.

BOOK III

CHAPTER I

Of India, distinguished into the Greater, Lesser, and Middle — Of the Manners and Customs of its Inhabitants — Of many remarkable and extraordinary Things to be observed there; and, in the first place, of the kind of Vessels employed in Navigation

Having treated, in the preceding parts of our work, of various provinces and regions, we shall now take leave of them, and proceed to the account of India, the admirable circumstances of which shall be related. We shall commence with a description of the ships employed by the merchants, which are built of fir-timber. They have a single deck, and below this the space is divided into about sixty small cabins, fewer or more, according to the size of the vessels, each of them affording accommodation for one merchant. They are provided with a good helm. They have four masts, with as many sails, and some of them have two masts which can be set up and lowered again, as may be found necessary. Some ships of the larger class have, besides (the cabins), to the number of thirteen bulk-heads or divisions in the hold, formed of thick planks let into each other (*incastrati*, mortised or rabbeted). The object of these is to guard against accidents which may occasion the vessels to spring a leak, such as striking on a rock or receiving a stroke from a whale, a circumstance that not unfrequently occurs; for, when sailing at night, the motion through the waves causes a white foam that attracts the notice of the hungry animal. In expectation of meeting with food, it rushes violently to the spot, strikes the ship, and often forces in some part of the bottom. The water, running in at the place where the injury has been sustained, makes its way to the well, which is always kept clear. The crew, upon discovering the situation of the leak, immediately remove the goods from the division affected by the water, which, in consequence of the boards being so well fitted, cannot pass from one division to another. They then repair the damage, and return the goods to that place in the hold from whence they had been taken. The ships are all double-planked; that is, they have a course of sheathing-boards laid over the planking in every part. These are caulked with oakum both withinside and without, and are fastened with iron nails. They are not coated with pitch, as the country does not produce that article, but the bottoms are smeared over with the following preparation. The people take quick-lime and hemp, which latter they cut small, and with these, when pounded together, they mix oil procured from a certain tree, making of the whole a kind of unguent, which retains its viscous properties more firmly, and is a better material than pitch.

Ships of the largest size require a crew of three hundred men; others, two hundred; and some, one hundred and fifty only, according to their greater or less bulk. They carry from five to six thousand baskets (or mat bags) of pepper. In former times they were of greater burthen than they are at present; but the violence of the sea having in many places broken up the islands, and especially in some of the principal ports, there is a want of depth of water for vessels of such draught, and they have on that account been built, in latter times, of a smaller size. The vessels are likewise moved with oars or sweeps, each of which requires four men to work it. Those of the larger class are accompanied by two or three large barks, capable of containing about one thousand baskets of pepper, and are manned with sixty, eighty, or one hundred sailors. These small craft are often employed to tow the larger, when working their oars, or even under sail, provided the wind be on the quarter, but not when right aft, because, in that case, the sails of the larger vessel must becalm those of the smaller, which would, in consequence, be run down. The ships also carry with them as many as ten small boats, for the purpose of carrying out anchors, for fishing, and a variety of other services. They are slung over the sides, and lowered into the water when there is occasion to use them. The barks are in like manner provided with their small boats. When a ship, having been on a voyage for a year or more, stands in need of repair, the practice is to give her a course of sheathing over the original boarding, forming a third course, which is caulked and paid in the same manner as the others; and this, when she needs further repairs, is repeated, even to the number of six layers, after which she is condemned as unserviceable and not seaworthy. Having thus described the shipping, we shall proceed to the account of India; but in the first instance we shall speak of certain islands in the part of the ocean where we are at present, and shall commence with the island named Zipangu.

CHAPTER II

Of the Island of Zipangu

Zipangu is an island in the eastern ocean, situated at the distance of about fifteen hundred miles from the mainland, or coast of Manji. It is of considerable size; its inhabitants have fair complexions, are well made, and are civilised in their manners. Their religion is the worship of idols. They are independent of every foreign power, and governed only by their own kings. They have gold in the greatest abundance, its sources being inexhaustible, but as the king does not allow of its being exported, few merchants visit the country, nor is it frequented by much shipping from other parts. To this circumstance we are to attribute the extraordinary richness of the sovereign's palace, according to what we are told by those who have access to the place. The entire roof is covered with a plating of gold, in the same manner as we cover houses or more properly churches, with lead. The ceilings of the halls are of the same precious metal; many of the apartments have small tables of pure gold, of considerable thickness; and the windows also have golden ornaments. So vast, indeed, are the riches of the palace, that it is impossible to convey an idea of them. In this island there are pearls also, in large quantities, of a red (pink) colour, round in shape, and of great size, equal in value to, or even exceeding that of the white pearls. It is customary with one part of the inhabitants to bury their dead, and with another part to burn them. The former have a practice of putting one of these pearls into the mouth of the corpse. There are also found there a number of precious stones.

Of so great celebrity was the wealth of this island, that a desire was excited in the breast of the Grand Khan Kublai, now reigning, to make the conquest of it, and to annex it to his dominions. In order to effect this, he fitted out a numerous fleet, and embarked a large body of troops, under the command of two of his principal officers, one of whom was named Abbacatan, and the other Vonsancin. The expedition sailed from the ports of Zai-tun and Kin-sai, and, crossing the intermediate sea, reached the island in safety; but in consequence of a jealousy that arose between the two commanders, one of whom treated the plans of the other with contempt and resisted the execution of his orders, they were unable to gain possession of any city or fortified place, with the exception of one only, which was carried by assault, the garrison having refused to surrender. Directions were given for putting the whole to the sword, and in obedience thereto the heads of all were cut off, excepting of eight persons, who, by the efficacy of a diabolical charm, consisting of a jewel or amulet introduced into the right arm, between the skin and the flesh, were rendered secure from the effects of iron, either to kill or wound. Upon this discovery being made, they were beaten with a heavy wooden club, and presently died.

It happened, after some time, that a north wind began to blow with great force, and the ships of the Tartars, which lay near the shore of the island, were driven foul of each other. It was determined thereupon, in a council of the officers on board, that they ought to disengage themselves from the land; and accordingly, as soon as the troops were re-embarked, they stood out to sea. The gale, however, increased to so violent a degree that a number of the vessels foundered. The people belonging to them, by floating upon pieces of the wreck, saved themselves upon an island lying about four miles from the coast of Zipangu. The other ships, which, not being so near to the land, did not suffer from the storm, and in which the two chiefs were embarked, together with the principal officers, or those whose rank entitled them to command a hundred thousand or ten thousand men, directed their course homewards, and returned to the Grand Khan. Those of the Tartars who remained upon the island where they were wrecked, and who amounted to about thirty thousand men, finding themselves left without shipping, abandoned by their leaders, and having neither arms nor provisions, expected nothing less than to become captives or to perish; especially as the island afforded no habitations where they could take shelter and refresh themselves. As soon as the gale ceased and the sea became smooth and calm, the people from the main island of Zipangu came over with a large force, in numerous boats, in order to make prisoners of these shipwrecked Tartars, and having landed, proceeded in search of them, but in a straggling, disorderly manner. The Tartars, on their part, acted with prudent circumspection, and, being concealed from view by some high land in the centre of the island, whilst the enemy were hurrying in pursuit of them by one road, made a circuit of the coast by another, which brought them to the place where the fleet of boats was at anchor. Finding these all abandoned, but with their colours flying, they instantly seized them and pushing off from the island, stood for the principal city of Zipangu, into which, from the appearance of the colours, they were suffered to enter unmolested. Here they found few of the inhabitants besides women, whom they retained for their own use, and drove out all others. When the king was apprised of what had taken place, he was much afflicted, and immediately gave directions for a strict blockade of the city, which was so effectual that not any person was suffered to enter or to escape from it, during six months that the siege continued. At the expiration of this time, the Tartars, despairing of succour, surrendered upon the condition of their lives being spared. These events took place in the course of the year 1264. The Grand Khan having learned some years after that the unfortunate issue of the expedition was to be attributed to the dissension between the two commanders, caused the head of one of them to be cut off; the other he sent to the savage island of Zorza, where it is the custom to execute criminals in the following manner. They are wrapped round both arms, in the hide of a buffalo fresh taken from the beast, which is sewed tight. As this dries, it compresses the body to such a degree that the sufferer is incapable of moving or in any manner helping himself, and thus miserably perishes.

CHAPTER III

Of the nature of the Idols Worshipped in Zipangu, and of the People being addicted to eating Human Flesh

In this island of Zipangu and the others in its vicinity, their idols are fashioned in a variety of shapes, some of them having the heads of oxen, some of swine, of dogs, goats, and many other animals. Some exhibit the appearance of a single head, with two countenances; others of three heads, one of them in its proper place, and one upon each shoulder. Some have four arms, others ten, and some an hundred; those which have the greatest number being regarded as the most powerful, and therefore entitled to the most particular worship. When they are asked by Christians wherefore they give to their deities these diversified forms, they answer that their fathers did so before them. 'Those who preceded us,' they say, 'left them such, and such shall we transmit them to our posterity.' The various ceremonies practised before these idols are so wicked and diabolical that it would be nothing less than impiety and an abomination to give an account of them in this our book. The reader should, however, be informed that the idolatrous inhabitants of these islands, when they seize the person of an enemy who has not the means of effecting his ransom for money, invite to their house all their relations and friends, and putting their prisoner to death, dress and eat the body, in a convivial manner, asserting that human flesh surpasses every other in the excellence of its flavour.

CHAPTER IV

*Of the Sea of Chin, between this Island and the Province of
Manji*

It is to be understood that the sea in which the island of Zipangu is
situated is called the Sea of Chin, and so extensive is this eastern sea,
that according to the report of experienced pilots and mariners who
frequent it, and to whom the truth must be known, it contains no
fewer than seven thousand four hundred and forty islands, mostly
inhabited. It is said that of the trees which grow in them, there are
none that do not yield a fragrant smell. They produce many spices
and drugs, particularly lignum-aloes and pepper, in great abundance,
both white and black. It is impossible to estimate the value of the gold
and other articles found in the islands; but their distance from the
continent is so great, and the navigation attended with so much
trouble and inconvenience, that the vessels engaged in the trade, from
the ports of Zai-tun and Kin-sai, do not reap large profits, being
obliged to consume a whole year in their voyage, sailing in the winter
and returning in the summer. For in these regions only two winds
prevail; one of them during the winter, and the other during the
summer season; so that they must avail themselves of the one for the
outward, and of the other for the homeward-bound voyage. These
countries are far remote from the continent of India. In terming this
sea the Sea of Chin, we must understand it, nevertheless, to be a part
of the ocean; for as we speak of the English Sea, or of the Egean Sea,
so do the eastern people of the Sea of Chin and of the Indian Sea;
whilst all of them are comprehended under the general term of the
ocean. We shall here cease to treat further of these countries and
islands, as well on account of their lying so far out of the way, as of
my not having visited them personally, and of their not being under
the dominion of the Grand Khan. We return now to Zai-tun.

CHAPTER V

Of the Gulf of Keinan, and of its Rivers

Departing from the port of Zai-tun, and steering a westerly course, but inclining to the south, for fifteen hundred miles, you pass the gulf named Keinan, which extends to the distance of two months' navigation, along its northern shore, where it bounds the southern part of the province of Manji, and from thence to where it approaches the countries of Ania, Toloman, and many others already mentioned. Within this gulf there are a multitude of islands, for the most part well inhabited, about the coasts of which much gold-dust is collected from the sea, at those places where the rivers discharge themselves. Copper also and many other articles are found there, and with these a trade is carried on, the one island supplying what another does not produce. They traffic also with the people of the continent, exchanging their gold and copper for such necessaries as they may require. In the most of these islands grain is raised in abundance. This gulf is so extensive and the inhabitants so numerous, that it appears like another world.

CHAPTER VI

Of the Country of Ziamba, of the King of that Country, and of his becoming Tributary to the Grand Khan

We now resume our former subject. Upon leaving Zai-tun and navigating fifteen hundred miles across this gulf, as has been mentioned, you arrive at a country named Ziamba, which is of great extent, and rich. It is governed by its own kings, and has its peculiar language. The inhabitants are worshippers of idols. An annual tribute, in elephants and lignum-aloes, is paid to the Grand Khan, the occasion and circumstances of which shall be related. About the year 1268, Kublai, having received accounts of the great wealth of this kingdom, resolved upon the measure of sending a large force, both of infantry and cavalry, to effect the conquest of it, and the country was accordingly invaded by a powerful army, placed under the command of one of his generals, named Sogatu. The king, whose name was Accambale, and who was far advanced in years, feeling himself incapable of making resistance in the field to the forces of the Grand Khan, retired to his strongholds, which afforded him security, and he there defended himself valiantly. The open towns, however, and habitations on the plains, were in the meantime overrun and laid waste, and the king, perceiving that his whole territory would be ruined by the enemy, sent ambassadors to the Grand Khan for the purpose of representing that, being himself an old man who had always preserved his dominions in a state of tranquillity and peace, he was anxious to save them from the destruction with which they were threatened, and, upon the condition of the invading army being withdrawn, he was willing to pay yearly an honorary tribute of elephants and sweet-scented wood. Upon receiving this proposal, the Grand Khan, from motives of compassion, immediately sent orders to Sogatu for his retreat from thence with the force under his command, and directed him to proceed to the conquest of other countries, which was executed without delay. From that time the king has annually presented to the Grand Khan, in the form of tribute, a very large quantity of lignum-aloes, together with twenty of the largest and handsomest elephants to be found in his districts. Thus it was that the king of Ziamba became the subject of the Grand Khan.

Having related the foregoing, we shall now mention some circumstances respecting this king and his country. In the first place it should be noticed that in his dominions no young woman can be given in marriage, until she has been first proved by the king. Those who prove agreeable to him he retains for some time, and when they are dismissed, he furnishes them with a sum of money, in order that they may be able to obtain, according to their rank in life, advantageous matches. Marco Polo, in the year 1280, visited this place, at which period the king had three hundred and twenty-six children, male and female. Most of the former had distinguished themselves as valiant soldiers. The country abounds with elephants and with lignum-aloes. There are also many forests of ebony of a fine black, which is worked into various handsome articles of furniture. No other circumstance requires particular mention. Leaving this place, we shall now speak of the island called Java Major.

CHAPTER VII

Of the Island of Java

Departing from Ziamba, and steering between south and south-east, fifteen hundred miles, you reach an island of very great size, named Java, which, according to the reports of some well-informed navigators, is the largest in the world, being in circuit above three thousand miles. It is under the dominion of one king only, nor do the inhabitants pay tribute to any other power. They are worshippers of idols. The country abounds with rich commodities. Pepper, nutmegs, spikenard, galangal, cubebs, cloves, and all the other valuable spices and drugs, are the produce of the island; which occasion it to be visited by many ships laden with merchandise, that yields to the owners considerable profit. The quantity of gold collected there exceeds all calculation and belief. From thence it is that the merchants of Zai-tun and of Manji in general have imported, and to this day import, that metal to a great amount, and from thence also is obtained the greatest part of the spices that are distributed throughout the world. That the Grand Khan has not brought the island under subjection to him, must be attributed to the length of the voyage and the dangers of the navigation.

CHAPTER VIII

Of the Islands of Sondur and Kondur, and of the Country of Lochac

Upon leaving the island of Java, and steering a course between south and south-west, seven hundred miles, you fall in with two islands, the larger of which is named Sondur, and the other Kondur. Both being uninhabited, it is unnecessary to say more respecting them. Having run the distance of fifty miles from these islands, in a south-easterly direction, you reach an extensive and rich province, that forms a part of the main land, and is named Lochac. Its inhabitants are idolaters. They have a language peculiar to themselves, and are governed by their own king, who pays no tribute to any other, the situation of the country being such as to protect it from any hostile attack. Were it assailable, the Grand Khan would not have delayed to bring it under his dominion. In this country sappan, or brezil wood, is produced in large quantities. Gold is abundant to a degree scarcely credible; elephants are found there; and the objects of the chase, either with dogs or birds, are in plenty. From hence are exported all those porcelain shells, which, being carried to other countries, are there circulated for money, as has been already noticed. Here they cultivate a species of fruit called *berchi*, in size about that of a lemon, and having a delicious flavour. Besides these circumstances there is nothing further that requires mention, unless it be that the country is wild and mountainous, and is little frequented by strangers, whose visits the king discourages, in order that his treasures and other secret matters of his realm may be as little known to the rest of the world as possible.

CHAPTER IX

Of the Island of Pentan, and of the Kingdom of Malaiur

Departing from Lochac, and keeping a southerly course for five hundred miles, you reach an island named Pentan, the coast of which is wild and uncultivated, but the woods abound with sweet-scented trees. Between the province of Lochac and this island of Pentan, the sea, for the space of sixty miles, is not more than four fathoms in depth, which obliges those who navigate it to lift the rudders of their ships (in order that they may not touch the bottom). After sailing these sixty miles, in a south-easterly direction, and then proceeding thirty miles further, you arrive at an island, in itself a kingdom, named Malaiur, which is likewise the name of its chief city. The people are governed by a king, and have their own peculiar language. The town is large and well-built. A considerable trade is there carried on in spices and drugs, with which the place abounds. Nothing else that requires notice presents itself. Proceeding onwards from thence, we shall now speak of Java Minor.

CHAPTER X

Of the Island of Java Minor

Upon leaving the island of Pentan, and steering in the direction of south-east for about one hundred miles, you reach the island of Java the Lesser. Small, however, as it may be termed by comparison, it is not less than two thousand miles in circuit. In this island there are eight kingdoms, governed by so many kings, and each kingdom has its own proper language, distinct from those of all the others. The people are idolaters. It contains abundance of riches, and all sorts of spices, lignum-aloes, sappan-wood for dyeing, and various other kinds of drugs, which, on account of the length of the voyage and the danger of the navigation, are not imported into our country, but which find their way to the provinces of Manji and Cathay.

We shall now treat separately of what relates to the inhabitants of each of these kingdoms; but in the first place it is proper to observe that the island lies so far to the southward as to render the north star invisible. Six of the eight kingdoms were visited by Marco Polo; and these he will describe, omitting the other two, which he had not an opportunity of seeing.

CHAPTER XI

Of the Kingdom of Felech, in the Island of Java Minor

We shall begin with the kingdom of Felech, which is one of the eight. Its inhabitants are for the most part idolaters, but many of those who dwell in the seaport towns have been converted to the religion of Mahomet, by the Saracen merchants who constantly frequent them. Those who inhabit the mountains live in a beastly manner; they eat human flesh, and indiscriminately all other sorts of flesh, clean and unclean. Their worship is directed to a variety of objects, for each individual adores throughout the day the first thing that presents itself to his sight when he rises in the morning.

CHAPTER XII

Of the Second Kingdom, named Basman

Upon leaving the last-mentioned kingdom, you enter that of Basman, which is independent of the others, and has its peculiar language. The people profess obedience to the Grand Khan, but pay him no tribute, and their distance is so great, that his troops cannot be sent to these parts. The whole island, indeed, is nominally subject to him, and when ships pass that way the opportunity is taken of sending him rare and curious articles, and especially a particular sort of falcon.

In the country are many wild elephants and rhinoceroses, which latter are much inferior in size to the elephant, but their feet are similar. Their hide resembles that of the buffalo. In the middle of the forehead they have a single horn; but with this weapon they do not injure those whom they attack, employing only for this purpose their tongue, which is armed with long, sharp spines, and their knees or feet; their mode of assault being to trample upon the person, and then to lacerate him with the tongue. Their head is like that of a wild boar, and they carry it low towards the ground. They take delight in muddy pools, and are filthy in their habits. They are not of that description of animals which suffer themselves to be taken by maidens, as our people suppose, but are quite of a contrary nature. There are found in this district monkeys of various sorts, and vultures as black as crows, which are of a large size, and pursue the quarry in a good style.

It should be known that what is reported respecting the dried bodies of diminutive human creatures, or pigmies, brought from India, is an idle tale, such pretended men being manufactured in this island in the following manner. The country produces a species of monkey, of a tolerable size, and having a countenance resembling that of a man. Those persons who make it their business to catch them, shave off the hair, leaving it only about the chin, and those other parts where it naturally grows on the human body. They then dry and preserve them with camphor and other drugs; and having prepared them in such a mode that they have exactly the appearance of little men, they put them into wooden boxes, and sell them to trading people, who carry them to all parts of the world. But this is merely an imposition, the practice being such as we have described; and neither in India, nor in any other country, however wild (and little known), have pigmies been found of a form so diminutive as these exhibit. Sufficient having been said of this kingdom, which presents nothing else remarkable, we shall now speak of another, named Samara.

CHAPTER XIII

Of the Third Kingdom, named Samara

Leaving Basman, you enter the kingdom of Samara, being another of those into which the island is divided. In this Marco Polo resided five months, during which, exceedingly against his inclination, he was detained by contrary winds. The north star is not visible here, nor even the stars that are in the wain. The people are idolaters; they are governed by a powerful prince, who professes himself the vassal of the Grand Khan.

As it was necessary to continue for so long a time at this island Marco Polo established himself on shore, with a party of about 2,000 men; and in order to guard against mischief from the savage natives, who seek for opportunities of seizing stragglers, putting them to death, and eating them, he caused a large and deep ditch to be dug around him on the land side, in such manner that each of its extremities terminated in the port, where the shipping lay. This ditch he strengthened by erecting several blockhouses or redoubts of wood, the country affording an abundant supply of that material; and being defended by this kind of fortification, he kept the party in complete security during the five months of their residence. Such was the confidence inspired amongst the natives, that they furnished supplies of victuals and other necessary articles according to an agreement made with them.

No finer fish for the table can be met with in any part of the world than are found here. There is no wheat produced, but the people live upon rice. Wine is not made; but from a species of tree resembling the date-bearing palm they procure an excellent beverage in the following manner. They cut off a branch, and put over the place a vessel to receive the juice as it distils from the wound, which is filled in the course of a day and a night. So wholesome are the qualities of this liquor, that it affords relief in dropsical complaints, as well as in those of the lungs and of the spleen. When these shoots that have been cut are perceived not to yield any more juice, they contrive to water the trees, by bringing from the river, in pipes or channels, so much water as is sufficient for the purpose; and upon this being done, the juice runs again as it did at first. Some trees naturally yield it of a reddish, and others of a pale colour. The Indian nuts also grow here, of the size of a man's head, containing an edible substance that is sweet and pleasant to the taste, and white as milk. The cavity of this pulp is filled with a liquor clear as water, cool, and better flavoured and more delicate than wine or any other kind of drink whatever. The inhabitants feed upon flesh of every sort, good or bad, without distinction.

CHAPTER XIV

Of the Fourth Kingdom, named Dragoian

Dragoian is a kingdom governed by its own prince, and having its peculiar language. Its inhabitants are uncivilised, worship idols, and acknowledge the authority of the Grand Khan. They observe this horrible custom, in cases where any member of the family is afflicted with a disease: The relations of the sick person send for the magicians, whom they require, upon examination of the symptoms, to declare whether he will recover or not. These, according to the opinion suggested to them by the evil spirit, reply, either that he will recover or the contrary. If the decision be that he cannot, the relations then call in certain men, whose peculiar duty it is and who perform their business with dexterity, to close the mouth of the patient until he be suffocated. This being done, they cut the body in pieces, in order to prepare it as victuals; and when it has been so dressed, the relations assemble, and in a convivial manner eat the whole of it, not leaving so much as the marrow in the bones. Should any particle of the body be suffered to remain, it would breed vermin, as they observe; these vermin, for want of further sustenance, would perish, and their death would prove the occasion of grievous punishment to the soul of the deceased. They afterwards proceed to collect the bones, and having deposited them in a small, neat box, carry them to some cavern in the mountains, where they may be safe against the disturbance of wild animals. If they have it in their power to seize any person who does not belong to their own district, and who cannot pay for his ransom, they put him to death, and devour him.

CHAPTER XV

Of the Fifth Kingdom, named Lambri

Lambri, in like manner, has its own king and its peculiar language: the people also worship idols, and call themselves vassals of the Grand Khan. The country produces verzino (brezil or sappan wood) in great abundance, and also camphor, with a variety of other drugs. They sow a vegetable which resembles the sappan, and when it springs up and begins to throw out shoots, they transplant it to another spot, where it is suffered to remain for three years. It is then taken up by the roots, and used as a dye-stuff. Marco Polo brought some of the seeds of this plant with him to Venice, and sowed them there; but the climate not being sufficiently warm, none of them came up. In this kingdom are found men with tails, a span in length, like those of the dog, but not covered with hair. The greater number of them are formed in this manner, but they dwell in the mountains, and do not inhabit towns. The rhinoceros is a common inhabitant of the woods, and there is abundance of all sorts of game, both beasts and birds.

CHAPTER XVI

Of the Sixth Kingdom, named Fanfur, where Meal is procured from a certain Tree

Fanfur is a kingdom of the same island, governed by its own prince, where the people likewise worship idols, and profess obedience to the Grand Khan. In this part of the country a species of camphor, much superior in quality to any other, is produced. It is named the camphor of Fanfur, and is sold for its weight in gold. There is not any wheat nor other corn, but the food of the inhabitants is rice, with milk, and the wine extracted from trees in the manner that has been described in the chapter respecting Samara. They have also a tree from which, by a singular process, they obtain a kind of meal. The stem is lofty, and as thick as can be grasped by two men. When from this the outer bark is stripped, the ligneous substance is found to be about three inches in thickness, and the central part is filled with pith, which yields a meal or flour, resembling that procured from the acorn. The pith is put into vessels filled with water, and is stirred about with a stick, in order that the fibres and other impurities may rise to the top, and the pure farinaceous part subside to the bottom. When this has been done, the water is poured off, and the flour which remains, divested of all extraneous matter, is applied to use, by making it into cakes and various kinds of pastry. Of this, which resembles barley bread in appearance and taste, Marco Polo has frequently eaten, and some of it he brought home with him to Venice. The wood of the tree, in thickness about three inches (as has been mentioned), may be compared to iron in this respect, that when thrown into water it immediately sinks. It admits of being split in an even direction from one end to the other, like the bamboo cane. Of this the natives make short lances: were they to be of any considerable length, their weight would render it impossible to carry or to use them. They are sharpened at one end, and rendered so hard by fire that they are capable of penetrating any sort of armour, and in many respects are preferable to iron. What we have said on the subject of this kingdom (one of the divisions of the island) is sufficient. Of the other kingdoms composing the remaining part we shall not speak, because Marco Polo did not visit them. Proceeding further, we shall next describe a small island named Nocueran.

CHAPTER XVII

Of the Island of Nocueran

Upon leaving Java (minor) and the kingdom of Lambri, and sailing about one hundred and fifty miles, you fall in with two islands, one of which is named Nocueran, and the other Angaman. Nocueran is not under the government of a king, and the people are little removed from the conditions of beasts; all of them, both males and females, going naked, without a covering to any part of the body. They are idolaters. Their woods abound with the noblest and most valuable trees, such as the white and the red sandal, those which bear the Indian (coco) nuts, cloves, and sappan; besides which they have a variety of drugs. Proceeding further, we shall speak of Angaman.

CHAPTER XVIII

Of the Island of Angaman

Angaman is a very large island, not governed by a king. The inhabitants are idolaters, and are a most brutish and savage race, having heads, eyes, and teeth resembling those of the canine species. Their dispositions are cruel, and every person, not being of their own nation, whom they can lay their hands upon, they kill and eat. They have abundance and variety of drugs. Their food is rice and milk, and flesh of every description. They have Indian nuts, apples of paradise, and many other fruits different from those which grow in our country.

CHAPTER XIX

Of the Island of Zeilan

Taking a departure from the island of Angaman, and steering a course something to the southward of west, for a thousand miles, the island of Zeilan presents itself. This, for its actual size, is better circumstanced than any other island in the world. It is in circuit two thousand four hundred miles, but in ancient times it was still larger, its circumference then measuring full three thousand six hundred miles, as the Mappa-Mundi says. But the northern gales, which blow with prodigious violence, have in a manner corroded the mountains, so that they have in some parts fallen and sunk in the sea, and the island, from that cause, no longer retains its original size. It is governed by a king whose name is Sender-naz. The people worship idols, and are independent of every other state. Both men and women go nearly in a state of nudity, only wrapping a cloth round the middle part of their bodies. They have no grain besides rice and sesamé, of which latter they make oil. Their food is milk, rice, and flesh, and they drink the wine drawn from trees, which has already been described. There is here the best sappan-wood that can anywhere be met with. The island produces more beautiful and valuable rubies than are found in any other part of the world, and likewise sapphires, topazes, amethysts, garnets, and many other precious and costly stones. The king is reported to possess the grandest ruby that ever was seen, being a span in length, and the thickness of a man's arm, brilliant beyond description, and without a single flaw. It has the appearance of a glowing fire, and upon the whole is so valuable that no estimation can be made of its worth in money. The Grand Khan, Kublai, sent ambassadors to this monarch, with a request that he would yield to him the possession of this ruby; in return for which he should receive the value of a city. The answer he made was to this effect: that he would not sell it for all the treasure of the universe; nor could he on any terms suffer it to go out of his dominions, being a jewel handed down to him by his predecessors on the throne. The Grand Khan failed therefore to acquire it. The people of this island are by no means of a military habit, but, on the contrary, are abject and timid; and when there is occasion to employ soldiers, they are procured from other countries, in the vicinity of the Mahometans. Nothing else of a remarkable nature presenting itself, we shall proceed to speak of Maabar.

CHAPTER XX

Of the Province of Maabar

§ 1. Leaving the island of Zeilan, and sailing in a westerly direction sixty miles, you reach the great province of Maabar, which is not an island, but a part of the continent of the greater India, as it is termed, being the noblest and richest country in the world. It is governed by four kings, of whom the principal is named Sender-bandi. Within his dominions is a fishery for pearls, in the gulf of a bay that lies between Maabar and the island of Zeilan, where the water is not more than from ten to twelve fathoms in depth, and in some places not more than two fathoms. The business of the fishery is conducted in the following manner. A number of merchants form themselves into separate companies, and employ many vessels and boats of different sizes, well provided with ground-tackle, by which to ride safely at anchor. They engage and carry with them persons who are skilled in the art of diving for the oysters in which the pearls are enclosed. These they bring up in bags made of netting that are fastened about their bodies, and then repeat the operation, rising to the surface when they can no longer keep their breath, and after a short interval diving again. In this operation they persevere during the whole of the day, and by their exertions accumulate (in the course of the season) a quantity of oysters sufficient to supply the demands of all countries. The greater proportion of the pearls obtained from the fisheries in this gulf, are round, and of a good lustre. The spot where the oysters are taken in the greatest number is called Betala, on the shore of the mainland; and from thence the fishery extends sixty miles to the southward.

In consequence of the gulf being infested with a kind of large fish, which often prove destructive to the divers, the merchants take the precaution of being accompanied by certain enchanters belonging to a class of Brahmans, who, by means of their diabolical art, have the power of constraining and stupefying these fish, so as to prevent them from doing mischief; and as the fishing takes place in the daytime only, they discontinue the effect of the charm in the evening; in order that dishonest persons who might be inclined to take the opportunity of diving at night and stealing the oysters, may be deterred by the apprehension they feel of the unrestrained ravages of these animals. The enchanters are likewise profound adepts in the art of fascinating all kinds of beasts and birds. The fishery commences in the month of April, and lasts till the middle of May. The privilege of engaging in it is farmed of the king, to whom a tenth part only of the produce is allowed; to the magicians they allow a twentieth part, and consequently they reserve to themselves a considerable profit. By the time the period above mentioned is completed, the stock of oysters is exhausted; and the vessels are then taken to another place, distant full three hundred miles from this gulf, where they establish themselves in the month of September, and continue till the middle of October. Independently of the tenth of the pearls to which the king is entitled, he requires to have the choice of all such as are large and well-shaped; and as he pays liberally for them, the merchants are not disinclined to carry them to him for that purpose.

§2. The natives of this part of the country always go naked, excepting that they cover with a piece of cloth those parts of the body which modesty dictates. The king is no more clothed than the rest, except that he has a piece of richer cloth; but is honourably distinguished by various kinds of ornaments, such as a collar set with jewels, sapphires, emeralds, and rubies, of immense value. He also wears, suspended from the neck and reaching to the breast, a fine silken string containing one hundred and four large and handsome pearls and rubies. The reason for this particular number is, that he is required by the rules of his religion to repeat a prayer or invocation so many times, daily, in honour of his gods; and this his ancestors never failed to perform. The daily prayer consists of these words, *pacauca, pacauca, pacauca*, which they repeat one hundred and four times. On each arm he wears three gold bracelets, adorned with pearls and jewels; on three different parts of the leg, golden bands ornamented in the same manner; and on the toes of his feet, as well as on his fingers, rings of inestimable value. To this king it is indeed a matter of facility to display such splendid regalia, as the precious stones and the pearls are all the produce of his own dominions. He has at the least one thousand wives and concubines; and when he sees a woman whose beauty pleases him, he immediately signifies his desire to possess her. In this manner he appropriated the wife of his brother, who being a discreet and sensible man, was prevailed upon not to make it the subject of a broil, although repeatedly on the point of having recourse to arms. On these occasions their mother remonstrated with them, and exposing her breasts, said: 'If you, my children, disgrace yourselves by acts of hostility against each other, I shall instantly sever from my body these breasts from which you drew your nourishment'; and thus the irritation was allowed to subside.

The king retains about his person many knights, who are distinguished by an appellation, signifying 'the devoted servants of his majesty, in this world and the next'. These attend upon his person at court, ride by his side in processions, and accompany him on all occasions. They exercise considerable authority in every part of the realm. Upon the death of the king, and when the ceremony of burning his body takes place, all these devoted servants throw themselves into the same fire, and are consumed with the royal corpse; intending by this act to bear him company in another life. The following custom likewise prevails. When a king dies, the son who succeeds him does not meddle with the treasure which the former had amassed, under the impression that it would reflect upon his own ability to govern, if being left in full possession of the territory, he did not show himself as capable of enriching the treasury as his father was. In consequence of this prejudice it is supposed that immense wealth is accumulated by successive generations.

No horses being bred in this country, the king and his three royal brothers expend large sums of money annually in the purchase of them from merchants of Ormus, Diufar, Pecher, and Adem, who carry them thither for sale, and become rich by the traffic, as they import to the number of five thousand, and for each of them obtain five hundred saggi of gold, being equal to one hundred marks of silver. At the end of the year, in consequence, as it is supposed, of their not having persons properly qualified to take care of them or to administer the requisite medicines, perhaps not three hundred of these remain alive, and thus the necessity is occasioned for replacing them annually. But it is my opinion that the climate of the province is unfavourable to the race of horses, and that from hence arises the difficulty in breeding or preserving them. For food they give them flesh dressed with rice, and other prepared meats, the country not producing any grain besides rice. A mare, although of a large size, and covered by a handsome horse, produces only a small ill-made colt, with distorted legs, and unfit to be trained for riding.

The following extraordinary custom prevails at this place. When a man who has committed a crime, for which he has been tried and condemned to suffer death, upon being led to execution, declares his willingness to sacrifice himself in honour of some particular idol, his relations and friends immediately place him in a kind of chair, and deliver to him twelve knives of good temper and well sharpened. In this manner they carry him about the city, proclaiming, with a loud voice, that this brave man is about to devote himself to a voluntary death, from motives of zeal for the worship of the idol. Upon reaching the place where the sentence of the law would have been executed, he snatches up two of the knives, and crying out, 'I devote myself to death in honour of such an idol,' hastily strikes one of them into each thigh, then one into each arm, two into the belly, and two into the breast. Having in this manner thrust all the knives but one into different parts of his body, repeating at every wound the words that have been mentioned, he plunges the last of them into his heart, and immediately expires. As soon as this scene has been acted, his relations proceed, with great triumph and rejoicing, to burn the body; and his wife, from motives of pious regard for her husband, throws herself upon the pile, and is consumed with him. Women who display this resolution are much applauded by the community, as, on the other hand, those who shrink from it are despised and reviled.

§3. The greater part of the idolatrous inhabitants of this kingdom show particular reverence to the ox; and none will from any consideration be induced to eat the flesh of oxen. But there is a particular class of men termed gaui, who although they may eat of the flesh, yet dare not to kill the animal; but when they find a carcase, whether it has died a natural death or otherwise, the gaui eat of it; and all descriptions of people daub their houses with cow-dung. Their mode of sitting is upon carpets on the ground; and when asked why they sit in that manner, they reply that a seat on the earth is honourable; that as we are sprung from the earth, so we shall again return to it; that none can do it sufficient honour, and much less should any despise the earth. These gaui and all their tribe are the descendants of those who slew Saint Thomas the Apostle, and on this account no individual of them can possibly enter the building where the body of the blessed apostle rests, even were the strength of ten men employed to convey him to the spot, being repelled by the supernatural power of the holy corpse.

The country produces no other grain than rice and sesamé. The people go to battle with lances and shields, but without clothing, and are a despicable unwarlike race. They do not kill cattle nor any kind of animals for food, but when desirous of eating the flesh of sheep or other beasts, or of birds, they procure the Saracens, who are not under the influence of the same laws and customs, to perform the office. Both men and women wash their whole bodies in water twice every day, that is, in the morning and the evening. Until this ablution has taken place they neither eat nor drink; and the person who should neglect this observance, would be regarded as a heretic. It ought to be noticed, that in eating they make use of the right hand only, nor do they ever touch their food with the left. For every cleanly and delicate work they employ the former, and reserve the latter for the base uses of personal abstersion, and other offices connected with the animal functions. They drink out of a particular kind of vessel, and each individual from his own, never making use of the drinking pot of another person. When they drink they do not apply the vessel to the mouth, but hold it above the head, and pour the liquor into the mouth, not suffering the vessel on any account to touch the lips. In giving drink to a stranger, they do not hand their vessel to him, but, if he is not provided with one of his own, pour the wine or other liquor into his hands, from which he drinks it, as from a cup.

Offences in this country are punished with strict and exemplary justice, and with regard to debtors the following customs prevail. If application for payment shall have been repeatedly made by a creditor, and the debtor puts him off from time to time with fallacious promises, the former may attach his person by drawing a circle round him, from whence he dare not depart until he has satisfied his creditor, either by payment, or by giving adequate security. Should he attempt to make his escape, he renders himself liable to the punishment of death, as a violater of the rules of justice.

Messer Marco when he was in this country on his return homeward, happened to be an eyewitness of a remarkable transaction of this nature. The king was indebted in a sum of money to a certain foreign merchant, and although frequently importuned for payment, amused him for a long time with vain assurances. One day when the king was riding on horseback, the merchant took the opportunity of describing a circle round him and his horse. As soon as the king perceived what had been done, he immediately ceased to proceed, nor did he move from the spot until the demand of the merchant was fully satisfied. The bystanders beheld what passed with admiration, and pronounced that king to merit the title of most just, who himself submitted to the laws of justice.

These people abstain from drinking wine made from grapes; and should a person be detected in the practice, so disreputable would it be held, that his evidence would not be received in court. A similar prejudice exists against persons frequenting the sea, who, they observe, can only be people of desperate fortunes, and whose testimony, as such, ought not to be admitted. They do not hold fornication to be a crime. The heat of the country is excessive, and the inhabitants on that account go naked. There is no rain excepting in the months of June, July, and August, and if it was not for the coolness imparted to the air during these three months by the rain, it would be impossible to support life.

In this country there are many adepts in the science denominated physiognomy, which teaches the knowledge of the nature and qualities of men, and whether they tend to good or evil. These qualities are immediately discerned upon the appearance of the man or woman. They also know what events are portended by meeting certain beasts or birds. More attention is paid by these people to the flight of birds than by any others in the world, and from whence they predict good or bad fortune. In every day of the week there is one hour which they regard as unlucky, and this they name *choiach*; thus, for example, on Monday the (canonical) hour of *mi-tierce*, on Tuesday the hour of *tierce*, on Wednesday the hour of *none*; and on these hours they do not make purchases, nor transact any kind of business, being persuaded that it would not be attended with success. In like manner they ascertain the qualities of every day throughout the year, which are described and noted in their books. They judge of the hour of the day by the length of a man's shadow when he stands erect. When an infant is born, be it a boy or a girl, the father or the mother makes a memorandum in writing of the day of the week on which the birth took place; also of the age of the moon, the name of the month, and the hour. This is done because every future act of their lives is regulated by astrology. As soon as a son attains the age of thirteen years, they set him at liberty, and no longer suffer him to be an inmate in his father's house; giving him to the amount, in their money, of twenty to twenty-four groats. Thus provided, they consider him as capable of gaining his own livelihood, by engaging in some kind of trade and thence deriving a profit. These boys never cease to run about in all directions during the whole course of the day, buying an article in one place, and selling it in another. At the season when the pearl fishery is going on, they frequent the beach, and make purchases from the fishermen or others, of five, six, or more (small) pearls, according to their means, carrying them afterwards to the merchants, who, on account of the heat of the sun, remain sitting in their houses, and to whom they say: 'These pearls have cost us so much; pray allow such a profit on them as you may judge reasonable.' The merchants then give something beyond the price at which they had been obtained. In this way likewise they deal in many other articles, and become excellent and most acute traders. When business is over for the day, they carry to their mothers the provisions necessary for their dinners, which they prepare and dress for them; but these never eat anything at their fathers' expense.

§4. Not only in this kingdom, but throughout India in general, all the beasts and birds are unlike those of our own country, excepting the quails, which perfectly resemble ours; the others are all different. There are bats as large as vultures, and vultures as black as crows, and much larger than ours. Their flight is rapid, and they do not fail to seize their bird.

In their temples there are many idols, the forms of which represent them of the male and the female sex; and to these, fathers and mothers dedicate their daughters. Having been so dedicated, they are expected to attend whenever the priests of the convent require them to contribute to the gratification of the idol; and on such occasions they repair thither, singing and playing on instruments, and adding by their presence to the festivity. These young women are very numerous, and form large bands. Several times in the week they carry an offering of victuals to the idol to whose service they are devoted, and of this food they say the idol partakes. A table for the purpose is placed before it, and upon this the victuals are suffered to remain for the space of a full hour; during which damsels never cease to sing, and play, and exhibit wanton gestures. This lasts as long as a person of condition would require for making a convenient meal. They then declare that the spirit of the idol is content with its share of the entertainment provided, and, ranging themselves around it, they proceed to eat in their turn; after which they repair to their respective homes. The reason given for assembling the young women, and performing the ceremonies that have been described, is this: The priests declare that the male divinity is out of humour with and incensed against the female, refusing to have connection or even to converse with her; and that if some measure were not adopted to restore peace and harmony between them, all the concerns of the monastery would go to ruin, as the grace and blessing of the divinities would be withheld from them. For this purpose it is, they expect the votaries to appear in a state of nudity, with only a cloth round their waists, and in that state to chant hymns to the god and goddess. These people believe that the former often solaces himself with the latter.

The natives make use of a kind of bedstead, or cot, of very light cane-work, so ingeniously contrived that when they repose on them, and are inclined to sleep, they can draw close the curtains about them by pulling a string. This they do in order to exclude the tarantulas, which bite grievously, as well as to prevent their being annoyed by fleas and other small vermin; whilst at the same time the air, so necessary for mitigating the excessive heat, is not excluded. Indulgences of this nature, however, are enjoyed only by persons of rank and fortune; others of the inferior class lie in the open streets.

In this province of Maabar is the body of the glorious martyr, Saint Thomas the Apostle, who there suffered martyrdom. It rests in a small city, not frequented by many merchants, because unsuited to the purposes of their commerce; but, from devout motives, a vast number both of Christians and Saracens resort thither. The latter regard him as a great prophet, and name him Ananias, signifying a holy personage. The Christians who perform this pilgrimage collect earth from the spot where he was slain, which is of a red colour, and reverentially carry it away with them; often employing it afterwards in the performance of miracles, and giving it, when diluted with water, to the sick, by which many disorders are cured. In the year of our Lord

1288, a powerful prince of the country, who at the time of gathering the harvest had accumulated (as his proportion) a very great quantity of rice, and had not granaries sufficient wherein to deposit it all, thought proper to make use of the religious house belonging to the church of Saint Thomas for that purpose. This being against the will of those who had the guardianship of it, they beseeched him not to occupy in this manner a building appropriated to the accommodation of pilgrims who came to visit the body of this glorious saint. He, notwithstanding, obstinately persisted. On the following night the holy apostle appeared to him in a vision, holding in his hand a small lance, which he pointed at the throat of the king, saying to him: 'If thou dost not immediately evacuate my house which thou hast occupied, I shall put thee to a miserable death.' Awaking in a violent alarm, the prince instantly gave orders for doing what was required of him, declaring publicly that he had seen the apostle in a vision. A variety of miracles are daily performed there, through the interposition of the blessed saint. The Christians who have the care of the church possess groves of those trees which produce the Indian nuts, and from thence derive their means of subsistence, paying, as a tax to one of the royal brothers, a groat monthly for each tree. It is related that the death of this most holy apostle took place in the following manner. Having retired to a hermitage, where he was engaged in prayer, and being surrounded by a number of pea-fowls, with which bird the country abounds, an idolater of the tribe of the Gaui, before described, who happened to be passing that way, and did not perceive the holy man, shot an arrow at a peacock, which struck the apostle in the side. Finding himself wounded, he had time only to thank the Lord for all his mercies, and into His hands he resigned his spirit.

In this province the natives, although black, are not born of so deep a dye as they afterwards attain by artificial means, esteeming blackness the perfection of beauty. For this purpose, three times every day, they rub the children over with oil of sesamé. The images of their deities they represent black, but the devil they paint white, and assert that all the demons are of that colour. Those amongst them who pay adoration to the ox, take with them, when they go to battle, some of the hair of a wild bull, which they attach to the manes of their horses, believing its virtue and efficacy to be such that everyone who carries it about with him is secure from all kind of danger. On this account the hair of the wild bull sells for a high price in these countries.

CHAPTER XXI

Of the Kingdom of Murphili or Monsul

The kingdom of Murphili is that which you enter upon leaving the kingdom of Maabar, after proceeding five hundred miles in a northerly direction. Its inhabitants worship idols, and are independent of any other state. They subsist upon rice, flesh, fish, and fruits. In the mountains of this kingdom it is that diamonds are found. During the rainy season the waters descend in violent torrents amongst the rocks and caverns, and when these have subsided the people go to search for diamonds in the beds of the rivers, where they find many. Messer Marco was told that in the summer, when the heat is excessive and there is no rain, they ascend the mountains with great fatigue, as well as with considerable danger from the number of snakes with which they are infested. Near the summit, it is said, there are deep valleys, full of caverns and surrounded by precipices, amongst which the diamonds are found; and here many eagles and white storks, attracted by the snakes on which they feed, are accustomed to make their nests. The persons who are in quest of the diamonds take their stand near the mouths of the caverns, and from thence cast down several pieces of flesh, which the eagles and storks pursue into the valley, and carry off with them to the tops of the rocks. Thither the men immediately ascend, drive the birds away, and recovering the pieces of meat, frequently find diamonds sticking to them. Should the eagles have had time to devour the flesh, they watch the place of their roosting at night, and in the morning find the stones amongst the dung and filth that drops from them. But you must not suppose that the good diamonds come among Christians, for they are carried to the Grand Khan, and to the kings and chiefs of that country. In this country they manufacture the finest cottons that are to be met with in any part of India. They have cattle enough, and the largest sheep in the world, and plenty of all kinds of food.

CHAPTER XXII

Of the Province of Lac, Loac, or Lar

Leaving the place where rests the body of the glorious apostle Saint Thomas, and proceeding westward, you enter the province of Lar, from whence the Brahmins, who are spread over India, derive their origin. These are the best and most honourable merchants that can be found. No consideration whatever can induce them to speak an untruth, even though their lives should depend upon it. They have also an abhorrence of robbery or of purloining the goods of other persons. They are likewise remarkable for the virtue of continence, being satisfied with the possession of one wife. When any foreign merchant, unacquainted with the usages of the country, introduces himself to one of these, and commits to his hands the care of his adventure, this Brahmin undertakes the management of it, disposes of the goods, and renders a faithful account of the proceeds, attending scrupulously to the interests of the stranger, and not demanding any recompense for his trouble, should the owner uncourteously omit to make him the gratuitous offer. They eat meat, and drink the wine of the country. They do not, however, kill any animal themselves, but get it done by the Mahometans. The Brahmins are distinguished by a certain badge consisting of a thick cotton thread, which passes over the shoulder and is tied under the arm, in such a manner that the thread appears upon the breast and behind the back. The king is extremely rich and powerful, and has much delight in the possession of pearls and valuable stones. When the traders from Maabar present to him such as are of superior beauty, he trusts to their word with respect to the estimation of their value, and gives them double the sum that each is declared to have cost them. Under these circumstances, he has the offer of many fine jewels. The people are gross idolaters, and much addicted to sorcery and divination. When they are about to make a purchase of goods, they immediately observe the shadow cast by their own bodies in the sunshine; and if the shadow be as large as it should be, they make the purchase that day.

Moreover, when they are in any shop for the purpose of buying anything, if they see a tarantula, of which there are many there, they take notice from which side it comes, and regulate their business accordingly. Again, when they are going out of their houses, if they hear anyone sneeze, they return into the house, and stay at home. They are very abstemious in regard to eating, and live to an advanced age. Their teeth are preserved sound by the use of a certain vegetable which they are in the habit of masticating. It also promotes digestion, and conduces generally to the health of the body.

Amongst the natives of this region there is a class peculiarly devoted to a religious life, who are named *tingui*, and who in honour of their divinities lead most austere lives. They go perfectly naked, not concealing any part of their bodies, and say there can be no shame in that state of nudity in which they came into the world; and with respect to what are called the parts of shame, they observe that, not being with them the organs of sin, they have no reason to blush at their exposure.

They pay adoration to the ox, and carry a small figure of one, of gilt brass or other metal, attached to their foreheads. They also burn the bones of oxen, reduce them to powder, and with this make an unguent for the purpose of marking various parts of the body, which they do in a reverential manner. If they meet a person with whom they are upon cordial terms, they smear the centre of his forehead with some of these prepared ashes. They do not deprive any creature of life, not even a fly, a flea, or a louse, believing them to be animated with souls; and to feed upon any animal they would consider as a heinous sin. They even abstain from eating vegetables, herbs, or roots, until they have become dry; holding the opinion that these also have souls. They make no use of spoons nor of platters, but spread their victuals upon the dried leaves of the Adam's apple, called likewise apples of paradise. When they have occasion to ease nature, they go to the sea-beach, and having dropped their burden in the sand, immediately scatter it in all directions, to prevent its giving birth to vermin, whose consequent death by hunger would load their consciences with a grievous offence. They live to a great age, some of them even to a hundred and fifty years, enjoying health and vigour, although they sleep upon the bare earth. This must be attributed to their temperance and chastity. When they die, their bodies are burned, in order for the same reason that they might not breed worms.

CHAPTER XXIII

Of the Island of Zeilan

I am unwilling to pass over certain particulars which I omitted when before speaking of the island of Zeilan, and which I learned when I visited that country in my homeward voyage. In this island there is a very high mountain, so rocky and precipitous that the ascent to the top is impracticable, as it is said, excepting by the assistance of iron chains employed for that purpose. By means of these some persons attain the summit, where the tomb of Adam, our first parent, is reported to be found. Such is the account given by the Saracens. But the idolaters assert that it contains the body of Sogomon-barchan, the founder of their religious system, and whom they revere as a holy personage. He was the son of a king of the island, who devoted himself to an ascetic life, refusing to accept of kingdoms or any other wordly possessions, although his father endeavoured, by the allurements of women, and every other imaginable gratification, to divert him from the resolution he had adopted. Every attempt to dissuade him was in vain, and the young man fled privately to this lofty mountain, where, in the observance of celibacy and strict abstinence, he at length terminated his mortal career. By the idolaters he is regarded as a saint. The father, distracted with the most poignant grief, caused an image to be formed of gold and precious stones, bearing the resemblance of his son, and required that all the inhabitants of the island should honour and worship it as a deity. Such was the origin of the worship of idols in that country; but Sogomon-barchan is still regarded as superior to every other. In consequence of this belief, people flock from various distant parts in pilgrimage to the mountain on which he was buried. Some of his hair, his teeth, and the basin he made use of, are still preserved, and shown with much ceremony. The Saracens, on the other hand, maintain that these belonged to the prophet Adam, and are in like manner led by devotion to visit the mountain.

It happened that, in the year 1281, the Grand Khan heard from certain Saracens who had been upon the spot, the fame of these relics belonging to our first parent, and felt so strong a desire to possess them, that he was induced to send an embassy to demand them of the king of Zeilan. After a long and tedious journey, his ambassadors at length reached the place of their destination, and obtained from the king two large back-teeth, together with some of the hair and a handsome vessel of porphyry. When the Grand Khan received intelligence of the approach of the messengers, on their return with such valuable curiosities, he ordered all the people of Kanbalu to march out of the city to meet them, and they were conducted to his presence with great pomp and solemnity. Having mentioned these particulars respecting the mountain of Zeilan, we shall return to the kingdom of Maabar, and speak of the city of Kael.

CHAPTER XXIV

Of the City of Kael

Kael is a considerable city, governed by Astiar, one of the four brothers, kings of the country of Maabar, who is rich in gold and jewels, and preserves his country in a state of profound peace. On this account it is a favourite place of resort for foreign merchants, who are well received and treated by the king. Accordingly all the ships coming from the west – as from Ormus, Chisti, Adem, and various parts of Arabia – laden with merchandise and horses, make this port, which is besides well situated for commerce. The prince maintains in the most splendid manner not fewer than three hundred women.

All the people of this city, as well as the natives of India in general, are addicted to the custom of having continually in their mouths the leaf called *tembul*; which they do, partly from habit, and partly from the gratification it affords. Upon chewing it, they spit out the saliva to which it gives occasion. Persons of rank have the leaf prepared with camphor and other aromatic drugs, and also with a mixture of quick-lime. I have been told that it is extremely conducive to health. If it is an object with any man to affront another in the grossest and most contemptuous manner, he spits the juice of this masticated leaf in his face. Thus insulted, the injured party hastens to the presence of the king, states the circumstances of his grievance, and declares his willingness to decide the quarrel by combat. The king thereupon furnishes them with arms, consisting of a sword and small shield; and all the people assemble to be spectators of the conflict, which lasts till one of them remains dead on the field. They are, however, forbidden to wound with the point of the sword.

CHAPTER XXV

Of the Kingdom of Koulam

Upon leaving Maabar and proceeding five hundred miles towards the south-west, you arrive at the kingdom of Koulam. It is the residence of many Christians and Jews, who retain their proper language. The king is not tributary to any other. Much good sappan-wood grows there, and pepper in great abundance, being found both in the woody and the open parts of the country. It is gathered in the months of May, June, and July; and the vines which produce it are cultivated in plantations. Indigo also, of excellent quality and in large quantities, is made here. They procure it from an herbaceous plant, which is taken up by the roots and put into tubs of water, where it is suffered to remain till it rots; when they press out the juice. This, upon being exposed to the sun, and evaporated, leaves a kind of paste, which is cut into small pieces of the form in which we see it brought to us.

The heat during some months is so violent as to be scarcely supportable; yet the merchants resort thither from various parts of the world, such, for instance, as the kingdom of Manji and Arabia, attracted by the great profits they obtain both upon the merchandise they import, and upon their returning cargoes. Many of the animals found here are different from those of other parts. There are tigers entirely black; and various birds of the parrot kind, some of them as white as snow, with the feet and the beak red; others whose colours are a mixture of red and azure, and others of a diminutive size. The peacocks also are handsomer and larger than ours, as well as of a different form, and even the domestic fowls have a peculiar appearance. The same observation will apply to the fruits. The cause of such diversity, it is said, is the intense heat that prevails in these regions. Wine is made from the sugar yielded by a species of palm. It is extremely good, and inebriates faster than the wine made from grapes. The inhabitants possess abundance of everything necessary for the food of man excepting grain, of which there is no other kind than rice; but of this the quantity is very great. Among them are many astrologers and physicians, well versed in their art. All the people, both male and female, are black, and, with the exception of a small piece of cloth attached to the front of their bodies, they go quite naked. Their manners are extremely sensual, and they take as wives their relations by blood, their mothers-in-law, upon the death of their fathers, and the widows of their deceased brothers. But this, as I have been informed, is the state of morals in every part of India.

CHAPTER XXVI

Of Komari

Komari is a province where a part of our northern constellation, invisible at Java, and to within about thirty miles of this place, may be just seen, and where it appears to be the height of a cubit above the horizon. The country is not much cultivated, being chiefly covered with forests, which are the abode of a variety of beasts, especially apes, so formed, and of such a size, as to have the appearance of men. There are also long-tailed monkeys, very different from the former in respect to magnitude. Tigers, leopards, and lynxes abound.

CHAPTER XXVII

Of the Kingdom of Dely

Leaving the province of Komari, and proceeding westward three hundred miles, you reach the kingdom of Dely, which has its proper king and peculiar language. It does not pay tribute to any other state. The people worship idols. There is no harbour for shipping, but a large river with a safe entrance. The strength of the country does not consist in the multitude of its inhabitants, nor in their bravery, but in the difficulty of the passes by which it must be approached, and which render its invasion by an enemy nearly impossible. It produces large quantities of pepper and ginger, with many other articles of spicery. Should a vessel be accidentally driven within the mouth of its river, not having intended to make that port, they seize and confiscate all the goods she may have on board, saying: 'It was your intentions to have gone elsewhere, but our gods have conducted you to us, in order that we may possess your property.' The ships from Manji arrive here before the expiration of the fine-weather season, and endeavour to get their cargoes shipped in the course of a week, or a shorter time if possible; the roadstead being unsafe, in consequence of sand-banks along the coast, which often prove dangerous, however, well provided they may be with large wooden anchors, calculated for riding out hard gales of wind. The country is infested with tigers, and many other ferocious animals.

CHAPTER XXVIII

Of Malabar

Malabar is an extensive kingdom of the Greater India, situated towards the west; concerning which I must not omit to relate some particulars. The people are governed by their own king, who is independent of every other state, and they have their proper language. In this country the north star is seen about two fathoms above the horizon. As well here as in the kingdom of Guzzerat, which is not far distant, there are numerous pirates, who yearly scour these seas with more than one hundred small vessels, seizing and plundering all the merchant ships that pass that way. They take with them to sea their wives and children of all ages, who continue to accompany them during the whole of the summer's cruise. In order that no ships may escape them, they anchor their vessels at the distance of five miles from each other; twenty ships thereby occupying a space of a hundred miles. Upon a trader's appearing in sight of one of them, a signal is made by fire or by smoke; when they all draw close together, and capture the vessel as she attempts to pass. No injury is done to the persons of the crew; but as soon as they have made prize of the ships, they turn them on shore, recommending to them to provide themselves with another cargo, which, in case of their passing that way again, may be the means of enriching their captors a second time.

In this kingdom there is vast abundance of pepper, ginger, cubebs, and Indian nuts; and the finest and most beautiful cottons are manufactured that can be found in any part of the world. The ships from Manji bring copper as ballast; and besides this, gold brocades, silks, gauzes, gold and silver bullion, together with many kinds of drugs not produced in Malabar; and these they barter for the commodities of the province. There are merchants on the spot who ship the former for Aden, from whence they are transported to Alexandria.

Having now spoken of the kingdom of Malabar, we shall proceed to describe that of Guzzerat, which borders on it. Should we attempt to treat of all the cities of India, the account would be prolix, and prove tiresome. We shall, therefore, touch only upon those respecting which we have particular information.

CHAPTER XXIX

Of the Kingdom of Guzzerat

The kingdom of Guzzerat, which is bounded on the western side by the Indian Sea, is governed by its own king, and has its peculiar language. The north-star appears from hence to have six fathoms of altitude. This country affords harbour to pirates of the most desperate character, who, when in their cruises they seize upon a travelling merchant, immediately oblige him to drink a dose of sea-water, which by its operation on his bowels, discovers whether he may not have swallowed pearls or jewels, upon the approach of an enemy, in order to conceal them.

Here there is great abundance of ginger, pepper, and indigo. Cotton is produced in large quantities from a tree that is about six yards in height, and bears during twenty years; but the cotton taken from trees of that age is not adapted for spinning, but only for quilting. Such, on the contrary, as is taken from trees of twelve years old, is suitable for muslins and other manufactures of extraordinary fineness. Great numbers of skins of goats, buffaloes, wild oxen, rhinoceroses, and other beasts are dressed here; and vessels are loaded with them, and bound to different parts of Arabia. Coverlets for beds are made of red and blue leather, extremely delicate and soft, and stitched with gold and silver thread; upon these the Mahometans are accustomed to repose. Cushions also, ornamented with gold wire in the form of birds and beasts, are the manufacture of this place; and in some instances their value is so high as six marks of silver. Embroidery is here performed with more delicacy than in any other part of the world. Proceeding further, we shall now speak of the kingdom named Kanan.

CHAPTER XXX

Of the Kingdom of Kanan

Kanan is a large and noble kingdom, situated towards the west. We say towards the west, because Messer Marco's journey being from the eastern side, he speaks of the countries in the direction in which he found them. It is governed by a prince, who does not pay tribute to any other. The people are idolaters and have a peculiar language. Neither pepper nor ginger grows here, but the country produces a sort of incense, in large quantities, which is not white, but on the contrary of a dark colour. Many ships frequent the place in order to load this drug, as well as a variety of other articles. They likewise take on board a number of horses, to be carried for sale to different parts of India.

CHAPTER XXXI

Of the Kingdom of Kambaia

This also is an extensive kingdom, situated towards the west, governed by its own king, who pays no tribute to any other, and having its proper language. The people are idolaters. In this country the north-star is seen still higher than in any of the preceding, in consequence of its lying further to the north-west. The trade carried on is very considerable, and a great quantity of indigo is manufactured. There is abundance of cotton cloth, as well as of cotton in the wool. Many skins well dressed are exported from hence, and the returns are received in gold, silver, copper, and tutty. There not being anything else deserving of notice, I shall proceed to speak of the kingdom of Servenath.

CHAPTER XXXII

Of the Kingdom of Servenath

Servenath, likewise, is a kingdom lying towards the west, the inhabitants of which are idolaters, are governed by a king who pays no tribute, have their peculiar language, and are a well-disposed people. They gain their living by commerce and manufactures, and the place is frequented by a number of merchants, who carry thither their articles of merchandise, and take away those of the country in return. I was informed, however, that the priests who serve in the temples of the idols are the most perfidious and cruel that the world contains. We shall now proceed to speak of the kingdom named Kesmacoran.

CHAPTER XXXIII

Of the Kingdom of Kesmacoran

This is an extensive country, having its proper king and its peculiar language. Some of the inhabitants are idolaters, but the greater part are Saracens. They subsist by trade and manufactures. Their food is rice and wheat, together with flesh and milk, which they have in abundance. Many merchants resort thither, both by sea and land. This is the last province of the Greater India, as you proceed to the north-west; for, as it begins at Maabar, so it terminates here. In describing it, we have noticed only the provinces and cities that lie upon the sea-coast; for were we to particularise those situated in the interior of the land, it would render our work too prolix. We shall now speak of certain islands, one of which is termed the Island of Males, and the other, the Island of Females.

CHAPTER XXXIV

Of the Islands of Males and of Females

Distant from Kesmacoran about five hundred miles towards the south, in the ocean, there are two islands within about thirty miles from each other, one of which is inhabited by men, without the company of women, and is called the island of males, and the other by women, without men, which is called the island of females. The inhabitants of both are of the same race, and are baptised Christians, but hold the law of the Old Testament. The men visit the island of females, and remain with them for three successive months, namely, March, April, and May, each man occupying a separate habitation along with his wife. They then return to the island of males, where they continue all the rest of the year, without the society of any female. The wives retain their sons with them until they are of the age of twelve years, when they are sent to join their fathers. The daughters they keep at home until they become marriageable, and then they bestow them upon some of the men of the other island. This mode of living is occasioned by the peculiar nature of the climate, which does not allow of their remaining all the year with their wives, unless at the risk of falling a sacrifice. They have their bishop, who is subordinate to the see of the island of Soccotera. The men provide for the subsistence of their wives by sowing the grain but the latter prepare the soil and gather in the harvest. The island likewise produces a variety of fruits. The men live upon milk, flesh, rice, and fish. Of these they catch an immense quantity, being expert fishermen. Both when fresh taken and when salted, the fish are sold to the traders resorting to the island, but whose principal object is to purchase ambergris of which a quantity is collected there.

CHAPTER XXXV

Of the Island of Soccotera

Upon leaving these islands, and proceeding five hundred miles in a southerly direction, you reach the island of Soccotera, which is very large, and abounds with the necessaries of life. The inhabitants find much ambergris upon their coasts, which is voided from the entrails of whales. Being an article of merchandise in great demand, they make it a business to take these fish; and this they do by means of a barbed iron, which they strike into the whale so firmly that it cannot be drawn out. To the iron (harpoon) a long line is fastened, with a buoy at the end, for the purpose of discovering the place where the fish, when dead, is to be found. They then drag it to the shore, and proceed to extract the ambergris from its belly, whilst from its head they procure several casks of (spermaceti) oil.

All the people, both male and female, go nearly naked, having only a scanty covering before and behind, like the idolaters who have been described. They have no other grain than rice, upon which, with flesh and milk, they subsist. Their religion is Christianity, and they are duly baptised, and are under the government, as well temporal as spiritual, of an archbishop, who is not in subjection to the pope of Rome, but to a patriarch who resides in the city of Baghdad, by whom he is appointed, or, if elected by the people themselves, by whom their choice is confirmed. Many pirates resort to this island with the goods they have captured, and which the natives purchase of them without any scruple, justifying themselves on the ground of their being plundered from idolaters and Saracens. All ships bound to the province of Aden touch here, and make large purchases of fish and of ambergris, as well as of various kinds of cotton goods manufactured on the spot.

The inhabitants deal more in sorcery and witchcraft than any other people, although forbidden by their archbishop, who excommunicates and anathematises them for the sin. Of this, however, they make little account; and if any vessel belonging to a pirate should injure one of theirs, they do not fail to lay him under a spell, so that he cannot proceed on his cruise until he has made satisfaction for the damage; and even although he should have had a fair and leading wind, they have the power of causing it to change, and thereby of obliging him, in spite of himself, to return to the island. They can, in like manner, cause the sea to become calm, and at their will can raise tempests, occasion shipwrecks, and produce many other extraordinary effects, that need not be particularised. We shall now speak of the island of Madagascar.

CHAPTER XXXVI

Of the great Island of Madagascar

Leaving the island of Soccotera, and steering a course between south and south-west for a thousand miles, you arrive at the great island of Madagascar, which is one of the largest and most fertile in the world. In circuit it is three thousand miles. The inhabitants are Saracens, or followers of the law of Mahomet. They have four sheikhs, which in our language may be expressed by 'elders', who divide the government amongst them. The people subsist by trade and manufacture, and sell a vast number of elephants' teeth, as those animals abound in the country, as they do also in that of Zenzibar, from whence the exportation is equally great. The principal food eaten at all seasons of the year is the flesh of camels. That of the other cattle serves them also for food, but the former is preferred, as being both the most wholesome and the most palatable of any to be found in this part of the world. The woods contain many trees of red sandal, and, in proportion to the plenty in which it is found, the price of it is low. There is also much ambergris from the whales; and as the tide throws it on the coast, it is collected for sale. The natives catch lynxes, tigers, and a variety of other animals, such as stags, antelopes, and fallow deer, which afford much sport; as do also birds, which are different from those of our climates.

The island is visited by many ships from various parts of the world, bringing assortments of goods consisting of brocades and silks of various patterns, which are sold to the merchants of the island, or bartered for goods in return; upon all of which they make large profits. There is no resort of ships to the other numerous islands lying further south, this and the island of Zenzibar alone being frequented. This is the consequence of the sea running with such prodigious velocity in that direction, as to render their return impossible. The vessels that sail from the coast of Malabar for this island, perform the voyage in twenty or twenty-five days, but in their returning voyage are obliged to struggle for three months; so strong is the current of water, which constantly runs to the southward.

The people of the island report that at a certain season of the year, an extraordinary kind of bird, which they call a rukh, makes its appearance from the southern region. In form it is said to resemble the eagle, but it is incomparably greater in size; being so large and strong as to seize an elephant with its talons, and to lift it into the air, from whence it lets it fall to the ground, in order that when dead it may prey upon the carcase. Persons who have seen this bird assert that when the wings are spread they measure sixteen paces in extent, from point to point; and that the feathers are eight paces in length, and thick in proportion. Messer Marco Polo, conceiving that these creatures might be griffins, such as are represented in paintings, half birds and half lions, particularly questioned those who reported their having seen them as to this point; but they maintained that their shape was altogether that of birds, or, as it might be said, of the eagle. The Grand Khan having heard this extraordinary relation, sent messengers to the island, on the pretext of demanding the release of one of his servants who had been detained there, but in reality to examine into the circumstances of the country, and the truth of the wonderful things told of it. When they returned to the presence of his majesty, they brought with them (as I have heard) a feather of the rukh, positively affirmed to have measured ninety spans, and the quill part to have been two palms in circumference. This surprising exhibition afforded his majesty extreme pleasure, and upon those by whom it was presented he bestowed valuable gifts. They were also the bearers of the tusk of a wild boar, an animal that grows there to the size of a buffalo, and it was found to weigh fourteen pounds. The island contains likewise camelopards, asses, and other wild animals, very different from these of our country. Having said what was necessary on this subject, we shall now proceed to speak of Zenzibar.

CHAPTER XXXVII

Of the Island of Zenzibar

Beyond the island of Madagascar lies that of Zenzibar, which is reported to be in circuit two thousand miles. The inhabitants worship idols, have their own peculiar language, and do not pay tribute to any foreign power. In their persons they are large, but their height is not proportioned to the bulk of their bodies. Were it otherwise, they would appear gigantic. They are, however, strongly made, and one of them is capable of carrying what would be a load for four of our people. At the same time, he would require as much food as five. They are black, and go naked, covering only the private parts of the body with a cloth. Their hair is so crisp, that even when dipped in water it can with difficulty be drawn out. They have large mouths, their noses turn up towards the forehead, their ears are long, and their eyes so large and frightful, that they have the aspect of demons. The woman are equally ill-favoured, having wide mouths, thick noses, and large eyes. Their hands, and also their heads, are out of proportion large. There are in this island the most ill-favoured women in the world; with large mouths and thick noses, and ill-favoured breasts, four times as large as those of other women. They feed on flesh, milk, rice, and dates. They have no grape vines, but make a sort of wine from rice and sugar, with the addition of some spicy drugs, very pleasant to the taste, and having the intoxicating quality of the other. In this island elephants are found in vast numbers, and their teeth form an important article of trade. With respect to these quadrupeds it should be observed, that their mode of copulating is the reverse of that of the brute creation in general, in consequence of the position of the female organ, and follows that of the human species.

In this country is found also the giraffe or camelopard, which is a handsome beast. The body is well-proportioned, the fore-legs long and high, the hind-legs short, the neck very long, the head small, and in its manners it is gentle. Its prevailing colour is light, with circular reddish spots. Its height (or length of the neck), including the head, is three paces. The sheep of the country are different from ours, being all white excepting their heads, which are black; and this also is the colour of the dogs. The animals in general have a different appearance from ours. Many trading ships visit the place, which barter the goods they bring for elephants' teeth and ambergris, of which much is found on the coasts of the island, in consequence of the sea abounding with whales.

The chiefs of the island are sometimes engaged in warfare with each other, and their people display much bravery in battle and contempt of death. They have no horses, but fight upon elephants and camels. Upon the backs of the former they place castles, capable of containing from fifteen to twenty men, armed with swords, lances, and stones, with which weapons they fight. Previously to the combat they give draughts of wine to their elephants, supposing that it renders them more spirited and more furious in the assault.

CHAPTER XXXVIII

Of the multitude of Islands in the Indian Sea

In treating of the provinces of India, I have described only the principal and most celebrated; and the same has been done with respect to the islands, the number of which is quite incredible. I have heard, indeed, from mariners and eminent pilots of these countries, and have seen in the writings of those who have navigated the Indian seas, that they amount to no fewer than twelve thousand seven hundred, including the uninhabited with the inhabited islands. The division termed the Greater India extends from Maabar to Kesmacoran, and comprehends thirteen large kingdoms, of which we have enumerated ten. The Lesser India commences at Ziampa, and extends to Murfili, comprehending eight kingdoms, exclusive to those in the islands, which are very numerous. We shall now speak of the Second or Middle India, which is called Abascia.

CHAPTER XXXIX

Of the Second or Middle India, named Abascia (or Abyssinia)

Abascia is an extensive country, termed the Middle or Second India. Its principal king is a Christian. Of the others, who are six in number, and tributary to the first, three are Christians and three are Saracens. I was informed that the Christians of these parts, in order to be distinguished as such, make three signs or marks (on the face), namely, one on the forehead, and one on each cheek, which latter are imprinted with a hot iron – and this may be considered as a second baptism with fire, after the baptism with water. The Saracens have only one mark, which is on the forehead, and reaches to the middle of the nose. The Jews, who are likewise numerous here, have two marks, and these upon the cheeks.

The capital of the principal Christian king is in the interior of the country. The dominions of the Saracen princes lie towards the province of Aden. The conversion of these people to the Christian faith was the work of the glorious apostle, St Thomas, who having preached the gospel in the kingdom of Nubia, and converted its inhabitants, afterwards visited Abascia, and there, by the influence of his discourses and the performance of miracles, produced the same effect. He subsequently went to abide in the province of Maabar; where, after converting an infinite number of persons, he received, as we have already mentioned, the crown of martyrdom, and was buried on the spot. These people of Abascia are brave and good warriors, being constantly engaged in hostility with the soldan of Aden, the people of Nubia, and many others whose countries border upon theirs. In consequence of this unceasing practice in arms, they are accounted the best soldiers in this part of the world.

In the year 1288, as I was informed, this great Abyssinian prince adopted the resolution of visiting in person the holy sepulchre of Christ in Jerusalem, a pilgrimage that is every year performed by vast numbers of his subjects; but he was dissuaded from it by the officers of his government, who represented to him the dangers to which he would be exposed in passing through so many places belonging to the Saracens, his enemies. He then determined upon sending thither a bishop as his representative, a man of high reputation for sanctity, who, upon his arrival at Jerusalem, recited the prayers and made the offerings which the king had directed. Returning, however, from that city, through the dominions of the soldan of Aden, the latter caused him to be brought into his presence, and endeavoured to persuade him to become a Mahometan. Upon his refusing with becoming firmness to abandon the Christian faith, the soldan, making light of the resentment of the Abyssinian monarch, caused him to be circumcised, and then suffered him to depart. Upon his arrival, and making a report of the indignity and violence to which he had been subjected, the king immediately gave orders for assembling an army, at the head of which he marched, for the purpose of exterminating the soldan; who on his part called to his assistance two Mahometan princes, his neighbours, by whom he was joined with a very large force. In the conflict that ensued, the Abyssinian king was victorious, and having taken the city of Aden, he gave it up to pillage, in revenge for the insult he had sustained in the person of his bishop.

The inhabitants of this kingdom live upon wheat, rice, flesh, and milk. They extract oil from sesame, and have abundance of all sorts of provisions. In the country there are elephants, lions, camelopards, and a variety of other animals, such as wild asses, and monkeys that have the figure of men, together with many birds, wild and domestic. It is extremely rich in gold, and much frequented by merchants, who obtain large profits. We shall now speak of the province of Aden.

CHAPTER XL

Of the Province of Aden

The province of Aden is governed by a king, who bears the title of soldan. The inhabitants are all Saracens, and utterly detest the Christians. In this kingdom there are many towns and castles, and it has the advantage of an excellent port, frequented by ships arriving from India with spices and drugs. The merchants who purchase

them with the intention of conveying them to Alexandria, unlade
them from the ships in which they were imported, and distribute
the cargoes on board of other smaller vessels or barks, with which
they navigate a gulf of the sea for twenty days, more or less,
according to the weather they experience. Having reached their
port, they then load their goods upon the backs of camels, and
transport them overland (thirty days' journey) to the river Nile,
where they are again put into small vessels, called *jerms*, in which
they are conveyed by the stream of that river to Kairo, and from
thence, by an artificial canal, named Kalizene, at length to Alexandria. This is the least difficult, and the shortest route the merchants
can take with their goods, the produce of India, from Aden to that
city. In this port of Aden, likewise, the merchants ship a great
number of Arabian horses, which they carry for sale to all the
kingdoms and islands of India, obtaining high prices for them, and
making large profits.

The soldan of Aden possesses immense treasures, arising from the
imposts he lays, as well upon the merchandise that comes from India,
as upon that which is shipped in his port as the returning cargo; this
being the most considerable mart in all that quarter for the exchange
of commodities, and the place to which all trading vessels resort. I was
informed that when the soldan of Babylon led his army the first time
against the city of Acre, and took it, this city of Aden furnished him
with thirty thousand horses and forty thousand camels, stimulated by
the rancour borne against the Christians. We shall now speak of the
city of Escier.

CHAPTER XLI

Of the City of Escier

The ruler of this city is a Mahometan, who governs it with exemplary
justice, under the superior authority of the sultan of Aden. Its distance
from thence is about forty miles to the south-east. Subordinate to it
there are many towns and castles. Its port is good, and it is visited by
many trading ships from India, which carry back a number of

excellent horses, highly esteemed in that country, and sold there at considerable prices.

This district produces a large quantity of white frankincense of the first quality, which distils, drop by drop, from a certain small tree that resembles the fir. The people occasionally tap the tree, or pare away the bark, and from the incision the frankincense gradually exudes, which afterwards becomes hard. Even when an incision is not made, an exudation is perceived to take place, in consequence of the excessive heat of the climate. There are also many palm trees, which produce good dates in abundance. No grain excepting rice and millet is cultivated in this country, and it becomes necessary to obtain supplies from other parts. There is no wine made from grapes; but they prepare a liquor from rice, sugar, and dates, that is a delicious beverage. They have a small breed of sheep, the ears of which are not situated like those in others of the species; two small horns growing in the place of them, and lower down, towards the nose, there are two orifices that serve the purpose of ears.

These people are great fishermen, and catch the tunny in such numbers, that two may be purchased for a Venetian groat. They dry them in the sun; and as, by reason of the extreme heat, the country is in a manner burnt up, and no sort of vegetable is to be seen, they accustom their cattle, cows, sheep, camels, and horses, to feed upon dried fish, which being regularly served to them, they eat without any signs of dislike. The fish used for this purpose are of a small kind, which they take in vast quantities during the months of March, April, and May, and when dried, they lay up in their houses for the food of their cattle. These will also feed upon the fresh fish, but are more accustomed to eat them in the dried state. In consequence also of the scarcity of grain, the natives make a kind of biscuit of the substance of the larger fish, in the following manner: they chop it into very small particles, and moisten the preparation with a liquor rendered thick and adhesive by a mixture of flour, which gives to the whole the consistence of paste. This they form into a kind of bread, which they dry and harden by exposure to a burning sun. A stock of this biscuit is laid up to serve them for the year's consumption. The frankincense before mentioned is so cheap in the country as to be purchased by the governor at the rate of ten besants (gold ducats) the quintal, who sells it again to the merchants at forty besants. This he does under the direction of the soldan of Aden, who monopolises all that is produced in the district at the above price, and derives a large profit from the re-sale. Nothing further presenting itself at this place, we shall now speak of the city of Dulfar.

CHAPTER XLII

Of the City of Dulfar

Dulfar is a large and respectable city or town, at the distance of twenty miles from Escier, in a south-easterly direction. Its inhabitants are Mahometans, and its ruler also is a subject of the soldan of Aden. This place lies near the sea, and has a good port, frequented by many ships. Numbers of Arabian horses are collected here from the inland country, which the merchants buy up and carry to India, where they gain considerably by disposing of them. Frankincense is likewise produced here, and purchased by the merchants. Dulfar has other towns and castles under its jurisdiction. We shall now speak of the gulf of Kalayati.

CHAPTER XLIII

Of the City of Kalayati

Kalayati is a large town situated near a gulf which has the name of Kalatu, distant from Dulfar about fifty miles towards the south-east. The people are followers of the law of Mahomet, and are subjects to the melik of Ormus, who, when he is attacked and hard pressed by another power, has recourse to the protection afforded by this city, which is so strong in itself, and so advantageously situated, that it has never yet been taken by an enemy. The country around it not yielding any kind of grain, it is imported from other districts. Its harbour is good, and many trading ships arrive there from India, which sell their piece-goods and spiceries to great advantage, the demand being considerable for the supply of towns and castles lying at a distance from the coast. These likewise carry away freights of horses, which they sell advantageously in India.

The fortress is so situated at the entrance of the gulf of Kalatu, that no vessel can come in or depart without its permission. Occasionally it happens that the melik of this city, who is under certain engagements with, and is tributary to the king of Kermain, throws off his allegiance in consequence of the latter's imposing some unusual contribution. Upon his refusing to pay the demand, and an army being sent to compel him, he departs from Ormus, and makes his stand at Kalayati, where he has it in his power to prevent any ship from entering or sailing. By this obstruction of the trade the king of Kermain is deprived of his duties, and being thereby much injured in his revenue, is constrained to accommodate the dispute with the melik. The strong castle at this place constitutes, as it were, the key, not only of the gulf, but also of the sea itself, as from thence the ships that pass can at all times be discovered. The inhabitants in general of this country subsist upon dates and upon fish, either fresh or salted, having constantly a large supply of both; but persons of rank, and those who can afford it, obtain corn for their use from other parts. Upon leaving Kalayati, and proceeding three hundred miles towards the north-east, you reach the island of Ormus.

CHAPTER XLIV

Of Ormus

Upon the island of Ormus there is a handsome and large city, built close to the sea. It is governed by a melik, which is a title equivalent to that of lord of the marches with us, and he has many towns and castles under his authority. The inhabitants are Saracens, all of them professing the faith of Mahomet. The heat that reigns here is extreme; but in every house they are provided with ventilators, by means of which they introduce air to the different floors, and into every apartment, at pleasure. Without this resource it would be impossible to live in the place. We shall not now say more of this city, as in a former book we have given an account of it, together with Kisi and Kerman.

Having thus treated sufficiently at length of those provinces and cities of the Greater India which are situated near the sea-coast, as well as of some of the countries of Ethiopia, termed the Middle India, I shall now, before I bring the work to a conclusion, step back, in order to notice some regions lying towards the north, which I omitted to speak of in the preceding books.

It should be known, therefore, that in the northern parts of the world there dwell many Tartars, under a chief of the name of Kaidu, who is of the race of Chingis-khan, and nearly related to Kublai, the Grand Khan. He is not the subject of any other prince. The people observe the usages and manners of their ancestors, and are regarded as genuine Tartars. These Tartars are idolaters, and worship a god whom they call Naagai, that is, the god of earth, because they think and believe that this their god has dominion over the earth, and over all things that are born of it; and to this their false god they make idols and images of felt, as is described in a former book. Their king and his armies do not shut themselves up in castles or strong places, nor even in towns; but at all times remain in the open plains, the valleys, or the woods, with which this region abounds. They have no corn of any kind, but subsist upon flesh and milk, and live amongst each other in perfect harmony; their king, to whom they all pay implicit obedience, having no object dearer to him than that of preserving peace and union amongst his subjects, which is the essential duty of a sovereign. They possess vast herds of horses, cows, sheep, and other domestic animals. In these northern districts are found bears of a white colour, and of prodigious size, being for the most part about twenty spans in length. There are foxes also whose furs are entirely black, wild asses in great numbers, and certain small animals named rondes, which have most delicate furs, and by our people are called zibelines or sables. Besides these there are various small beasts of the marten or weasel kind, and those which bear the name of Pharaoh's mice. The swarms of the latter are incredible; but the Tartars employ such ingenious contrivances for catching them, that none can escape their hands.

In order to reach the country inhabited by these people, it is necessary to perform a journey of fourteen days across a wide plain, entirely uninhabited and desert − a state that is occasioned by innumerable collections of water and springs, that render it an entire marsh. This, in consequence of the long duration of the cold season, is frozen over, excepting for a few months of the year, when the sun dissolves the ice, and turns the soil to mud, over which it is more difficult and fatiguing to travel than when the whole is frozen. For the purpose, however, of enabling the merchants to frequent their country, and purchase their furs, in which all their trade consists, these people have exerted themselves to render the marshy desert passable for travellers, by erecting at the end of each day's stage a wooden house, raised some height above the ground, where persons are stationed, whose business it is to receive and accommodate the merchants, and on the following day to conduct them to the next station of this kind; and thus they proceed from stage to stage, until they have effected the passage of the desert. In order to travel over the frozen surface of the ground, they construct a sort of vehicle, not unlike that made use of by the natives of the steep and almost inaccessible mountains in the vicinity of our own country, and which is termed a *tragula* or sledge. It is without wheels, is flat at bottom, but rises with a semicircular curve in front, by which construction it is fitted for running easily upon the ice. For drawing these small carriages they keep in readiness certain animals resembling dogs, and which may be called such, although they approach to the size of asses. They are very strong and inured to the draught. Six of them, in couples, are harnessed to each carriage, which contains only the driver who manages the dogs, and one merchant, with his package of goods. When the day's journey has been performed he quits it, together with that set of dogs, and thus changing both, from day to day, he at length accomplishes his journey across the desert, and afterwards carries with him (in his return) the furs that find their way, for sale, to our part of the world.

CHAPTER XLV

Of those Countries which are termed the Region of Darkness

Beyond the most distant part of the territory of those Tartars from whence the skins that have been spoken of are procured, there is another region which extends to the utmost bounds of the north, and is called the Region of Darkness, because during most part of the winter months the sun is invisible, and the atmosphere is obscured to the same degree as that in which we find it just about the dawn of day, when we may be said to see and not to see. The men of this country are well made and tall, but of a very pallid complexion. They are not united under the government of a king or prince, and they live without any established laws or usages, in the manner of the brute creation. Their intellects also are dull, and they have an air of stupidity. The Tartars often proceed on plundering expeditions against these people, to rob them of their cattle and goods. For this purpose they avail themselves of those months in which the darkness prevails, in order that their approach may be unobserved; but, being unable to ascertain the direction in which they should return homeward with their booty, they provide against the chance of going astray by riding mares that have young foals at the time, which latter they suffer to accompany the dams as far as the confines of their own territory, but leave them, under proper care, at the commencement of the gloomy region. When their works of darkness have been accomplished, and they are desirous of revisiting the region of light, they lay the bridles on the necks of their mares, and suffer them freely to take their own course. Guided by maternal instinct, they make their way directly to the spot where they had quitted their foals; and by these means the riders are enabled to regain in safety the places of their residence.

The inhabitants of this (polar) region take advantage of the summer season, when they enjoy continual daylight, to catch vast multitudes of ermines, martens, arcolini, foxes, and other animals of that kind, the furs of which are more delicate, and consequently more valuable, than those found in the districts inhabited by the Tartars, who, on that account, are induced to undertake the plundering expeditions that have been described. During the summer, also, these people carry their furs to the neighbouring countries, where they dispose of them in a manner highly advantageous; and, according to what I have been told, some of them are transported even as far as to the country of Russia; of which we shall proceed to speak in this the concluding part of our work.

CHAPTER XLVI

Of the Province of Russia

The province of Russia is of vast extent, is divided into many parts, and borders upon that northern tract which has been described as the Region of Darkness. Its inhabitants are Christians, and follow the Greek ritual in the offices of their Church. The men are extremely well-favoured, tall, and of fair complexions; the women are also fair and of a good size, with light hair, which they are accustomed to wear long. The country pays tribute to the king of the Western Tartars, with whose dominions it comes in contact on its eastern border. Within it are collected in great abundance the furs of ermines, arcolini, sables, martens, foxes, and other animals of that tribe, together with much wax. It contains several mines, from whence a large quantity of silver is procured. Russia is an exceedingly cold region, and I have been assured that it extends even as far as the Northern Ocean, where, as has been mentioned in a preceding part of the work, jerfalcons and peregrine falcons are taken in vast numbers, and from thence are carried to various parts of the world.

CHAPTER XLVII

Of Great Turkey

In Great Turkey there is a king called Kaidu, who is the nephew of the Grand Khan, for he was son of the son of Ciagatai, who was brother to the Grand Khan. He possesses many cities and castles, and is a very great lord. He is Tartar, and his men also are Tartar, and they are good warriors, which is no wonder, for they are all men brought up to war; and I tell you that this Kaidu never gave obedience to the Grand Khan, without first making great war. And you must know that this Great Turkey lies to the north-west when we leave Ormus, by the way already mentioned. Great Turkey is beyond the River Ion, and stretches out northward to the territory of the Grand Khan. This Kaidu has already fought many battles with the people of the Grand Khan, and I will relate to you how he came to quarrel with him. You must know for a truth that Kaidu sent word one day to the Grand Khan that he wanted his part of what they had obtained by conquest, claiming a part of the province of Cathay and of that of Manji. The Grand Khan told him that he was quite willing to give him his share, as he had done to his other sons, if he, on his part, would repair to his court and attend his council as often as he sent for him; and the Grand Khan willed further, that he should obey him like the others his sons and his barons; and on this condition the Grand Khan said that he would give him part of their conquest (of China). Kaidu, who distrusted his uncle the Grand Khan, rejected this condition, saying that he was willing to yield him obedience in his own country, but that he would not go to his court for any consideration, as he feared lest he should be put to death. Thus originated the quarrel between the Grand Khan and Kaidu, which led to a great war, and there were many great battles between them. And the Grand Khan posted an army round the kingdom of Kaidu, to prevent him or his people from committing any injury to his territory or people. But, in spite of all these precautions of the Grand Khan, Kaidu invaded his territory, and fought many times with the forces sent to oppose him. Now King Kaidu, by exerting himself, could bring into the field a hundred thousand horsemen, all good men, and well trained to war and battle. And, moreover, he had with him many barons of the lineage of the emperor, that is of Chingis-khan, who was the founder of the empire. We will now proceed to narrate certain battles between Kaidu and the Grand Khan's people; but first we will describe their mode of fighting. When they go to war, each is obliged to carry with him sixty arrows, thirty of which are of a smaller size, intended for shooting at a distance, but the other thirty are larger, and have a broad blade; these they use near at hand, and strike their enemies in the faces and arms, and cut the strings of their bows, and do great damage with them. And when they have discharged all their arrows, they take their swords and maces, and give one another heavy blows with them.

In the year 1266, this King Kaidu, with his cousins, one of whom was called Jesudar, assembled a vast number of people, and attacked two of the Grand Khan's barons, who also were cousins of King Kaidu, though they held their lands of the Grand Khan. One of these was named Tabai or Ciban. They were sons of Ciagatai, who had received Christian baptism, and was own brother to the Grand Khan Kublai. Well, Kaidu with his people fought with these his two cousins, who also had a great army, for on both sides there were about a hundred thousand horsemen. They fought very hard together, and there were many slain on both sides; but at last King Kaidu gained the victory, and did great damage to the others. But the two brothers, the cousins of King Kaidu, escaped without hurt, for they had good horses, which bore them away with great swiftness. Having thus gained the victory, Kaidu's pride and arrogance increased; and he returned into his own country, where he remained full two years in peace, without any hostilities between him and the Grand Khan. But at the end of two years Kaidu again assembled a great army. He knew that the Grand Khan's son, named Nomogan, was at Kara-korum, and that with him was George the grandson of Prester John, which two barons had also a very great army of horsemen. King Kaidu, having assembled his host, marched from his own country, and, without any occurrence worth mentioning, arrived in the neighbour-hood of Kara-korum, where the two barons, the son of the Grand Khan and the grandson of Prester John, were with their army. The latter, instead of being frightened, prepared to meet them with the utmost ardour and courage; and having assembled their whole army, which consisted of not less than sixty thousand horsemen, they marched out and established their camp very well and orderly at a distance of about ten miles from King Kaidu, who was encamped with his men in the same plain. Each party remained in their camp till the third day, preparing for battle in the best way they could, for their numbers were about equal, neither exceeding sixty thousand horsemen, well armed with bows and arrows, and a sword, mace, and shield to each. Both armies were divided into six squadrons of ten thousand men each, and each having its commander. And when the two armies were drawn up in the field, and waited only for the signal to be given by sounding the nacar, they sang and sounded their instruments of music in such a manner that it was wonderful to hear. For the Tartars are not allowed to commence a battle till they hear the nacars of their lord begin to sound, but the moment it sounds they begin to fight; and it is their custom, while thus waiting the signal of battle, to sing and sound their two-corded instruments very sweetly, and make great solace. As soon as the sound of the nacars was heard, the battle began, and they put their hands to their bows, and placed the arrows to the strings. In an instant the air was filled with arrows like rain, and you might see many a man and many a horse struck down dead, and the shouting and the noise of the battle was so great, that one could hardly have heard God's thunder. In truth, they fought like mortal enemies. And truly, as long as they had any arrows left, those who were able ceased not to shoot; but so many were slain and mortally wounded, that the battle commenced propitiously for neither party. And when they had exhausted their arrows, they placed the bows in their cases, and seized their swords and maces, and, rushing upon each other, began to give terrible blows with them. Thus they began a very fierce and dreadful battle, with such execution upon each other, that the ground was soon covered with corpses. Kaidu especially performed great feats of arms, and but for his personal prowess, which restored courage to his followers, they were several times nearly defeated. And on the other side, the son of the Grand Khan and the grandson of Prester John also behaved themselves with great bravery. In a word, this was one of the most sanguinary battles that had ever taken place among the Tartars; for it lasted till nightfall; and in spite of all their efforts, neither party could drive the other from the field, which was covered with so many corpses that it was a pity to see, and many a lady that day was made a widow, and many a child an orphan. And when the sun set, both parties gave over fighting, and returned to their several camps to repose during the night. Next morning, King Kaidu, who had received information that the Grand Khan had sent a very powerful army against him, put his men under arms at daybreak, and, all having mounted, he ordered them to proceed homewards. Their opponents were so weary with the previous day's battle, that they made no attempt to follow them, but let them go without molestation. Kaidu's men continued their retreat, until they came to Samarcand, in Great Turkey.

CHAPTER XLVIII

What the Grand Khan said of the Injuries done to him by Kaidu

Now the Grand Khan was greatly enraged against Kaidu, who was always doing so much injury to his people and his territory, and he said in himself, that if he had not been his nephew, he should not have escaped an evil death. But his feelings of relationship hindered him from destroying him and his land; and thus Kaidu escaped from the hands of the great khan. We will now leave this matter, and we will tell you a strange history of King Kaidu's daughter.

CHAPTER XLIX

Of the Daughter of King Kaidu, how strong and valiant she was

You must know, then, that King Kaidu had a daughter named, in the Tartar language, Aigiarm, which means shining moon. This damsel was so strong, that there was no young man in the whole kingdom who could overcome her, but she vanquished them all. Her father the king wished to marry her; but she declined, saying, that she would never take a husband till she met with some gentleman who should conquer her by force, upon which the king, her father, gave her a written promise that she might marry at her own will. She now caused it to be proclaimed in different parts of the world, that if any young man would come and try his strength with her, and should overcome her by force, she would accept him for her husband. This proclamation was no sooner made, than many came from all parts to try their fortune. The trial was made with great solemnity. The king took his place in the principal hall of the palace, with a large company of men and women; then came the king's daughter, in a dress of cendal, very richly adorned, into the middle of the hall; and next came the young man, also in a dress of cendal. The agreement was, that if the young man overcame her so as to throw her by force to the ground, he was to have her for wife; but if, on the contrary, he should be overcome by the king's daughter, he was to forfeit to her a hundred horses. In this manner the damsel gained more than ten thousand horses, for she could meet with no one able to conquer her, which was no wonder, for she was so well-made in all her limbs, and so tall and strongly built, that she might almost be taken for a giantess. At last, about the year 1280, there came the son of a rich king, who was very beautiful and young; he was accompanied with a very fine retinue, and brought with him a thousand beautiful horses. Immediately on his arrival, he announced that he was come to try his strength with the lady. King Kaidu received him very gladly, for he was very desirous to have this youth for his son-in-law, knowing him to be the son of the king of Pamar; on which account, Kaidu privately told his daughter that he wished her on this occasion to let herself be vanquished. But she said she would not do so for anything in the world. Thereupon the king and queen took their places in the hall, with a great attendance of both sexes, and the king's daughter presented herself as usual, and also the king's son, who was remarkable no less for his beauty than for his great strength. Now when they were brought into the hall, it was, on account of the superior rank of the claimant, agreed as the conditions of the trial, that if the young prince were conquered, he should forfeit the thousand horses he had brought with him as his stake. This agreement having been made, the wrestling began; and all who were there, including the king and queen, wished heartily that the prince might be the victor, that he might be the husband of the princess. But, contrary to their hopes, after much pulling and tugging, the king's daughter gained the victory, and the young prince was thrown on the pavement of the palace, and lost his thousand horses. There was not one person in the whole hall who did not lament his defeat. After this the king took his daughter with him into many battles, and not a cavalier in the host displayed so much valour; and at last the damsel rushed into the midst of the enemy, and seizing upon a horseman, carried him off to her own people. We will now quit this episode, and proceed to relate a great battle which fell out between Kaidu and Argon, the son of Abaga the lord of the east.

CHAPTER L

How Abaga sent Argon his Son with an Army

Now Abaga, the lord of the east, held many provinces and many lands, which bordered on the territory of King Kaidu, on the side towards the tree which is called in the book of Alexander, Arbor Secco. And Abaga, in consequence of the damages done to his land by King Kaidu, sent his son Argon with a very great number of horsemen into the country of the Arbor Secco, as far as the River Ion, where they remained to protect the country against King Kaidu's people. In this manner Argon and his men remained in the plain of the Arbor Secco, and garrisoned many cities and castles thereabouts. Thereupon King Kaidu assembled a great number of horsemen, and gave the command of them to his brother Barac, a prudent and brave man, with orders to fight Argon. Barac promised to fulfil his commandment, and to do his best against Argon and his army; and he marched with his army, which was a very numerous one, and proceeded for many days without meeting with any accident worth mentioning, till he reached the River Ion, where he was only ten miles distant from the army of Argon. Both sides immediately prepared for battle, and in a very fierce engagement, which took place three days afterwards, the army of Barac was overpowered, and pursued with great slaughter over the river.

CHAPTER LI

How Argon succeeded his Father in the Sovereignty

Soon after this victory, Argon received intelligence that his father Abaga was dead, for which he was very sorrowful, and he set out with all his host on his way to his father's court, a distance of forty days' journey, in order to receive the sovereignty. Now Abaga had a brother named Acomat Soldan, who had become a Saracen, and who no sooner heard of his brother Abaga's death, than he formed the design of seizing the succession for himself, considering that Argon was at too great a distance to prevent him. He therefore collected a powerful army, went direct to the court of his brother Abaga, and seized upon the sovereignty. There he found such an immense quantity of treasure as could hardly be believed, and by distributing this very lavishly among Abaga's barons and knights, he gained so far upon their hearts, that they declared they would have no other lord but him. Moreover, Acomat Soldan showed himself a very good lord, and made himself beloved by everybody. But he had not long enjoyed his usurped power, when news came that Argon was approaching with a very great host. Acomat showed no alarm, but courageously summoned his barons and others, and within a week he had assembled a vast number of cavalry, who all declared that they were ready to march against Argon, and that they desired nothing more than to take him and put him to death.

CHAPTER LII

How Acomat went with his Host to fight Argon

When Acomat Soldan had collected full sixty thousand horsemen, he set out on his way to encounter Argon and his people, and at the end of ten days' march he halted, having received intelligence that the enemy was only five days' march from him, and equal in number to his own army. Then Acomat established his camp in a very great and fair plain, and announced his intention of awaiting his enemy there, as a favourable place for giving battle. As soon as he arranged his camp, he called together his people, and addressed them as follows: 'Lords,' said he, 'you know well how I ought to be liege lord of all which my brother Abaga held, because I was the son of his father, and I assisted in the conquest of all the lands and territories we possess. It is true that Argon was the son of my brother Abaga, and that some pretend that the succession would go of right to him; but, with all respect to those who hold this opinion, I say that they are in the wrong, for as his father held the whole of so great a lordship, it is but just that I should have it after his death, who ought rightly to have had half of it during his life, though by my generosity he was allowed to retain the whole. But since it is as I tell you, pray, let us defend our right against Argon, that the kingdom and lordship may remain to us all; for I assure you that all I desire for myself is the honour and renown, while you have the profit and the goods and lordships through all our lands and provinces. I will say no more, for I know that you are wise men and love justice, and that you will act for the honour and good of us all.' When he had ended, all the barons, and knights, and others who were there, replied with one accord that they would not desert him as long as they had life in their bodies, and that they would aid him against all men whatever, and especially against Argon, adding that they feared not but they should take him and deliver him into his hands. After this, Acomat and his army remained in their camp, waiting the approach of the enemy.

CHAPTER LIII

*How Argon held Council with his Barons before encountering
Acomat*

To return to Argon; as soon as he received certain intelligence of the
movements of Acomat, and knew that he was encamped with so
large an army, he was greatly affected, but he thought it wise to show
courage and ardour before his men. Having called all his barons and
wise counsellors into his tent, for he was encamped also in a very fair
spot, he addressed them as follows: 'Fair brothers and friends,' said he,
'you know well how tenderly my father loved you; while alive he
treated you as brothers and sons, and you know how in many battles
you were with him, and how you helped him to conquer the land he
possessed. You know, too, that I am the son of him who loved you
so much, and I myself love you as though you were my own body. It
is just and right, therefore, that you aid me against him who comes
contrary to justice and right to disherit us of our land. And you know
further how he is not of our law, but that he has abandoned it, and
has become a Saracen and worships Mahomet, and it would ill
become us to let Saracens have lordship over Tartars. Now, fair
brethren and friends, all these reasons ought to give you courage and
will to do your utmost to prevent such an occurrence; wherefore I
implore each of you to show himself a valiant man, and to put forth
all his ardour that we may conquer in the battle, and that the
sovereignty may belong to you and not to Saracens. And truly
everyone ought to reckon on victory, since justice is on our side, and
our enemies are in the wrong. I will say no more, but again to
implore every one of you to do his duty.'

CHAPTER LIV

How the Barons replied to Argon

When the barons and knights who were present had heard Argon's address, each resolved that he would prefer death in the battle to defeat; and while they stood silent, reflecting on his words, one of the great barons rose and spoke thus: 'Fair Sir Argon, fair Sir Argon,' said he; 'we know well that what you have said to us is the truth, and therefore I will be spokesman for all your men who are with you to fight this battle, and tell you openly that we will not fail you as long as we have life in our bodies, and that we would rather all die than not obtain the victory. We feel confident that we shall vanquish your enemies, on account of the justice of our cause, and the wrong which they have done; and therefore I counsel that we proceed at once against them, and I pray all our companions to acquit themselves in such a manner in this battle, that all the world shall talk of them.' When this man had ended, all the others declared that they were of his opinion, and the whole army clamoured to be led against the enemy without delay. Accordingly, early next morning, Argon and his people began their march with very resolute hearts, and when they reached the extensive plain in which Acomat was encamped, they established their camp in good order at a distance of about ten miles from him. As soon as he had encamped, Argon sent two trusty messengers on a mission to his uncle.

CHAPTER LV

How Argon sent his Messengers to Acomat

When these two trusty messengers, who were men of very advanced age, arrived at the enemy's camp, they dismounted at Acomat's tent, where he was attended by a great company of his barons, and having entered it, they saluted him courteously. Acomat, who knew them well, received them with the same courtesy, told them they were welcome, and made them sit down before him. After they had remained seated a short space, one of the messengers rose up on his feet and delivered his message as follows: 'Fair Sir Acomat,' said he, 'your nephew Argon wonders much at your conduct in taking from him his sovereignty, and now again in coming to engage him in mortal combat; truly this is not well, nor have you acted as a good uncle ought to act towards his nephew. Wherefore he informs you by us that he prays you gently, as that good uncle and father, that you restore him his right, so that there be no battle between you, and he will show you all honour, and you shall be lord of all his land under him. This is the message which your nephew sends you by us.'

CHAPTER LVI

Acomat's Reply to the Message of Argon

When Acomat Soldan had heard the message of his nephew Argon, he replied as follows: 'Sir Messenger,' said he, 'what my nephew says amounts to nothing, for the land is mine and not his; I conquered it as well as his father; and therefore tell my nephew that if he will, I will make him a great lord, and I will give him land enough, and he shall be as my son, and the highest in rank after me. And if he will not, you may assure him that I will do all in my power to put him to death.

Now this is what I will do for my nephew, and no other thing or other arrangement shall you ever have from me.' When Acomat had concluded, the messengers asked again, 'Is this all the answer which we shall have?' 'Yes,' said he, 'you shall have no other as long as I live.' The messengers immediately departed, and riding as fast as they could to Argon's camp, dismounted at his tent and told him all that had passed. When Argon heard his uncle's message, he was so enraged, that he exclaimed in the hearing of all who were near him, 'Since I have received such injury and insult from my uncle, I will never live or hold land if I do not take such vengeance that all the world shall talk of it!' After these words, he addressed his barons and knights: 'Now we have nothing to do but to go forth as quickly as we can and put these faithless traitors to death; and it is my will that we attack them tomorrow morning, and do our utmost to destroy them.' All that night they made preparations for battle; and Acomat Soldan, who knew well by his spies what were Argon's designs, prepared for battle also, and admonished his people to demean themselves with valour.

CHAPTER LVII

The Battle between Argon and Acomat

Next morning, Argon, having called his men to arms and drawn them up skilfully in order of battle, addressed to them an encouraging admonition, after which they advanced towards the enemy. Acomat had done the same, and the two armies met on their way and engaged without further parley. The battle began with a shower of arrows so thick that it seemed like rain from heaven, and you might see everywhere the riders cast from the horses, and the cries and groans of those who lay on the earth mortally wounded were dreadful to hear. When they had exhausted their arrows, they took to their swords and clubs, and the battle became so fierce and the noise so great that you could hardly have heard God's thunder. The slaughter was very great on both sides; but at last, though Argon himself displayed extraordinary valour, and set an example to all his men, it was in vain, for fortune turned against him, and his men were compelled to fly, closely pursued by Acomat and his men, who made great havoc of them. And in the flight Argon himself was captured, upon which the pursuit was abandoned, and the victors returned to their camp and tents, glad beyond measure. Acomat caused his nephew, Argon, to be confined and closely guarded, and, being a man given to his pleasures, he returned to his court to enjoy the society of the fair ladies who were there, leaving the command of the army to a great melic, or chief, with strict orders to keep Argon closely guarded, and to follow him to court by short marches, so as not to fatigue his men.

CHAPTER LVIII

How Argon was liberated

Now it happened that a great Tartar baron, who was of great age, took pity on Argon, and said in himself that it was a great wickedness and disloyalty thus to hold their lord a prisoner, and that he would do his best to set him free. He began by persuading many other barons to adopt the same sentiments, and his personal influence, on account of his age and known character for justice and wisdom, was so great, that he easily gained them over to the enterprise, and they promised to be directed by him. The name of the leader of this enterprise was Boga, and the chief of his fellow-conspirators were named Elcidai, Togan, Tegana, Taga, Tiar Oulatai, and Samagar. With these, Boga went to the tent where Argon was confined, and told him that they repented of the part they had taken against him, and that in reparation of their error they had come to set him free and take him for their lord.

CHAPTER LIX

How Argon recovered the Sovereignty

When Argon heard Boga's words, he thought at first that they came to mock him, and was very angry and cross. 'Fair sirs,' said he, 'you sin greatly in making me an object of mockery, and ought to be satisfied with the wrong you have already done me in imprisoning your rightful lord. You know that you are behaving wrongfully, and therefore I pray go your way and mock me no more.' 'Fair Sir Argon,' said Boga, 'be assured that we are not mocking you at all, but what we say is quite true, and we swear to it upon our faith.' Then all the barons took an oath that they would hold him for their lord. And Argon on his side swore that he would never trouble them for what was past, but that he would hold them all as dear as his father Abaga had done. And as soon as these mutual oaths had been taken, they took Argon out of prison, and received him as their lord. Then Argon told them to shoot their arrows at the tent in which the melic who had the command of the army was, and they did so, and thus the melic was slain. This melic was named Soldan, and was the greatest lord after Acomat. Thus Argon recovered the sovereignty.

CHAPTER LX

How Argon caused his Uncle Acomat to be put to death

And when Argon found that he was assured of the sovereignty, he gave orders to the army to commence its march towards the court. It happened one day that Acomat was at court in his principal palace making great festivity, when a messenger came to him and said: 'Sir, I bring you news, not such as I would, but very evil. Know that the barons have delivered Argon and raised him to the sovereignty, and have slain Soldan, your dear friend; and I assure you that they are hastening hither to take and slay you; take counsel immediately what is best to be done.' When Acomat heard this, he was at first so overcome with astonishment and fear that he knew not what to do or say; but at last, like a brave and prudent man, he told the messenger to mention the news to no one, and hastily ordered his most trusty followers to arm and mount their horses; telling nobody whither he was going, he took the route to go to the Sultan of Babilonia, believing that there his life would be safe. At the end of six days he arrived at a pass which could not be avoided, the keeper of which knew that it was Acomat, and perceived that he was seeking safety by flight. This man determined to take him, which he might easily do, as he was slightly attended. When Acomat was thus arrested, he made great entreaty, and offered great treasure to be allowed to go free; but the keeper of the pass, who was a zealous partisan of Argon, replied that all the treasure in the world should not hinder him from doing his duty towards his rightful lord. He accordingly placed Acomat under a strong guard, and marching with him to the court, arrived there just three days after Argon had taken possession of it, who was greatly mortified that Acomat had escaped. When, therefore, Acomat was delivered to him a prisoner, he was in the greatest joy imaginable, and commanding the army to be assembled immediately, without consulting with anybody, he ordered one of his men to slay his uncle, and to throw his body into such place as it would never be seen again, which order was immediately executed. Thus ended the affair between Argon and his uncle Acomat.

CHAPTER LXI

The Death of Argon

When Argon had done all this, and had taken possession of the principal palace with the sovereignty, all the barons who had been in subjection to his father came to perform their homages as to their lord, and obeyed it as such in everything. And after this, Argon sent Casan, his son, with full thirty thousand horsemen, to the Arbor Secco, which is in that country, to protect his land and people. Argon thus recovered his sovereignty in the year 1286 of the incarnation of Jesus Christ, and Acomat had held the sovereignty two years. Argon reigned six years, at the end of which he died, as was generally said, by poison.

CHAPTER LXII

How Quiacatu seized upon the Sovereignty after the Death of Argon

When Argon was dead, his uncle, named Quiacatu, seized upon the sovereignty, which he was enabled to do with the more ease in consequence of Casan being so far distant as the Arbor Secco. Casan was greatly angered when he heard of the death of his father and of the usurpation of Quiacatu, but he could not leave his post at that moment for fear of his enemies He threatened, however, that he would find the occasion to revenge himself as signally as his father had done upon Acomat. Quiacatu held the sovereignty, and all were obedient to him except those who were with Casan; and he took the wife of his nephew Argon and held her as his own, and enjoyed himself much with the ladies, for he was excessively given to his pleasures. Quiacatu held the sovereignty two years, at the end of which he was carried off by poison.

CHAPTER LXIII

How Baidu seized upon the Sovereignty after the Death of Quiacatu

When Quiacatu was dead, Baidu, who was his uncle, and a Christian, seized upon the sovereignty, and all obeyed him except Casan and the army with him. This occurred in the year 1294. When Casan learnt what had occurred, he was more furious against Baidu than he had been against Quiacatu, and, threatening to take such vengeance on him as should be talked of by everybody, he resolved that he would delay no longer, but march immediately against him. He accordingly provisioned his army, and commenced his march. When Baidu knew for certain that Casan was coming against him, he assembled a vast number of men, and marched forwards full ten days, and then encamped and waited for him to give battle. On the second day Casan appeared, and immediately there began a fierce battle, which ended in the entire defeat of Baidu, who was slain in the combat. Casan now assumed the sovereignty, and began his reign in the year 1294 of the Incarnation. Thus did the kingdom of the Eastern Tartars descend from Abaga to Casan, who now reigns.

CHAPTER LXIV

Of the Lords of the Tartars of the West

The first lord of the Tartars of the West was Sain, who was a very great and powerful king. He conquered Russia, and Comania, and Alania, and Lac, and Mengiar, and Zic, and Gucia, and Gazaria. All these provinces were conquered by King Sain. Before this conquest, they were all Comanians, but they were not under one government; and through their want of union they lost their lands, and were dispersed into different parts of the world; and those who remained were all in a state of serfdom to King Sain. After King Sain reigned King Patu, after him King Berca, next King Mungletemur, then King Totamongur, and lastly Toctai, who now reigns. Having thus given you a list of the kings of the Tartars of the West, we will tell you of a great battle that fell out between Alau, the lord of the East, and Berca, the lord of the West, as well as the cause of the battle, and its result.

CHAPTER LXV

Of the War between Alau and Berca, and the Battle they fought

In the year 1261 there arose a great quarrel between King Alau, lord of the Tartars of the East, and Berca, king of the Tartars of the West, on account of a province which bordered on each of their territories, which both claimed, and each was too proud to yield it to the other. They mutually defied each other, each declaring that he would go and take it, and he would see who dared hinder him. When things had come to this point, each summoned his followers to his banner, and they exerted themselves to such a degree that within six months each had assembled full three hundred thousand horsemen, very well furnished with all things appertaining to war according to their usage. Alau, lord of the East, now began his march with all his forces, and they rode many days without meeting with any adventure worth mentioning. At length they reached an extensive plain, situated between the Iron Gates and the Sea of Sarain, in which they encamped in good order, and there was many a rich pavilion and tent. And there Alau said he would wait to see what course Berca would follow, as this spot was on the borders of the two territories.

CHAPTER LXVI

How Berca and his Host went to meet Alau

Now when King Berca had made all his preparations, and knew that Alau was on his march, he also set out on his way, and in due time reached the same plain where his enemies awaited him, and encamped at about ten miles' distance from him. Berca's camp was quite as richly decked out as that of Alau, and his army was more numerous, for it numbered full three hundred and fifty thousand horsemen. The two armies rested two days, during which Berca called his people together, and addressed them as follows:'Fair sirs,' said he, 'you know certainly that since I came into possession of the land I have loved you like brothers and sons, and many of you have been in many great battles with me, and you have assisted me to conquer a great part of the lands we hold. You know that I share everything I have with you, and you ought in return to do your best to support my honour, which hitherto you have done. You know what a great powerful man Alau is, and how in this quarrel he is in the wrong, and we are in the right, and each of you ought to feel assured that we shall conquer him in battle, especially as our number exceeds his; for we know for certain that he has only three hundred thousand horsemen, while we have three hundred and fifty thousand as good men as his and better. For all these reasons, then, you must see clearly that we shall gain the day, but since we have come so great a distance only to fight this battle, it is my will that we give battle three days hence, and we will proceed so prudently and in such good order that we cannot fail of success, and I pray you all to show yourselves on this occasion men of courage, so that all the world shall talk of your deeds. I say no more than that I expect every one of you to be well prepared for the day appointed.'

CHAPTER LXVII

Alau's Address to his Men

When Alau knew certainly that Berca was come with so great an army, he also assembled his chiefs, and addressed them as follows: 'Fair brothers, and sons, and friends,' said he, 'you know that all my life I have prized you and assisted you, and hitherto you have assisted me to conquer in many battles, nor ever were you in any battle where we failed to obtain the victory, and for that reason are we come here to fight this great man Berca; and I know well that he has more men than we have, but they are not so good, and I doubt not but we shall put them all to flight and discomfiture. We know by our spy that they intend to give battle three days hence, of which I am very glad, and I pray you all to be ready on that day, and to demean yourselves as you used to do. One thing only I wish to impress upon you, that it is better to die on the field in maintaining our honour, than to suffer discomfiture; so let each of you fight so that our honour may be safe, and our enemies discomfited and slain.'

Thus each of the kings encouraged his men, and waited for the day of the battle, and all prepared for it in the best way they could.

CHAPTER LXVIII

Of the great Battle between Alau and Berca

When the day fixed for the battle arrived, Alau rose early in the morning, and called his men to arms, and marshalled his army with the utmost skill. He divided it into thirty squadrons, each squadron consisting of ten thousand horsemen; and to each he gave a good leader and a good captain. And when all this was duly arranged, he ordered his troops to advance, which they did at a slow pace, until they came half-way between the two camps, where they halted and waited for the enemy. On the other side, King Berca had drawn up his army, which was arranged in thirty-five squadrons, exactly in the same manner as that of Alau's, and he also ordered his men to advance, which they did within half a mile of the others. There they made a short halt, and then they moved forward again till they came to the distance of about two arbalest shots of each other. It was a fair plain, and wonderfully extensive, as it ought to be, when so many thousands of men were marshalled in hostile array, under the two most powerful warriors in the world, who moreover were near kinsmen, for they were both of the imperial lineage of Chingis-khan. After the two armies had remained a short while in face of each other, the nacars at length sounded, upon which both armies let fly such a shower of arrows at each other that you could hardly see the sky, and many were slain, man and horse. When all their arrows were exhausted, they engaged with swords and maces, and then the battle was so fierce that the noise was louder than the thunder of heaven, and the ground was covered with corpses and reddened with blood. Both the kings distinguished themselves by their valour, and their men were not backward in imitating their example. The battle continued in this manner till dusk, when Berca began to give way, and fled, and Alau's men pursued furiously, cutting down and slaying without mercy. After they had pursued a short distance, Alau recalled them, and they returned to their tents, laid aside their arms, and dressed their wounds; and they were so weary with fighting, that they gladly sought repose. Next morning Alau ordered the bodies of the dead to be buried, enemies as well as friends, and the loss was so great on both sides that it would be impossible to describe it. After this was done, Alau returned to his country with all his men who had survived the battle.

CHAPTER LXIX

How Totamangu was Lord of the Tartars of the West

You must know that in the West there was a king of the Tartars named Mongutemur, and the sovereignty descended to Tolobuga, who was a young bachelor, and a very powerful man, named Totamangu, slew Tolobuga, with the assistance of another king of the Tartars, named Nogai. Thus Totamangu obtained the sovereignty by the aid of Nogai, and, after a short reign, he died, and Toctai, a very able and prudent man, was chosen king. Meanwhile the two sons of Tolobuga had grown to be now capable of bearing arms, and they were wise and prudent. The two brothers assembled a very fair company, and went to the court of Toctai, and presented themselves with so much courtesy and humility on their knees that Toctai welcomed them, and told them to stand up. Then the eldest said to the king, 'Fair Sir Toctai, I will tell you in the best way I can why we are come to court. You know that we are the sons of Tolobuga, who was slain by Totamangu and Nogai. Of Totamangu, I have nothing to say, since he is dead; but we claim justice on Nogai for the slaughter of our father, and we pray you as a righteous lord to grant it us. This is the object of our visit to your court.'

CHAPTER LXX

How Toctai Sent for Nogai to Court

When Toctai had heard the youth, he knew that what he said was true, and he replied, 'Fair friend, I will willingly yield to your demand of justice upon Nogai, and for that purpose we will summon him to court, and do everything which justice shall require.' Then Toctai sent two messengers to Nogai, and ordered him to come to court to answer to the sons of Tolobuga for the death of their father; but Nogai laughed at the message, and told the messengers he would not go. When Toctai heard Nogai's message, he was greatly enraged, and said in the hearing of all who were about him, 'With the aid of God, either Nogai shall come before me to do justice to the sons of Tolobuga, or I will go against him with all my men and destroy him.' He then sent two other messengers, who rode in all haste to the court of Nogai, and on their arrival they presented themselves before him and saluted him very courteously, and Nogai told them they were welcome. Then one of the messengers said: 'Fair sir, Toctai sends you word that if you do not come to his court to render justice to the sons of Tolobuga, he will come against you with all his host, and do you all the hurt he can both to your property and person; therefore resolve what course you will pursue, and return him an answer by us.' When Nogai heard Toctai's message, he was very angry, and replied to the messenger as follows: 'Sir messenger,' said he, 'now return to your lord and tell him from me, that I have small fear of his hostility; and tell him further, that if he should come against me, I will wait for him at the entrance of my territory, for I will meet him half-way. This is the message you shall carry back to your lord.' The messenger hastened back, and when Toctai received this answer, he immediately sent his messengers to all parts which were under his rule, and summoned his people to be ready to go with him against King Nogai, and he had soon collected a great army. When Nogai knew certainly that

Toctai was preparing to come against him with so large a host, he also made great preparation, but not so great as Toctai, because, though a great and powerful king, he was not so great or powerful as the other.

CHAPTER LXXI

How Toctai proceeded against Nogai

When Toctai's army was ready, he commenced his march at the head of two hundred thousand horsemen, and in due time reached the fine and extensive plain of Nerghi, where he encamped to wait for his opponent. With him were the two sons of Tolobuga, who had come with a fair company of horsemen to avenge the death of their father. Nogai also was on his march, with a hundred and fifty thousand horsemen, all young and brave men, and much better soldiers than those of Toctai. He arrived in the plain where Toctai was encamped two days after him, and established his camp at a distance of ten miles from him. Then King Toctai assembled his chiefs, and said to them: 'Sirs, we are come here to fight King Nogai and his men, and we have great reason to do so, for you know that all this hatred and rancour has arisen from Nogai's refusal to do justice to the sons of Tolobuga; and since our cause is just, we have every reason to hope for victory. Be therefore of good hope; but at all events I know that you are all brave men, and that you will do your best to destroy our enemies.' Nogai also addressed his men in the following terms: 'Fair brothers and friends,' said he, 'you know that we have gained many great and hard-fought battles, and that we have overcome better men than these. Therefore be of good cheer. We have right on our side; for you know well that Toctai was not my superior to summon me to his court to do justice to others. I will only further urge you to demean yourselves so in this battle that we shall be talked of everywhere, and that ourselves and our heirs will be the more respected for it.' Next day they prepared for battle. Toctai drew up his army in twenty squadrons, each with a good leader and captain; and Nogai's army was formed in fifteen squadrons. After a long and desperate battle, in which the two kings, as well as the two sons of Tolobuga, distinguished themselves by their reckless valour, the army of Toctai was entirely defeated, and pursued from the field with great slaughter by Nogai's men, who, though less numerous, were much better soldiers than their opponents. Full sixty thousand men were slain in this battle, but King Toctai, as well as the two sons of Tolobuga, escaped.

WORDSWORTH CLASSICS
OF WORLD LITERATURE